Crisis in the Canadas: 1838-1839

Other Pioneer Books

AUTHENTIC LETTERS FROM UPPER CANADA
Edited by the Rev. Thomas Radcliff, introduced by James Talman

OLD TORONTO
*Excerpts from John Ross Robertson's 'Landmarks of Toronto',
edited by E. C. Kyte*

IN SEARCH OF THE MAGNETIC NORTH
John Henry Lefroy's letters, edited by George Stanley

JOURNEYS TO THE ISLAND OF ST. JOHN
(Prince Edward Island). Edited by D. C. Harvey

EARLY TRAVELLERS IN THE CANADAS
Edited by Gerald Craig

SIXTEEN YEARS IN THE INDIAN COUNTRY
The journal of Daniel Williams Harmon, edited by W. Kaye Lamb

A JOURNEY TO THE NORTHERN OCEAN
By Samuel Hearne, edited by Richard Glover

LIFE IN THE CLEARINGS
By Susanna Moodie, edited by Robert L. McDougall

WITH BURGOYNE FROM QUEBEC
A journal by Thomas Anburey, edited by Sydney Jackman

THE LETTERS AND JOURNALS OF SIMON FRASER, 1806-1808
Edited by W. Kaye Lamb

Crisis in the Canadas: 1838-1839

THE GREY JOURNALS
AND LETTERS

Edited by William Ormsby

PIONEER

BOOKS

1964

MACMILLAN OF CANADA

TORONTO

Printed in Canada for The Macmillan Company of Canada Limited,
70 Bond Street, Toronto,
by the T. H. Best Printing Company Limited

To W. Kaye Lamb

INTRODUCTION

The lookouts strained their eyes for a glimpse of land as H.M.S. *Malabar* made her way cautiously through the dense fog. Just a fortnight before, on April 24, 1838, she had sailed from the Cove of Cork bound for Quebec with the 71st Light Infantry. After a remarkably good passage, land had been sighted on May 5th. Now, three days later, Captain Harvey believed his ship was well into the Gulf of St. Lawrence and both the fog and the danger of floating ice made extreme caution essential. At noon the sun broke through briefly and he was able to fix his position accurately between Anticosti Island and Cape Rosier. On deck the men amused themselves attempting to catch small birds that flocked about the ship.

The *Malabar* was a crowded vessel. The 520 officers and men of the 71st Regiment, together with the forty-two women and eighty-six children who accompanied them, had been assigned the entire lower deck, from which the guns had been removed. The ship's company of 500 had been moved to the main deck. Lieutenant-Colonel the Honourable Charles Grey, the regiment's commanding officer, and his wife, Caroline, had been given the captain's cabin for the voyage.

On May 9th, as he gazed at the Canadian shore in the distance, Colonel Grey's thoughts may have turned to his grandfather, the 1st Earl Grey, who had served with Wolfe at Rochefort in 1757, and had commanded a British brigade during the American Revolution. Although he was not yet thirty-five, **Grey** himself had enjoyed a varied career. As a child he developed an adventurous spirit and an intense love of the outdoors playing among the perilous rocks on the coast at Howick, the family estate about forty miles north of Newcastle. In 1820, at the age of sixteen, he entered the army as a second-lieutenant in the Rifle Brigade. By purchase and exchange he advanced in ten years to the rank of lieutenant-colonel and saw service with the 23rd Welsh Fusiliers, the 43rd Light Infantry and the 60th Rifles. He was a lieutenant-colonel, unattached, from 1830 until 1833 when, by means of an exchange, he joined the 71st Light Infantry.

The rising tide of reform which swept his father into office as Prime Minister in 1830 also carried Charles Grey into the realm of active politics. Throughout the four years of his father's administration he served as his private secretary, and in 1831 he was elected to represent High Wycombe in the House of Commons. He successfully retained that seat against Benjamin Disraeli in the election of 1834. Grey did not play an active role in the House of Commons, but on occasion he displayed that spirit of independence which the 2nd Earl Grey had encouraged in his sons. In 1833 he aligned himself with the liberal element of the Whig party and declined to support the government's Irish Church Bill because it contained no provision for the alienation of the Church's extensive land holdings.

Colonel Grey did not find the same satisfaction in politics as his elder brother, Henry, Viscount Howick, who had been Under-Secretary of State for the Colonies during his father's administration and was now Secretary at War in Lord Melbourne's cabinet. In 1837, when the accession of Queen Victoria made a new election necessary, Grey decided to retire from parliamentary life and accepted an appointment as equerry-in-waiting. He hoped to be able to combine his military career with a civil one in the royal household for a few years, and to continue in the latter when he retired on half-pay.

The 71st Regiment had been ordered to Canada as a result of the rebellions that had broken out in Upper and Lower Canada at the end of 1837. The actual insurrections had been short, but many rebel leaders had taken refuge in the United States. There was every possibility of serious trouble if they were able to rally their forces and raise support south of the border.

Despite obvious similarities in the backgrounds of the rebellions in the two provinces there was one significant difference. The Upper Canadian reform movement was primarily a reaction against the attempt to establish a privileged class and a privileged church. Among their major grievances the reformers listed the monopolization of patronage by the Family Compact, the clergy reserves, the lack of proper financial controls, and the failure to provide adequate roads in many areas although large sums were spent on the Welland Canal. In Lower Canada the reform movement was essentially an expression of French Canada's determination to survive. Papineau and his followers were reformers only in so far as their immediate objectives were concerned. They sought effective control of the legislature in order to protect the French-Canadian way of life from the threat posed by the progressive English-speaking mercantile class. The French Canadian saw internal improvements, immigration, land settlement companies, and registry offices as devices designed to anglicize Lower Canada and thereby deprive his descendants of their heritage.

The basic cause of the rebellions in both provinces was the fact that under the constitution of 1791 a popular majority in the elected assembly was powerless to effect its will against the opposition of an appointed legislative council. Regardless of the support a reform measure might receive in the assembly it could not become law until it had also been passed by the council. The power of the upper house was further strengthened by the governor's practice of choosing most of his executive council from among its members. The legislative councils soon became the core of local oligarchies derisively known as the *Château*

Clique in Lower Canada and as the Family Compact in Upper Canada.

Upon finding their measures blocked by the legislative councils, the reformers entered into a contest to gain control of the purse. After the Whigs took office in 1830 the imperial government looked more sympathetically upon the Canadian reformers and, as a conciliatory gesture, control of the proceeds of the Quebec Revenue Act was turned over to the provincial legislatures in 1831. The Whigs expected that in return the provinces would provide permanent civil lists covering the salaries of the governor, the judiciary, and the executive council. A Tory majority in the Upper Canadian assembly accepted the concession and passed a civil list, but William Lyon Mackenzie attacked it vigorously as an 'everlasting salary bill'. In Lower Canada, Louis Joseph Papineau led a reform majority in the assembly which refused even to consider providing permanent salaries for a clique of appointed officials who they believed were opposed to French-Canadian interests.

The reformers in both provinces had originally looked to England for constitutional reform which would give effective power to the assembly. Before the War of 1812, Pierre Bédard had tentatively pointed to a solution based on the British principle of holding the executive responsible to the lower house. This concept was more fully developed by Dr. William Warren Baldwin and his son Robert during the decade before the rebellions. By the mid-1830s, however, Papineau and Mackenzie had emerged as leaders of radical groups that rejected the British parliamentary system in favour of the American model with its predominance of elective institutions. Their appeals to the spirit of the American Revolution caused moderate reformers to draw back and the two radical leaders were left to proceed on the road to rebellion.

Although the Whigs could not accede to the extreme demands of Papineau and Mackenzie, they still sought to solve the Canadian problem by means of conciliation. Lord Gosford was sent out to offer the Lower Canadian assembly further financial concessions in return for a modest civil list. In Upper Canada Sir John Colborne, who had been tardy in forwarding information concerning Mackenzie's *Seventh Report on Grievances* to England, was replaced by Sir Francis Bond Head.

Head made a promising beginning when he persuaded Robert Baldwin and two of his colleagues to accept appointments in the executive council. For a brief moment it appeared that a solution would be found through the concession of responsible government, but the Lieutenant-Governor soon made it clear that he did not consider himself bound to consult his council and they resigned in a body. The assembly supported the council's action by refusing to vote supplies, and Head, eager to accept their challenge, dissolved the legislature. In the ensuing election he made effective use of the loyalty cry and a strong Tory majority was returned. The reformers' exasperation was complete.

In Lower Canada Lord Gosford's charm enabled him to establish cordial social relations with many prominent French Canadians, but his efforts to obtain a civil list were rebuffed by the assembly. When it was disclosed, in 1836, that his instructions forbade the concession of an elected executive council or any of the reformers' other extreme demands, Gosford's faint hopes of eventual success evaporated. The assembly became even more intransigent and would vote supplies only on a short-term basis.

With Gosford's failure, the Whigs abandoned their policy of conciliation and, under Lord John Russell's leadership, prepared to adopt sterner measures. In March 1837, Russell introduced his Ten Resolutions, which were clearly intended as an ultimatum to the reformers in both provinces. Neither responsible government nor an elected upper house would be conceded. Control of the crown revenue would be surrendered only after a permanent civil list had been provided. Moreover, if the assembly sought to paralyze government by refusing to pass supplies, the governor was authorized to make necessary expenditures without their approval.

The Russell resolutions produced an immediate reaction in the Canadas. Mackenzie's newspaper, which had been extolling American institutions for a year, now called for open resistance. At the end of July the reformers issued a virtual declaration of independence and Mackenzie began to draft a constitution. In Lower Canada Papineau made no plans for armed resistance, but his inflammatory addresses to excited public meetings left room for no alternative course. The Lower Canadian legislature met in August, but when the assembly refused to pass supplies they were dismissed after having been in session just one week. A further stage was reached in early autumn as the *patriotes* began to organize the *Fils de la liberté* in Montreal. On October 23rd an assembly was held at St. Charles and the initial steps were taken to prepare for a provisional government.

Rebellion had become inevitable, and yet when it actually broke out it seemed almost an anticlimax to the events that preceded it. During the month of October the *patriotes* began organizing and drilling the rural population in the Richelieu Valley and north of Montreal. Sir John Colborne, who had remained in Canada as Commander of the Forces, felt obliged to take the precaution of requesting the lieutenant-governors of Upper Canada and Nova Scotia to send him any regular troops that could be spared. On November 6th the steadily mounting tension in Montreal culminated in a street brawl between the loyalist Doric Club and the *Fils de la liberté*. The victorious Doric Club paraded through the city threatening to attack Papineau. A few days later the French-Canadian leader left Montreal, hoping thus to avoid further violence. On the assumption that he had gone to raise an armed force, orders were issued to arrest him and his leading associates for high treason.

Less than a week later Colborne informed Head that the 'whole French Population of this province are now united against the Government.' In many sections, he added, they were not only organized but 'have already taken the lead in active operations by sending out parties of three or four hundred armed persons that run over the District and force every individual to join them.'[1] On November 17th the *patriotes* proceeded to take direct action. An escort of the Montreal Mounted Police, returning from St. Johns with two prisoners, was ambushed outside Longueuil and the prisoners released.

The fighting began on November 23rd at St. Denis, where the rebels successfully resisted Colonel Gore's advance towards St. Charles. This victory was nullified two days later, however, when Colonel Wetherall defeated and dispersed the main rebel force at St. Charles. Papineau and several other rebel leaders were forced to take refuge in the United States. The immediate danger of a serious insurrection disappeared when the remaining rebel concentration north of Montreal was crushed in a bloody battle at St. Eustache on December 14th.

The rebellion in Upper Canada was even less dramatic than its Lower Canadian counterpart. By sending virtually all of the regular troops to Lower Canada, Sir Francis Bond Head provided Mackenzie and his followers with an opportunity to attack Toronto and overthrow the government. A rebel force gathered at Montgomery's Tavern north of the city, but from the beginning its chances of success were impaired by conflicting orders and indecision. On December 7th Colonels FitzGibbon and Mac-Nab led a hastily assembled militia contingent up Yonge Street and dispersed the rebels after a skirmish which lasted less than half an hour.

Charles Grey very possibly had discussed the background of the Canadian rebellions with his brother Henry. Lord Howick had taken an active interest in the colonies and had tried, in 1830 and 1831, to reduce the privileges accorded to the Church of England in North America. Under his sponsorship, legislation

---

1 Public Archives of Canada, Record Group 8, C 1272, p. 28, Colborne to Head, November 12, 1837.

was passed in the House of Commons placing the proceeds of
the Quebec Revenue Act at the disposal of the provincial legislatures. He had been critical of the coercive policy embodied in
Russell's Ten Resolutions and had suggested that an alternative
might be found if J. A. Roebuck, the London Agent of the Lower
Canadian assembly, could be persuaded to introduce an acceptable measure. After the rebellions had taken place he conferred
with Roebuck on possible solutions for the Canadian problem.
Lord Howick felt that the imperial government should show
that it was prepared to return to a policy of conciliation, and
he therefore sought to couple the suspension of the Lower
Canadian constitution with provision for a constituent assembly.

For a time Charles Grey had considered coming to Canada on
the staff of his brother-in-law, John George Lambton, 1st Earl
of Durham. When Durham was appointed to investigate the
cause of the rebellions, he had offered to make Grey his military
secretary. Grey's first inclination was to refuse the appointment,
but he found it difficult to come to a decision. If he accepted, he
would probably be able to retain his position in the royal household and he could take his wife to Canada with him. If he
declined, he would probably be required to accompany his
regiment abroad in the autumn. He would have preferred to
see the regiment posted to Canada and to arrange for Caroline
to come out with Lord Durham's suite, but preliminary inquiries
convinced him that this was out of the question. He knew that
his father would advise against accepting Durham's offer, for
Lord Grey had found his son-in-law a most difficult colleague
in his reform administration. He regarded as a gross understate-
ment his son's observation that 'the chief reason *against* going
is the danger of Lambton getting into hot water with the military authorities, in which case, as his military secretary, I
should be in a very unpleasant situation'.[2] His uneasiness increased when Charles added in the same letter, 'I never felt
so doubtful as to what I ought to do. I am rather inclined to

[2] Charles Grey to 2nd Earl Grey, January 22, 1838.

go with Lambton. I *believe* he will get on very well, and it gives me an opportunity, which may not again occur, of getting on half-pay in a satisfactory manner.' Upon further consideration of his father's objections and all the other factors involved, Grey reluctantly decided not to accept Durham's offer. Having reached this difficult decision, he was pleasantly surprised to find that his problem had solved itself – the 71st Regiment was ordered to Canada after all. In the end there was no need to send Caroline out with Lord Durham as he was able to obtain suitable quarters for her on the *Malabar*.

Grey arrived in Canada on May 14, 1838, and stayed until July 5, 1839. During that time he undertook a special mission to Washington, accompanied Lord Durham on his visit to Upper Canada, and took part in the suppression of the second outbreak of rebellion in Lower Canada. The events which he witnessed are recorded with interesting comments and observations in three journals covering the periods April 20 to December 19, 1838; January 1 to March 31, 1839; and June 5 to August 16, 1839. The first and third of these are in the Grey of Howick Collection at the University of Durham. The second journal is in the Public Archives of Canada, together with photostatic copies of the other two. An additional journal, kept briefly from June 1 to July 18, 1841, during Grey's second tour of duty in Canada, is also in the Public Archives. The account presented in the journals is amplified by a series of thirty-four letters which Grey wrote to his father while he was in Canada. The original letters are in the Grey of Howick Collection at Durham, but the Public Archives has photographic copies.

Grey was a unique observer of the events which transpired during his fourteen months in Canada. He knew the Durham family intimately and thus was able to provide interesting background details, yet, because he was not in his brother-in-law's confidence, he was able to report Lord Durham's activities with a considerable degree of detachment. Moreover, his knowledge of the political situation in England permitted him to see the Durham mission in a larger setting. He was involved in a special mission to Washington and the suppression of the second rebellion, and his record of these events has a depth and vitality to be found only in an eye-witness account.

Grey showed remarkable perception in his analysis of the Lower Canadian situation, but he also revealed a blind spot common to most English observers. Like Durham, he soon realized that the Lower Canadian rebellion was actually a racial conflict and his ingrained sense of British superiority automatically aligned him with the English-speaking minority. Although he had real sympathy for the French Canadians who suffered from the severity with which the second rebellion was crushed, he was incapable of understanding or appreciating French Canada's will to survive as a separate cultural entity.

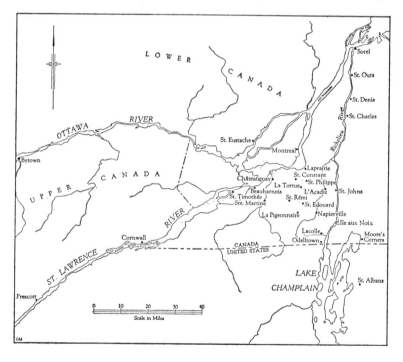

For Grey, there could be but one solution to the Lower Canadian problem – French Canada must be submerged and assimilated in a legislative union of Upper and Lower Canada. He accurately predicted that there was more to be feared from a dissatisfied English minority than from the French Canadians, but to him this only reinforced the argument in favour of a legislative union. In his opinion, alternative plans were unrealistic, and the scheme for a federal union of British North America, which Durham was reported to favour, was totally impracticable. He was both surprised and delighted when, contrary to all previous indications, his brother-in-law recommended a legislative union. He could not foresee that in the united legislature French-Canadian members would successfully resist assimilation and that ultimately a new federal concept would emerge.

This volume includes only the journal entries and letters written while Grey was in Canada. A summary has been substituted for the full text of the journal covering the first three months of 1839, which records only routine events. Brief journal entries and introductory paragraphs of letters that convey no information have been deleted. Every effort has been made to reproduce Grey's words accurately, but for the sake of clarity and uniformity some liberties have been taken with the text. Modern punctuation has been used in place of the numerous dashes, irregular commas, and periods in the original. Whenever possible the rank and regiment of military personnel referred to in the text are given in the index.

CHAPTER I

Arrival in Canada

At 5.30 a.m. May 14, 1838, H.M.S. 'Malabar' weighed anchor as the flood tide surged up the St. Lawrence. Navigational hazards had forced her to stop for the night forty-five miles below Quebec, but now the air of anticipation that always accompanies the end of a voyage pervaded the ship. The troops on board were eager to set foot in Canada and the pilot was sure they would reach Quebec by noon.

With a good breeze the vessel made rapid progress on the last short leg of the journey, but just seven miles from Quebec the wind died. For a time it seemed unlikely that Quebec would be sighted before dark. At last the breeze freshened and with billowing sails the 'Malabar' soon covered the remaining distance. Quebec came into view about three o'clock with its numerous tin roofs glinting brightly in the sun. As the vessel came to anchor a band on board struck up 'Auld Lang Syne' and spectators on shore cheered enthusiastically.

In a short time the Deputy Quartermaster-General, Colonel Gore, and Lord Durham's military secretary, Colonel Couper,[1] came on board to welcome Colonel Grey and his regiment to Canada. Grey was momentarily disappointed to hear that the regiment was to be sent on to Montreal, but he soon revised his opinion upon learning of the crowded conditions in Quebec

---

[1] When Grey declined the appointment of military secretary, Lord Durham selected Lieutenant-Colonel George Couper, who had previously served in Canada in that capacity on the staff of Sir James Kempt.

where the new barracks had not yet been completed.

At Couper's invitation Grey accompanied him on shore to inspect the preparations made in anticipation of Lord Durham's arrival. He agreed that the House of Assembly which had been taken over as Durham's headquarters was the only possible building for the purpose, but could not refrain from expressing the fear that this might be seized upon later as a grievance. Couper assured him, however, that all parties had endorsed his selection.

During the voyage Grey had grown accustomed to the fresh sea air and he soon began to feel uncomfortably warm in the bright spring sun. After a brief tour with Couper he was not sorry to return on board for dinner. The next morning, before taking Caroline on shore, he wrote a letter to his father to inform him of their safe arrival.

Quebec,
May 15, 1838.

My Dear Father,

The sailing of the *Apollo* and *Edinburgh* for England tomorrow gives me an opportunity of writing to announce our safe arrival here and our intended departure tomorrow for Montreal.

It was impossible to have a better or finer passage than we had after our second start – only twelve hours foul wind till we arrived inside the island of Anticosti at the mouth of the river – only two days rather rough, when the ship rolled a good deal, and consequently very little sickness – bright sunny weather till we got to the Banks, and very warm. On the banks, though it got cold, we had, what is very rare, bright clear weather with the exception of half a day. In short everything favoured us and we were just ten days from land to land – fourteen fairly into the St. Lawrence, and six days in the river, most of the time becalmed, making in all twenty days to Quebec. We found all the ships with the Guards arrived four days before us, having had equally good passages. The *Inconstant*, which sailed first, having made the longest [passage] in consequence of having to wait eight days till she could get through the Ice. We still saw a great deal when we came, but we luckily hit the passage near the shore of Newfoundland – for sixty miles the ice appearing very thick to the Southward of us. We were also lucky enough to see a very pretty Iceberg about 150 feet high. It is quite clear that we left England quite soon enough, for the *Inconstant* proves that we could not have got into the river a week sooner.

I am in hopes we are to remain at Montreal and, if so, I shall be very glad to go there for the Brigade of Guards completely fills Quebec and it is impossible to find a hole to lay one's head in. I shall endeavour to find out today, as Sir John Colborne is just landed from Montreal, and if I can I will find out what is intended about us.

Colonel Couper took me yesterday to the House of Assembly, which is appropriated for Lambton,[2] and he also showed me the old Government House and the other places which had been suggested for him. It certainly is the *only* place that has the least chance of suiting him and Colonel Couper tells me that, so far from giving offence, it was the *wish* of both Parties that he should take it.

Colonel Couper says the Party feeling is stronger than can be imagined here and that he sees no possibility of bringing them together. At the same time I think he seems pretty sanguine in his expectation that Lambton will be able to settle everything, as far as it is possible to settle it, in less than a year and a half. The Canadian party,[3] he says, is at this moment prepared to make very large concessions, and would at once give up all the

---

[2] Colonel Couper had selected as Lord Durham's residence and headquarters the new wing of the Bishop's Palace which had served as the House of Assembly until the suspension of the Lower Canadian constitution. Durham arrived at Quebec on May 27th before this accommodation was ready and was forced to reside at the Globe Hotel until June 9th.

[3] The French Canadians.

hitherto disputed points and also the tenure laws. The union of the Provinces is what they dread beyond measure and this is what the more violent of the English party are most clamorous for. *Both* parties say there is nothing for it but to keep up an overpowering force here for three or four years at least, to keep all sides in awe – and the report is that Sir John Colborne has applied for three additional Regiments. In the meantime the Country is perfectly tranquil and things are better on the American frontier of upper Canada, though there is still excitement enough to have made it advisable to send two more Regiments into upper Canada. In Maine, however, things do not look quite so well for the report is that the people of that Province have taken it into their own hands and have pushed a road across the disputed Territory.

I do not think I have heard anything else worth repeating except that it is expected that Papineau, who is said to be at Albany, will return to this country the moment the suspension of the Habeas Corpus Act ceases, which it will do in August, and that there is no Canadian Jury who will give a verdict against him.

I am now going down to bring Caroline on shore, having got a carriage lent to take her round the town, after which we shall return on board to dinner. We get into Steamers tomorrow and in eighteen hours hope to get to Montreal. I have already written to try and secure rooms at the Hotel for a day or two till I can get into the House which Colonel Couper has taken for Lambton, which he has written to desire may be given up to me as soon as possible. It is an unfurnished house, but I have enough to make us comfortable, and I take for granted Lambton will not object to my going in for the time.

I will add a few lines in the evening if I can, but lest I should not be able, pray give our best love to my Mother and all at home, and believe me ever, My Dear Father,

Your most affectionate son,
C. Grey.

TUESDAY, MAY 15

Colonel Gore lends Arthur Lennox and myself his carriage, and we take our wives on shore to see the views. Little enough to see. The *view from Cape Diamond magnificent* and the French church rather worth seeing, *but the town is nothing – the streets are narrow and ill paved and there are no fine buildings.* We tried to get into the Country and drove about a mile across the Plains of Abraham, which, with the exception of the Race Course, is all enclosed, but the road was so bad we had to turn back. The sun very hot. Lunched at the Globe Hotel with Colonel Couper and returned on board to dinner.

Sir John Colborne arrived at half past twelve. I went to the Quay to see him land. [He was] received with a guard of honour which, (being furnished by the guards who stand upon their privileges!) does not present Arms! General Macdonell[4] and the Heads of Departments also meet him on the Quay. Introduced to him but hear nothing of our destination. Write letters to go by the *Apollo*, which expects to sail tomorrow.

H.M.S. *Malabar*,

Tuesday Evening.

I add one line, my Dear Father, to say that I have heard nothing farther. We are to be at St. Helen's Island, opposite Montreal, which they tell me is perfectly beautiful and has, what I think, the advantage of being separated from the Town. I believe too that unless things get worse we are to remain there. I was introduced today to Sir John Colborne, but had no conversation with him, and I think it best to ask no questions about the Regiment but to obey orders.

I do not think I ever was much more disappointed than I was by the sail up the St. Lawrence. After the first 30 miles there is nothing very striking in the scenery on either side and the

---

[4] Major-General Sir James Macdonell, Officer Commanding at Quebec.

woods, of which one has heard so much, consist of the most miserable trees, crowded together, and drawn up into whips. The situation of Quebec and the view from the Citadel are certainly perfect, but it must be anything but an enjoyable place. In summer the tin roofs must be perfectly insupportable. You cannot drive over the roads above one mile out of the Town, at least we tried today and were forced to turn back, it was so rough, and in winter – seven months of the year – I cannot imagine much enjoyment with the thermometer constantly below zero. I am told Montreal is much less severe both for heat and cold and I only hope we may stay there.

The wind is come back to the East tonight and if it lasts I do not think the *Apollo* will sail tomorrow, but as we sail tomorrow evening for Montreal I cannot keep my letter open.

I hope soon to hear of you all and trust that somebody will write to me every opportunity. Once more give my best love to all, and believe me,

Your most affectionate son,
C. Grey.

WEDNESDAY, MAY 16

We are to proceed this evening at eight o'clock in the *British America* Steamer for Montreal, there to be stationed on the Island of St. Helen's. The baggage goes in a barge towed by another Steamer, the *Canada*, which also takes two large merchant barks in tow. *These Vessels particularly the Canada are magnificent. In the British America the Cabins are nine feet high and the Saloon*, or gentlemen's apartment, where everybody meets at breakfast and dinner, *is 90 feet long*. The great objection is that the gentlemen's berths are open all round the Saloon, and that Ladies cannot comfortably come to breakfast. However, there are very good private Cabins, and no difficulty in getting breakfast there. It rains nearly all day with a thick fog, and the *Apollo* is unable to sail. She drops down, however, with the tide about half a mile into the fairway, and will proceed tomorrow at daylight. At a quarter past seven the Steamer comes alongside. At a quarter before nine we are all on board, and instantly start up the river, with cheers given and received, as a parting from the *Malabar*.

THURSDAY, MAY 17

The men being very crowded we were forced to keep one third on deck, tho' it was very cold. At eight this morning stop at Three Rivers for wood and Passengers – a very neat little village apparently, where the head Quarters of the 66th are stationed. The men receive us with loud cheers, which of course we return – no time to land. Reach *Sorel* about two – *45 miles from Montreal*. Remain here an hour to take in wood, and to give Captain Armstrong time to visit his wife. Lunch on shore with a detachment of the 66th with whom we had also exchanged cheers. Cheering seems to be the order of the day everywhere. It is a very neat village and forms the usual *summer residence of Sir John Colborne*. It is also the great Depôt of Steamers and new and old, there are several lying here, for which there is no employment. One, the *John Bull*, said to be the finest on the St. Lawrence. Reach Montreal at eight – an immense crowd on the beach, and cheering without end. Land and report myself to General Clitherow[5] and Colonel Wetherall,[6] and take up our quarters at *Rasco's Hotel*, where we find rooms ready. The Regiment to land on the Island tomorrow at daylight.

FRIDAY, MAY 18

The Regiment crosses in Bateaux beginning at six A.M., the last part of it getting over at half past eleven. It is a beautiful

---

5 Major-General John Clitherow, Officer Commanding, Montreal District.

6 Lieutenant-Colonel George Augustus Wetherall, 1st (or the Royal) Regiment of Foot, Officer Commanding the Montreal Garrison.

Island, or rather will be when the leaves are out, and when we get settled, and have a proper communication established with the shore, I have no doubt we shall like it, but at present *everything* is wanted.

SATURDAY, MAY 19

General Clitherow inspects us this morning at ten o'clock. The men *look* well, but we march past infamously – want of practice – cramped ground – and Companies 38 file instead of 24 to which we had been accustomed – our excuse. Booth, 43rd, there whom I was delighted to see. My old friends[7] are at Laprairie nine miles up from hence. They, as well as the 85th and 34th, are still without their baggage, having marched across by the Portages from New Brunswick.

SUNDAY, MAY 20

Go to the English Church and hear a violent sectarian sermon from Dr. Mathew, the Rector. He seems one of the Class of Men who do so much mischief both at home and abroad. Not to see too how he *violated the very doctrines he was endeavouring to lay down. After attacking the Catholic Religion, in a Catholic Country, in as violent a manner as was possible, he laid down forbearance towards those who differed from us as the distinguishing trait of Christianity*, and ended with a quotation from Scripture to the effect that we should guard our language, and say nothing to give offense either to Jew or Gentile! I forgot to mention that yesterday we went into the Cathedral, or French Church as they call [it] – a very handsome stone building, *which has already cost £77,000, and would cost near 20 more to complete it*. It is built of stone and would really be beautiful if the Towers 80 feet high . . . were finished, but as the Seminary of

[7] Grey was a captain in the 43rd Regiment from 1825 to 1828.

St. Sulpice, to whom it belongs, are already heavily in debt, there seems little chance of its being ever completed. The inside is not quite in such good taste, and the painted window is very bad. While we are looking at it, one of the Priests comes to us, who introduces us to the Superior and the others, who are most civil and insist upon showing us everything. The Superior is a *M. Quiblier*,[8] *who was most useful during the late troubles* in giving information. He also produced a map for Sir John Colborne, and pointed out the road by which he could march on St. Eustache without impediment; and by doing which and not taking the direct road, which led thro' woods and other obstacles, as the rebels expected, all their plans were disconcerted. He says, on the authority of the Curates of the different parishes, that 150 *at least*, were killed at St. Eustache. *If the Catholic Priests had not been loyal, the insurrection in all probability would not have been so easily put down*, and yet firebrands like Dr. Mathew must needs do their best to create a bad feeling among them. It is not *my* idea of religion.

THURSDAY, MAY 31

Employed every day either settling myself or the Regiment or returning the visits which we have received in shoals. I have got into the House taken for Edward Ellice[9] and am very comfortable. I only hope I may not be turned out again. There is a tank of water at the top of the House, which belongs to the water work Company, which *might* break thro' but I hope it is not likely.

8 Joseph Vincent Quiblier, a Sulpician priest who was sent to Canada by his order in 1825. He was Superior of the Seminary at Montreal from 1831 to 1846 and did much to organize a system of primary education for French Roman Catholics in the city.

9 Edward Ellice, Jr., the son of 'Bear' Ellice of Hudson's Bay Company fame, came out to Canada as Lord Durham's private secretary. Ellice did not remain with Durham throughout his mission but went to his father's seigniory at Beauharnois in July and was still there when the second insurrection broke out.

'Major-General Sir Charles Grey', after G. Thomas
From a copy presented to the Public Archives of Canada by J. Ross Robertson

'The Rt. Honble Charles Grey, Second Earl Grey'
(Lieut.-Col. Charles Grey's father)
From an engraving in the Public Archives of Canada

General Clitherow commands the Montreal District, and is very civil, but from what I see I am just as well pleased to escape his *active* superintendence by being on the Island of St. Helen's. There is a very good house taken for Lord Durham, from Mr. Bingham, in the same street as we live in, but it will not be ready for his reception before the 1st of September which I am sorry for, for I both *think Montreal a pleasanter place than Quebec* and a more appropriate one as being more central for the Seat of Government. The Montreal people are very anxious for him to come here and above all things for a union of the Provinces, which would make Montreal the Capital. I mean the English party, for the French are violent against such a measure, and I am also told that in Upper Canada the wish for it is by no means general. The only event which has happened since we arrived is *the duel and death of Major Warde*[10] *of the 6th* [sic] *Royal last Tuesday week.* I sat next him at dinner on Monday and before six the next morning he was shot. He had distinguished himself very much at St. Charles, where he had a horse shot under him, and was reckoned an excellent officer, and had obtained his rank young. Heard yesterday of the arrival of the *Hastings* — 33 days passage from Portsmouth, having sailed on the 24th April, the same day that we did. Send Sir Hew Dalrymple down to look after our Band, which is come out in her. He takes his place in the Steamer that sails at six for Quebec, but at seven he comes to my house, as we are at dinner, to say that she was detained an hour in consequence of the arrival of intelligence of the burning of the *Sir Robert Peel*, Steamer from Prescott to Toronto, on the American coast as she was stopping to take in wood. General Clitherow sends for me to say that my Regiment will probably be

10 Major Henry J. Warde, 1st (or the Royal) Regiment, was killed on May 22, 1838, in a duel with Robert Sweeney. According to one report Sweeney challenged Warde to a duel because of a note he had sent to Mrs. Sweeney. Another version states that remarks made by Warde to a female member of Sweeney's family were the cause. Public Archives of Canada, *Abraham Joseph's diary*, May 23, 1838. Warde was a member of the 1st, not the 6th, Regiment.

sent up in consequence, as it had been originally intended for the Upper Country by Sir John Colborne. This puts a stop to all our plans for making ourselves comfortable on the Island, which were in full operation. The account makes it out to be a regular act of Piracy. It appears that she touched about two in the morning at Wells Island, belonging to the States, and separated by a very narrow channel from the mainland, to take in wood and that while there 30 or 40 Ruffians disguised as Indians and negroes, and with blackened faces, suddenly rushed on board, turned everybody out at the point of the bayonets, without allowing time scarcely to put on their clothes – towed the Vessel into the Stream, plundered and set her on fire. No lives lost.

FRIDAY, JUNE I

It appears by the news received today that the American Government is active in endeavouring to take up the Pirates and that several have already been arrested. The excitement on our frontier is very great, and there are no troops between Kingston and Montreal. A Regiment will certainly be sent, or probably the 24th will be detained.

SATURDAY, JUNE 2

No further news. Pull up to Laprairie, where the 43rd are quartered, in a Thames wherry *which eight of us* have bought from the 32nd – two hours and five minutes doing it. A comfortable barrack, in an extensive plain, but the Regiment has not yet got its heavy baggage from New Brunswick. It arrived at Montreal just as we started.

SUNDAY, JUNE 3

An order arrives this morning from Quebec for the 85th to march tomorrow morning for Kingston and for the 43rd to come in from Laprairie. I am also ordered to proceed direct to

Quebec on her Majesty's service. That order gives rise to endless conjectures and most people seem to think I shall be sent to
Washington. I cannot see what other reason there can be for
sending for me. Attend high Mass in the Cathedral at half past
nine. Disappointed in the music – only one hymn tolerable.
Scotch Church in a barrack room to the Regiment after their
dinner. The extremes of pomp and of simplicity.

MONDAY, JUNE 4

Sir H[ew] Dalrymple returns with the band. From what he
says I am certainly going *somewhere*, so in all probability it is
to Washington. Determine to take Caroline with me to Quebec.
Embark in the *British America* at six. Mr. Arthur[11] on board,
son of Sir G[eorge] Arthur, on his way to Quebec with dispatches. Says our Volunteers at Prescott have fired into an
American Steamer, but it appears certainly to have arisen in
consequence of a mistake by the Sentries of the Volunteers in
their orders. Still, it is unfortunate. He confirms the statement
that the American Government is doing all it can to get hold of
the Pirates. They have taken thirteen, eleven of whom are
Canadians. It remains to be seen whether or not they are sincere by what they do with them, now they have got them.
They can scarcely let them off as they did Drs. Nelson and
Côté.[12] I am sorry to hear from Mr. Arthur that there is a great

11 Captain Frederick Leopold Arthur, 4th (or the King's Own) Regiment, was
   the son of Sir George Arthur, Lieutenant-Governor of Upper Canada, and
   was an A.D.C. on his father's staff.
12 Dr. Cyrille Hector Octave Côté played a major role in the agitation which
   preceded the rebellion in 1837. Upon the collapse of the rebellion he fled
   to Plattsburg, New York, where he endeavoured to organize an invasion
   of Canada. Dr. Robert Nelson, a brother of Dr. Wolfred Nelson, supported
   Papineau in the legislative assembly but did not participate in the insurrection of 1837. He joined the fugitive rebels in the United States, however,
   in 1838. Nelson and Côté crossed over to Canadian soil in February, 1838,
   planted a tree of liberty, and proclaimed Nelson President of the Republic
   of Canada before returning to the United States. They were subsequently
   arrested and stood trial at Windsor, Vermont, for violating American
   neutrality, but were acquitted. Both Nelson and Côté took a prominent
   part in the second rebellion.

deal more disaffection in Upper Canada than is supposed. Altogether, *the Frontier Population on both sides appears to be as bad as possible.*

TUESDAY, JUNE 5

Reach Sorel last night at half past ten and wait there till one taking in wood. Smoke a cigar in the meantime with the officers of the 66th stationed here. At Three Rivers take Colonel Baird of the same Regiment on board. He tells us that *Sir John Colborne went up last night in the Canada with all his staff. He is going as far as Kingston,* and his doing so will no doubt have a good effect. Arrive at Quebec at half past twelve. Raining very heavily. Walk up and get Lord Durham's carriage for Caroline. Find, as I expected, that I am to go straight to Washington with dispatches for Mr. Fox,[13] and with instructions to obtain, if possible, an interview with the President,[14] and *to point out to him the impossibility that Lord Durham, with the ample force at his disposal, would allow the present insecure state of things on the frontier to continue without making use of that force for the protection of her Majesty's subjects, should the American Government not take effectual measures itself.* I return to Montreal tomorrow at ten o'clock by the same Steamer I came down in.

Lord Durham holds a Levee at two in the Château. Immensely full, all parties vying who can be most assiduous. The House of Assembly will not be ready till Thursday and they are at present in the Globe Hotel, dining every day in the Château. I am delighted to find that the most cordial understanding exists between Lord Durham and Sir John Colborne, and that they are fully agreed as to the measures to be adopted in the Country. Lord Durham's proclamation on the burning of the *Sir Robert Peel* seems to have given unmixed satisfaction. It is firm and

[13] H. S. Fox, the British Minister at Washington.
[14] Martin Van Buren.

decided as respects the American Government without being offensive. He has also applied home for a reinforcement of 3,000 men.

Went on board the *Malabar*, after the Levee, which begins to look like a Man of War. Guns have taken our places in the fore Cabin and her main deck battery is once more in its place. Went thence with Captain Stanley on board the *Pique*, the finest frigate without any exception I ever saw and by Captain Boxer's account she is so. All the stories about her are so many lies. Dine at the Château at six. Most of the Suite dine on board the *Hastings*, and instead of 22, the usual number, we are only ten, including Captain Stanley and Mr. Arthur, Sir George's son, who is come down from the Upper Province with dispatches.

CHAPTER II

Mission to Washington

The uneasy state of the Canadian-American frontier made Charles Grey's mission urgent. After spending only one night in Quebec, he embarked the following morning in the 'British America' for Montreal as soon as he had received his instructions. To his annoyance he discovered that the steamer had two heavy vessels to tow up to Montreal and it was forty hours before he reached his destination.

As the vessel slowly made her way up the St. Lawrence, Grey contemplated his mission – the first diplomatic assignment he had ever undertaken. Would he be able to present Durham's message to President Van Buren with the proper finesse and the precise shades and undertones? What would his father think of his having become so closely involved with Durham? Could he anticipate success, and if not, what would be the consequence of his failure? If some means were not found to improve Anglo-American relations, there was a very definite possibility of war.

Upon reaching Montreal Grey hastily made his final preparations and obtained General Clitherow's permission for Sir Hew Dalrymple and Lord Aberdour, two of the junior officers in his regiment, to accompany him. On the morning of June 9th he set out for Washington.

SATURDAY, JUNE 9

Embark at nine in *Princess Victoria* Steamer which sails every morning at nine for Laprairie, from whence there is a railroad to St. Johns with which the Steamer is a connection. The fare is only one Dollar to St. Johns and the distance, 24 miles, is generally done in two hours. At St. Johns there is a delay of upwards of an hour, as the Steamer for Whitehall does not leave till near one. Early as the hour is, you are expected to dine before you embark, as you get nothing on board except Tea at eight o'clock. There is a Table d'hote at Mr. Mott's Hotel a little before twelve, where we consequently get a very bad dinner. There are very few passengers on board, and it is a general complaint, in consequence of the troubles, that there is nothing doing. Some of the large Steamers on the St. Lawrence, which are usually kept in full employment by Emigrants and other travellers, are laid up this year.

Leave Whitehall at a quarter before one and reach Burlington at ten, having touched at Isle aux Noix, Plattsburgh, Port Kent etc. We lie at the wharf a little more than half an hour discharging a quantity of Cargo. During this time a great number of people come down to the gentlemen's Cabin, and go to the Bar for something to drink, among them some Canadian Refugees, one of whom, a very gentlemanlike respectable young man, takes his passage on with us for Whitehall. There is a bar in all American Steamers in the fore part of the Gentlemen's Cabin where you can get anything to drink and it seems a common custom on the arrival of a Steamer in any place, for the idle wharf loungers to resort there, with a view of seeing who is on board. I hear that the Refugees have scattered more latterly, but there are still a great many in all the Vermont frontier villages. They are all ready to turn out again at any moment and they would be assisted by the great body of the labouring Population about here, who are mostly French Canadians. The Americans, as we hear from a respectable looking and intelligent man from Milton in Vermont, would lend them every assistance, merely from the feeling that *any* People who fight against the dominion of a distant Country must be right. There are evidently attempts making to renew agitation, for this American showed me a paper, the *Quotidienne* – which has been revived within the last three weeks, and is evidently written with the sole end of exciting the Canadians again, and enlisting in their favour the sympathies of the Americans – which he tells me, was put into his hand just before he sailed, he did not know by whom. I suspect much this Paper is unknown to the Authorities at Montreal. I have never seen it during the time I was there and among the Papers offered to me for sale I did not observe it. Keep the Paper. Leave Burlington at half past ten, and reach Whitehall at seven A.M. of [June 10th].

SUNDAY, JUNE 10

Make an agreement with a Mr. Hicks to send us through in an Extra Coach to Albany in time for the evening boat for New York, for which we are to pay $30, the proper fare being $12 or $3 each. Barely time to swallow our breakfasts, 'eating' as Mr. H[icks] expressed it 'Spry', when we are off. The first stage to Comstocks landing – seven miles. The road is beyond every idea I had ever before formed of an unmade road and nobody who has not tried can have any idea of what the jolting was. We do the distance in 55 minutes however, and no time whatever is lost in changing. This we found to be the effect, at all the stages, of the heavy extra fine we have agreed to pay, or rather paid, with the written understanding that we get back $18 if we do not reach Albany in time. Change again at Sandy Hill, 14 miles; Schuylerville, 15; the Borough, 16. Thence to Albany, 18, where we arrive just as the boat is shoving off, and have barely time to hustle our things on board. At one time between Schuy-

lerville and the Borough, the driver had nearly given it up, one
of the wheelers having knocked up, and being detained a quarter of an hour getting a fresh horse. Considering the extreme
heat of the day we do the distance wonderfully. The American
system of treating horses on a journey is very different from
ours. We halted twice doing each stage, and gave the four
horses each time two whole buckets full of water among them.
The drive is very pretty, particularly between Sandy Hill and
Schuylerville. The situation of Fort Edward, where we come
down upon the Hudson, is beautiful. The road hence goes all
the way along the river and is very interesting. We cross it
twice over long covered bridges and the Canal which runs by
its side, nearly 20 times. At Troy we cross it again in a ferry
boat, worked on both sides by two blind horses in a treadmill.

The Steamer, the *North America*, is immensely full and, as
we cannot get good berths, we prefer the deck all night to the
dreadful heat of the cabin with near 200 people sleeping in it.
Nothing can be finer than the scenery of the Hudson and I am
told that the lower part, which we passed in the night, is still
more worth seeing. Something goes wrong with our machinery
and we are delayed near two hours at Newburgh, in consequence of which we are just too late for the morning boat to
Amboy which starts at six precisely.

MONDAY, JUNE 11

We are forced in consequence to wait in New York for the
second boat which starts at twelve. At which hour we embark
in the *Trenton*, an old bad boat, for Amboy, from whence we
proceed to Philadelphia in cars by the railroad. Stopped while
at New York at the Astor House. An immense establishment,
where they are able, they say, to make up 400 beds – apparently
clean, and People civil. Walk about the town to the Quays etc.,
but without being able to enjoy it from the intense heat of the

day. Went on board the *Garrick*, a beautiful New York and Liverpool Packet – superbly fitted up, but it is all in vain. They may set in splendour, but the days of these sailing Packets are numbered. The *Great Western*[1] is hourly expected on her *second* voyage to New York since the 10th of April, and on both sides of the Atlantic several Steamers are building for the same service. I myself should infinitely prefer the *Garrick*, but I am afraid others are not of my mind. Meet Colonels Hope and Harcourt of the Guards on their way to Quebec with their wives. They arrived yesterday. Call upon the Consul and give him my letters. Buy a whalebone hat etc.

The Steamer reaches Amboy, 25 miles, about a quarter past two and we start directly in the train for Trenton and Philadelphia, changing at Trenton. It is a slow concern, not arriving till eight P.M. The prettiest Country today that I have seen since I left Montreal, particularly after we cross into Pennsylvania at Trenton. The Country enclosed – Fields large and well laid out and apparently in a high state of cultivation. The wood judiciously cleared away. In short it looks so like home that I am delighted. Then I do see some gentlemanlike looking places which I have hitherto in vain looked for. Before we reach Trenton we passed Joseph Bonaparte's[2] place which has the appearance of a fine English place and must be beautiful, tho' the situation of the House seems very bad. Arrive at Philadelphia at eight and walk an immense distance to the Mansion House Hotel which we have the pleasure of finding full when we get there, and we have to walk back almost as far to the Washington House. Get a very good supper here and clean beds, but it is so intensely hot, it is impossible to sleep.

[1] The *Great Western* was the first steamship especially designed for the transatlantic trade.

[2] Joseph Bonaparte's estate, Point Breeze, was on the banks of the Delaware near Bordentown, New Jersey. In travelling from Amboy to Philadelphia, Grey could not have passed it before reaching Trenton. He must either have been misinformed or have become confused regarding its location. Bonaparte, a brother of Napoleon, lived at Point Breeze from 1816 until he returned to Europe in 1832. He also held extensive lands in New York state.

New York,
June 11, 1838.

My Dear Father,

I arrived here this morning and have barely time, before I start again for Philadelphia, to write you a line to say that I am on my way to Washington with dispatches for Mr. Fox about the burning of the *Sir Robert Peel*, and the general state of disturbance in which the frontier is kept in consequence of the inactivity of the American Government. I have also orders, if possible, to see the President on the subject – with written instructions what I am to say to him, and I shall take care to say no more. I knew nothing of my being sent till it was arranged between Lambton and Sir J[ohn] Colborne. My name appeared in Orders to proceed to Quebec on Her Majesty's service. I got there last Tuesday and came away on Wednesday, and here I now am. I shall be in Washington tomorrow afternoon and, I hope, back at Quebec in a week from thence. If I had been consulted, I should have begged that my name might not appear as having anything to do with his commission – Attaché to the High Commission – nobody will know that it was only with reference to my being sent on this Mission, and I should certainly have protested against the Gazette, had I known of it beforehand.

So far Lambton has given great satisfaction. His proclamations, particularly the last which is firm and decided as regards the American Government without saying anything at which they have any right to take offence, are universally approved. I think he is prepared really to act, if these disturbances on the frontier continue, but I am in great hopes that we may soon see a termination put to them. I think in all probability the American Government will make greater exertions, in answer to his appeal to them; particularly now that the circumstances under which the *Sir Robert Peel* was burnt must convince them what a set of mere Robbers and Pirates these self-styled Patriots are, with whom they have been sympathizing. Then, on the other hand, Sir John Colborne is gone to the Upper Province with a view to getting the Volunteers disembodied again, at least to a great extent. There is no doubt, though it is certainly true that drillings by night have been constantly going on, at Buffalo and other places in the States, with the avowed object of revenging the loss of the *Caroline*,[3] that much of the excitement is kept up by these same volunteers, who are not willing to give up the regular pay and allowances they have been receiving. The fact I believe to be that on both sides of the Frontier in Upper Canada, they are a set of marauding Scoundrels who would desire nothing better than to keep up a sort of plundering warfare on each other. On our side we keep them back, but on the other the American Government either can't or won't, and this they should be made to do.

Lambton is very sanguine about his plan for the pacification of the Country. What it is I know not, but I fear much it does not go far enough. From what I hear I believe firmly that no concession will dispose the French Canadians one jot more to you; their object, even with those who are still loyal, is to secure eventually an independent and distinct 'Nation Canadienne'. Our object, it seems to me, ought to be to make the whole Country one People, and I do not believe it can be done in any way except by the union of the Provinces. Every Englishman at Montreal and everyone I have met, and I have met many on board the different Steamers, are unanimous and violent on this point. They say, and I own it appears to me with justice, that no form of representation *can* be devised which, in Lower Canada alone, can possibly give the English Colonists a fair share of influence without doing injustice to the French,

[3] The steamship *Caroline* was used to supply Mackenzie's rebel camp on Navy Island in the Niagara River. On December 29, 1837, a volunteer force under Captain Andrew Drew seized the vessel while it was tied up at Fort Schlosser, set it on fire, and let it go adrift. The *Caroline* sank in the rapids above Niagara Falls. The American government demanded compensation for the *Caroline* incident but eventually accepted an apology tendered by Lord Ashburton in 1842.

and that less than this Union consequently will *not* satisfy the English. They also say that even such a Union would be incomplete without doing as the Americans did when they bought Louisiana from the French – forcing everything to be done in English.

In the meantime whatever Lambton means to do, he tells me he has applied for 3,000 additional men. I hope he may get them for if we do *not* satisfy the English Party, my firm belief is that we shall have much more to apprehend from them than we have had from the French. We have distributed among them about 30,000 stand of Arms, which are for the most part still in their possession and would be available on either side. . . .

Louisa[4] and all the children were looking remarkably well and were in good spirits. Caroline stays with them till my return. My best love to my Mother and all my Brothers and Sisters.

Ever your most affectionate son,
C. Grey.

TUESDAY, JUNE 12

Embark at a quarter past six at the end of Dock Street in the *Telegraph* Steamer for Wilmington. This boat is just established in connection with the railroad from Wilmington to Baltimore and nothing can possibly be better managed. The whole distance from Philadelphia being done in little more than six hours, 100 miles. The sail down the Delaware is very pretty and the railroad goes thro' a very prettily wooded Country tho' not so well cultivated as that we saw yesterday. Cross several very wide Creeks, I believe near the head of the Chesapeake Bay, on long strong wooden bridges. Cross the Susquehanna in a Steamer and reach Baltimore a few minutes before

---

4 Lady Louisa Grey, 1st Countess of Durham, Lord Durham's wife and Charles Grey's sister.

one. Dine at half past two at the Exchange Hotel, which belongs to Joseph Bonaparte,[5] and get a *most excellent* dinner in
the *Ladies'* dining room. Leave Baltimore at four in the railroad
cars for Washington, which we reach at a quarter past six, 40
miles! It is impossible for anything to be better arranged or
more comfortable than the travelling in this Country. The Cars
and Steamers start invariably to a moment. They are very comfortable and there is not the slightest confusion or difficulty
about baggage. At the commencement of your journey it is all
put together and locked up in a baggage car which is transferred
from Steamers to the train, and from the train to Steamers,
without the slightest trouble on your part. And the travelling is
besides uncommonly cheap. The only drawback we experienced
was in the heat of the weather, and in the multitude of black
particles from the chimney. The engine is detached from the
train at the entrance of the large towns, and the cars are drawn
thro' by teams of horses, already harnessed to poles, which are
attached to the cars without a moment's loss of time. Nothing
could possibly exceed the beauty of the five teams of grey
horses which drew the cars out of Baltimore. One team in particular would have done honour to the Queen's Stud. Get three
bad and very hot bedrooms at Brown's Hotel. Drive up to Mr.
Fox's, near a mile and a half off on the road to Georgetown, and
leave my dispatches as he is not at home. Stroll out afterwards
and get excellent Ices at a Confectioner's of the name of Pickny.

WEDNESDAY, JUNE 13

Go with Aberdour at six in the morning to bathe in the Potomac – a muddy nasty place, but bathe notwithstanding. Walk

[5] No evidence has been found to indicate that Joseph Bonaparte owned the
Exchange Hotel and it seems most unlikely that he did. When planning a
visit to Baltimore in 1832 he requested his nephew, Jerome Napoleon
Bonaparte (Patterson), to make a reservation for him at Barnum's Hotel.
See Georges Bertin, *Joseph Bonaparte en Amérique* (Paris, 1893), pp. 395-6.

at twelve o'clock to Mr. Fox's and have a long conversation
with him. I am to go with him to the President in the evening.
Mr. Fox thinks that ultimately war must be the result of the
many questions of difficulty now pending between us and the
Americans. Dine tête-à-tête with him at six o'clock. While I am
with him before dinner he receives a communication from the
Secretary of State[6] to say that two Steamers have been taken
up to be employed, with 50 soldiers in each, on Lakes Ontario
and Erie in the preservation of the Peace of the frontier; that
other troops are ordered to Sackets Harbor with the view of
scouting the American position of the Thousand Islands; and
that General Macomb, the Commander-in-Chief of the American Army, is sent up to direct operations. Mr. Fox thinks this is
in anticipation of the communication they expect from Lambton, tho' he does not appear to place much faith in their real
exertions. The fact is, he says and I believe it, they have not the
power. *Their whole Army is under 6,000 men,* and they are
fully employed elsewhere.

Go to the President at half past eight. Find him alone. He is a
gentlemanlike old man and was excessively civil. He talked
without reserve. Told me to assure Lord Durham how anxious
he was to co-operate with him. Agreed in the danger arising
from the excitement existing on both sides, but seemed to think
the steps taken, which he recapitulated, would be effectual. Mr.
Fox pressed strongly upon him the necessity of having as strong
a force of regular troops as they could command as the only
means of restoring confidence, and nothing could be apparently
more satisfactory than the manner in which he took everything. He seemed perfectly aware that the only means of keeping quiet the People on our side was the confidence they had
that Lord Durham would afford them protection and that it
would be his duty to use the force at his disposal for that purpose if necessary.

6 John Forsyth.

THURSDAY, JUNE 14

Drive this morning to the President's to leave our cards. Afterwards go up to the Capitol. In the House of Representatives there was nothing interesting. The House struck me as being excessively comfortable and well arranged, and everything appeared to be conducted with great decorum. There is too much echo, however, for hearing. In the Senate, Mr. Webster was speaking on the Boundary question.[7] A very plain conversational style of speaking, but very clear, and, not knowing anything about the other side of the question, he appeared to me to make a very strong case. The Capitol is certainly handsome, tho' the Cupola is too heavy for it. It would have been better too, if it had stood square to the end of the long wide street that constitutes Washington. For though upwards of 20 wide streets are traced out at right angles to this street, and several others run parallel to it, they are merely traced out with a wooden house here and there and even in the Main Street there are many wide gaps between the houses. Dine at half past seven with Mr. Fox. The only guest besides ourselves is a Mr. McDonell from Upper Canada, sent here with dispatches from Sir G[eorge] Arthur. He was on board the *Sir Robert Peel* when she was burnt. We are all invited to dine with the President tomorrow.

FRIDAY, JUNE 15

At eight o'clock Aberdour and I start on hired horses to visit the great falls of the Potomac, about 15 miles off. The worst

[7] The Maine–New Brunswick boundary was inadequately defined in the Treaty of Paris of 1783 and, as a result, it became a contentious issue in Anglo-American relations. The question was submitted to the King of the Netherlands for arbitration in 1831 but his award was rejected by the United States. Daniel Webster was a particularly able exponent of the American case which claimed both the Aroostook Valley and the Lake Temiscouata–Madawaska area. Maine's attempt to evict New Brunswick lumbermen from the Aroostook Valley in 1839 resulted in the so-called 'Aroostook War'. The question was finally settled by the Webster-Ashburton Treaty in 1842.

beast I ever rode and nearly giving it up. A most *beautiful* ride
along the towing path of the Canal to the Crommelier Hotel at
the 14-mile stone where we put up our horses. Delighted with
the Falls and the whole ride, and enjoy my day of all things,
in spite of the heat.

Dine with the President, where we meet Mr. Forsyth, Secretary of State, Mr. Poinsett, Secretary at War, Mr. Dickerson,
Secretary of the Navy, Mr. Fox, etc. Have a very long and satisfactory conversation with Mr. Poinsett who says 'he will pledge
himself' that everything possible shall be done by the American
Government to preserve the peace of the frontier. The President
also desires me to assure Lord Durham, '*in the strongest manner*',
of his sincere desire to do all in his power to keep up a good
understanding between the two Countries. He denies most positively that there is any wish on the part of the American Government to obtain Canada. I see no reason to doubt what he
says, but unfortunately the American Government is one which
must always yield to circumstances, and can never take its own
line. At this moment especially, when Van Buren is a candidate
for another term of the Presidency, he will do, not what he may
perhaps think right, but what he may think most likely to secure
his re-election. I am told, however, that he has not the slightest
chance and that the reaction against the Jackson party is complete. Nothing could be more gentlemanlike than the dinner
which was quite in the English style.

SATURDAY, JUNE 16

Go to the Navy Yard this morning to return Commodore
Patterson's visit. He is very civil and takes us over the yard which
is principally used for the fabrication of stores. The only vessel
there is the *Fulton* Steamer, intended for Harbour defence and
which I should think a perfect failure. Her Engines are of
immense power – the action horizontal. But her Boilers are close
to the sides *above* water and completely exposed. From hence

we went to return General Jones' visit, the Adjutant General.
A Clerk from Mr. Poinsett brings me, while there, a copy of
the instructions to General Macomb, and also gives me a letter
to read from Governor Marcy giving an account of 'Bill
Johnston, the Pirate of the Thousand Isles'.[8] It appears that he
has fortified himself upon one of them, that he defies both Governments, and that he is determined not to be taken alive. His
followers are said to vary from 20 or 25, who are constantly
with him, to 120 who are *available*. Governor Marcy proposes
a joint effort against him on both sides, and urges most strongly
the employment of a sufficient regular force on the American
side as the only means of preserving the peace of the frontier.
Get my dispatches from Mr. Fox and start in the trains for
Baltimore at half past four. Arrive in that town at seven and
immediately take the Steamboat line for Philadelphia. One
Steamer taking you 64 miles to Frenchtown from whence you
cross in cars by the railroad to New Castle. Thence going in
another steamer . . . to Philadelphia.

SUNDAY, JUNE 17

Arrive at five A.M. at Philadelphia and at six go on by the
railroad via Trenton and Bordentown to New York or rather
Amboy, from whence we go by Steamer to the City, where we

---

[8] Before the War of 1812 Bill Johnston kept a prosperous little store in Kingston. When the war broke out he was called upon to serve with the
Frontenac militia. After he had served for a short time his brother volun-
teered to replace him and he was permitted to return to his store. His
brother deserted, however, and he was ordered back to his regiment. When
he refused to serve again he was charged with desertion and thrown into
prison. Henceforth his sympathies lay with the Americans. He was suspected of performing espionage service for the United States during the
war. After the war he removed to French Creek and engaged in smuggling,
and when the rebellion broke out he aligned himself with Mackenzie's
forces. Johnston's knowledge of the Thousand Islands region enabled him
to terrorize settlements along the Canadian shore of the St. Lawrence with
the threat of sudden raids. The burning of the *Sir Robert Peel* on May 30,
1838, was his most notorious exploit.

arrive about one o'clock, putting up as before at the Astor House.

In going from New York to Amboy we went between Staten Island and the main [land], but in returning we came outside Staten Island which is much more interesting. The view of the Bay as far as Sandy Hook and the sail up the Narrows is very fine. The *Great Western* arrived this morning *in 14 and a half days from Bristol*. She brings Papers from London of the 1st June. The chief news seems to be the death of Talleyrand on the 19 May, and the probability, from the mutual concessions of the Leaders, that the Irish Questions[9] may be settled this session. Go to evening Church at St. Pauls – a handsome church well filled, but the service sufficiently slovenly. The lessons are all different from ours and the prayers are much curtailed. Lord Aberdour dines with a Mr. Daer [?]. Sir Hew and I dine tête-à-tête at half past seven for in this great house, as elsewhere, there is no difficulty in getting dinners when you please, if you do not like the Table d'hôte.

New York,

June 17, 1838.

My Dear Father,

You will probably receive this letter announcing my arrival here on my way back to Quebec, before one which I wrote to you some days ago on my way through to Washington – as this goes home by the *Great Western* which arrived here this morning, and sails again for England on Thursday.

In my former letter I told you that I had been sent off at a moment's notice with dispatches from Lambton for Mr. Fox and

---

9 The Irish question centred on the land tithes claimed by the Anglican Church of Ireland. It was generally agreed that the extinction of the tithe system was desirable for it provided a link between sectarian and economic grievances in Ireland, but there was no agreement as to the means by which this should be accomplished.

with instructions also to see the President. The enclosed copy of Lambton's instructions will save the necessity of my detailing the nature of those instructions.

I will now endeavour, as shortly as I can, to tell you the result and I really believe that it has been advantageous. I arrived at Washington on the afternoon of the 12th July [June] and Mr. Fox immediately requested an interview for me with the President, which was fixed for the evening of the next day. On that day, previous to my interview, Mr. Fox received a communication from Mr. Forsyth to say that it might be as well to put him in possession of the measures which had been adopted by the United States Government for the purpose of securing the peace of the frontier, in order that he might make such use of the communication as he should think desirable. Mr. Fox said immediately that he was convinced this was done with the view of anticipating any demand which might be made on seeing the proclamation issued by Lambton, and hearing of my arrival. And this I think most probable, as you will see that the instructions to General Macomb – which were communicated to me yesterday by the Secretary at War, and of which I send you a copy – are only dated the same day.

At my interview with the President the next day I had not an opportunity of saying much, beyond bearing testimony to the excited state of the Canadian Frontier and the imminent danger there was of collision unless effectual measures were taken by the Authorities on both sides for keeping the peace. I felt that if I gave Lambton's private message in the presence of Mr. Fox, it would lose its character as a *friendly* representation, and therefore thought it best to wait for the chance of speaking to him by myself the next day when I was to dine with him. The next day, accordingly, I went early, and had an opportunity before anybody else came of telling the President that Lambton's object in sending me was to give him the direct assurance of his anxious wish to cultivate the most cordial relations with the

Government of the United States in the discharge of his duties as Governor General of Canada. But that his *first* duty was to afford efficient protection to Her Majesty's subjects – that he was the more bound to do this after the noble manner in which the population of Upper Canada had come forward, at a time when there was not a single regular soldier in the Province, in defence of the Queen's Government. That there was just cause for complaint when, at a time that the provinces themselves were perfectly tranquil, Her Majesty's Subjects had been kept in a constant state of excitement and alarm from attacks, or threatenings of attacks, and outrages by a Band of Desperadoes who had been allowed, almost without interruption, to assemble and concoct their measures within the American frontier. That if this state of things was allowed to continue, there was imminent danger of the Canadians, armed as they were to the number of upwards of 20,000 men, taking matters into their own hands in a manner which, with the best possible feelings towards each other, might make it impossible for the two Governments to avoid a rupture.

I had no difficulty in saying all this to the President who in fact anticipated everything; and desired me repeatedly to assure Lord Durham '*in the strongest manner*' of their sincere wish to prevent a recurrence of late events, and entered into a detail of the measures which had been adopted with this view, and which went to the full extent of what they had in their power, till the Bill, now before Congress, for increasing the Army should have passed into a Law. He said that nothing could be more untrue than that the United States Government had the slightest wish to foment disturbances in Canada – much less that they had any views upon those Provinces for annexing them to the Union. On the contrary that it was against their interests to do so. That as the Northern States now protested against the annexation of Texas, the Southern States would equally be opposed to any increase of Territory in the north, and that they had already

too many things on their hands not to wish to restore the peace
of the frontier.

After dinner, Mr. Poinsett, the Secretary at War, asked me to
speak to him, and certainly nothing could be more satisfactory
than all he said. He suggested that Our Authorities in Canada
should immediately communicate with General Macomb, to
whom he would write that he might expect such communication, and repeatedly 'pledged himself' that efficient measures
should be taken to the full extent of the means now at the disposal of the American Government, and of the additional means
which they expected on the passing of the Bills before Congress,
for the preservation of peace and the restoration of confidence –
and was most anxious that the Authorities on both sides should
act in co-operation, without which the desired result could
hardly be produced.

Mr. Fox is still doubtful of their being in earnest, I confess
I think without cause, but I have no doubt he is correct in
attributing their present activity to the tone of Lambton's proclamation, and to the large force which we have now got in
Canada. Mr. Poinsett was very anxious on this subject and
asked me the number of Regiments we had in the Country,
which I gave him, increasing, however, the strength of each
Regiment and adding that five more were expected, in which
perhaps I am not wrong as Lambton has applied for a reinforcement of 3,000 men.

On the whole, I cannot but think the American Government
is disposed to co-operate fairly. But from all the accounts I fear
there is still a great deal of disaffection in Upper Canada, and it
will be a service of some difficulty and danger rooting out
Mr. Johnston and his fellow Pirates from their Strongholds in
the Thousand Islands, but I hope a combined movement, which
General Macomb will have orders to agree to, may prove successful.

I expect to be sent up to Sackets Harbor, where General
Macomb is stationed, as soon as I have seen Lambton and Sir

John Colborne. At least Mr. Poinsett was anxious that I should, but if I can I shall avoid doing so and, as it is simply with a view to military operations and the stationing [of] an efficient military force at the different points necessary for the protection of the Steamers that ply on the Rivers and Lakes, I think Sir John's Military Secretary is the proper Person. But of course I shall not object. . . .

I have given you so long and twaddling an account of my 'Embassy' that I have not time to say much more. If it had not been for the intense heat of the weather – for two days the thermometer being over 90 in the shade – I should have enjoyed the trip of all things. Nothing can possibly exceed the Beauty of the Scenery and it is just the best time of the year for seeing it, but I must reserve my account of what I have seen in that way till I get back to Montreal. I propose returning there to my Regiment immediately after I get back to Quebec and hope to remain with it a month, at least, before I again leave it. The *Great Western* and *Sirius* both arrived today – the former in 15, the latter in 17 days from England. I see the *Sun* of the first June makes allusion both to some concession of Sir R[obert] Peel on the subject of the Irish Church and to some acknowledgement by Lord John Russell that the principle of the Appropriation Clause could not be acted upon at present. I am curious to know what this means.

I shall hope on my arrival at Montreal to receive letters, and trust that I shall hear that you are all well. With my best love to my Mother, etc., Believe me ever, My Dear Father,

Your most affectionate son,
C. Grey.

Pray excuse execrable paper, pens, and ink, if you find this very illegible. I am besides very sleepy having travelled all last night, but I am sure I should not have time to write if I waited till tomorrow.

[Enclosure 1]   Castle of St. Lewis,
   (*Copy*)   Quebec,
                                       June 9, 1838.

Sir,

I have to request that you will immediately proceed to Washington. On your arrival there you will deliver the enclosed Dispatch to Her Majesty's Minister.

I have requested Mr. Fox to ask for an interview for you with the President of the United States. You will be pleased to express to him my feelings of sincere respect for him and his Country. And assure him that in the discharge of my duty as Governor General of British North America I shall be most anxious to cultivate relations of Amity and Cordiality with the Government of the United States. You will acquaint him that I feel persuaded that he will view the outrage at Wells Island with feelings of as much indignation as myself, and that I confidently rely on the most prompt and efficacious means being taken by the American Authorities to bring the perpetrators of this heinous offence to condign punishment. At the same time you will make him understand that something more is required from the United States Government. That the redress of this particular outrage must also be accompanied by measures for the prevention in future of similar crimes. The British frontier cannot be left exposed to those perpetual attacks and this constant irritation, and I have a right to call on the American Government to fulfil the most sacred of all duties, the due observance of the faith of Treaties and the strict maintenance of the rights of Friendly powers.

I earnestly hope that the Executive Power on the American Government side will be effectually and promptly employed. In justice to those of Her Majesty's subjects, the insecurity of whose lives and properties in consequence of these repeated attacks proceeding from the United States is daily and hourly represented to me, I make this communication. In all circumstances and at all hazards I must afford them protection; and it would give me the sincerest pleasure to find that my task is rendered easier by the Co-operation of the American Government.

> I have the honour to be, Sir,
> Your obedient Servant,
> Durham.

[Enclosure 2]   Department of War,
  (*Copy*)   June 12, 1838.

Maj. Gen. Alexander Macomb,
  Commg. in Chief,
    U.S. Army.

Sir,

Desirous of adopting every measure in the power of the Government to maintain the treaty stipulations existing between the United States and Great Britain, and to restrain our own citizens, and others within our jurisdiction from committing outrages upon the persons and property of the subjects of Her Britannic Majesty, the President has instructed me to direct you to proceed, without unnecessary delay, to the frontier of Canada, and take the command there.

You will collect such regular force as can be drawn from other stations, without serious inconvenience to the public service, and distribute them so as to occupy the most exposed positions. These appear to be the neighborhood of Buffalo, Sackets Harbor, and the Country between it and Fort Covington, Champlain and Plattsburg in the state of New York, and Swanton, Derby and Troy on the frontier of Vermont.

Information having been communicated to the Department, by the Governor of New York, that a gang of desperate men have assembled in that part of the river St. Lawrence called the 'Thousand Islands' and within the territory of the United States, with the intention of committing hostilities upon that of a friendly power, you will proceed immediately to scour those Islands, first informing the British authorities in Canada of the object of the expedition. Under the Act of the 10th of March last, you are empowered to seize such arms and munitions of war as you may find there, and, under that of the 20th of April, 1818, to arrest all persons engaged in hostile expeditions against the peace of a friendly power.

From the respect for the laws hitherto so signally evinced by the Citizens of the United States on all occasions, it is apprehended that the border inhabitants of the Northern frontier are not generally acquainted with the enactments which may render their conduct penal. You will, therefore, on your arrival on the frontier, cause to be published and widely circulated copies of the laws of the United States under which you are authorized to adopt measures to repress all hostile acts against the territory of a friendly power, and to preserve the neutral Relations of the United States.

Having made known these laws to our own citizens, and to the Canadian subjects of Her Britannic Majesty who have lately taken up their residence within the limits of the United States, you will proceed to adopt all necessary measures to carry them into prompt and vigorous execution, using every exertion to detect the unlawful combinations against the peace of a neighboring and friendly power, and to prevent and repress any outrage that may be meditated or attempted against the persons or property of its subjects; and otherwise preserve inviolate, the good faith of this Government towards Great Britain.

The Governor of New York has advised this Department that he deemed it prudent to call out a small militia force and such force as has actually assembled at the place of rendezvous under this call, you are authorized to have mustered into the Service of the United States from the period of their assembling in order that they may be paid from that time by the United States. You will not, however, retain them one moment longer than is absolutely necessary, but have them discharged and paid as soon as they can be dispensed with in order that they may return to their homes, as this is a season of the year when it will be particularly onerous to them to be obliged to be absent on Military Service.

Very respectfully
Your most obedient Servant,
J. R. Poinsett.

MONDAY, JUNE 18

Walk all over the town. Go on board the *Great Western* which at this moment looks black and dirty enough. Write letters etc., and at five P.M., having dined at half past three at the Table d'hôte, start in the *De Witt Clinton* for Albany. A great many passengers, but I had fortunately secured berths in what I consider the best part of the ship – just amidships, at the foot of the companion, where additional tiers of berths cannot be put up, and where you get fresh air from above. She is an unpleasant vessel. The engine is of immense power and the vessel is too weak for it and her deck feels as if it was lifting up under your feet.

TUESDAY, JUNE 19

Arrive at Albany at four and immediately go on in a smaller Steamer to Troy, where we dress and breakfast at the Mansion House Hotel, and thence proceed in the railroad cars to Mechanicsville or the Borough. We there take the Canal boats for Whitehall, in order to avoid the dust and heat, and slow as it is, not getting in till ten o'clock, it is much more comfortable than the quick journey we made the other way in the Coach. We dine and sup tolerably well on board. Put up at the Clinton

House, Hitchcock's – a wretched place, and People tolerably un-
civil. There is another Inn at the entrance of the town which
looks much better.

WEDNESDAY, JUNE 20

Start in the *Winooski* Steamer at one for St. Johns and not
sorry to get away from Whitehall where there is nothing to
see. A little below Ticonderoga take in Colonel Chaplin of the
Coldstream Guards, his wife, Mrs. Howe, Captain and Mrs.
Taylor of the 85th, and an American gentleman, a Mr. Dutcher,
who had come from Albany by the way of Saratoga and Lake
George. By their account this must be much the pleasantest way
of travelling and the scenery on Lake George is said to be beautiful. M. LaFontaine,[10] a Canadian Refugee with his wife, also come
on board with the intention, I am told, of returning to Canada.
Mr. Dutcher is in some way employed for them. Make acquaintance on board with an old gentleman, a Mr. Elkanah Watson,
who lives at Port Kent [and] who was employed with Franklin
in his mission to Paris, and sent over by him to Lord Shelburne,
just previous to the acknowledgement of the Independence of
America. He showed me several letters from Washington etc.
and seems to have been a great man for internal improvement.
M. LaFontaine and his wife stop at Burlington.

THURSDAY, JUNE 21

Reach St. Johns at six o'clock. Aberdour and I bathe and,
after breakfast at Mr. Mott's at half past seven, start in the trains

10 Louis Hippolyte LaFontaine represented Terrebonne in the Lower Canadian
   assembly from 1830 until the suspension of the constitution in 1838. Although a strong supporter of Papineau, LaFontaine was opposed to the use
   of violence and appealed to Lord Gosford on the eve of the rebellion in an
   effort to prevent bloodshed. After the outbreak of rebellion he fled from
   Lower Canada and paid a brief visit to France. Upon his return in 1838,
   he was arrested but was released without being brought to trial. In 1848,
   with Robert Baldwin, he formed the first responsible ministry in the Province of Canada.

at nine and reach Montreal a few minutes before eleven – having been about twelve days. Take my place in the *St. George* Steamer which sails this evening at eight. Nothing new during my absence. Four men tried to desert – all Men of bad character – but were retaken. Colonel Chaplin and his party come to the Island to dinner at six o'clock, from whence we proceed on board the Steamer, the *St. George,* and sail for Quebec at half past eight. A violent thunderstorm with heavy rain shortly after nine o'clock and being driven off deck I turn in.

FRIDAY, JUNE 22

Wake at five o'clock as we stop at Three Rivers. Reach Quebec at twelve. The same ships of war here as I left plus the *Vestal,* and *Medea* Steamers. The last Cavalry transport arrived yester-day and the troops go up this evening. Make a verbal report of my mission to Lord Durham who desires me to make him a written one that he may send it home in the *Hercules* which is to sail immediately. Accompany him with the Admiral to Sir J[ohn] Colborne's and it is arranged that orders shall be sent up forthwith to Captain Sandom and Colonel Dundas, commanding at Kingston, to communicate at once with General Macomb with a view to joint operations against the Pirates. Sir John says if the Americans act sincerely as they promise to do, the whole thing will soon be put an end to. A large dinner in the evening.

CHAPTER III

Rumours and Unrest

Grey was glad to be back in Canada. He had acquitted himself well on his diplomatic assignment and he felt he was now entitled to withdraw to the relative obscurity of his regimental duties. He knew his brother-in-law's explosive temperament and he realized that if he became closely identified with the Durham mission he would unnecessarily jeopardize his career in the royal household. Any further special assignments were to be avoided if at all possible. In the meantime, he and his wife planned to spend a pleasant weekend in Quebec, sight-seeing and visiting, before returning to Montreal.

SATURDAY, JUNE 23

Ride out with Caroline, Mary Lambton[1] etc. on the other side of the St. Charles – a pretty ride, and very good view of Quebec. After breakfast write out my report, which is to go home by the *Pique* which the Admiral has this morning received orders to send home. The *Hercules* will consequently be detained a few days. Go on board the *Malabar* with Mr. Dutcher, the American I made acquaintance with on Lake Champlain, and afterwards to the *Pique*. Pay visits with Caroline on my return.

[1] Lady Mary Lambton, a daughter of Lord Durham and later the wife of Lord Elgin, Governor General of British North America from 1846 to 1854.

SUNDAY, JUNE 24

The *Pique* sails this morning, backing and filling down the river against a strong easterly wind, till she is able to clear Point Levis. Blowing hard and raining nearly all day. Prayers at home and do not stir out.

MONDAY, JUNE 25

Still blowing and drizzling. Put off my going in consequence and wait for the *Canada* which is expected to sail tomorrow. A fresh attempt of Bill Johnston's in the neighbourhood of Chippawa reported – eight Militia Lancers taken prisoners and one killed – *very doubtful.*[2]

Quebec,
June 25, 1838.

My Dear Father,

The order for the *Pique* to sail, which she did yesterday morning, was so sudden that having to write a report of my Mission to Washington to Lambton, I had not time to write to you to announce my return on Friday last, and to thank you for the letter which I found waiting my arrival. As the *Hercules*, however, sails today or tomorrow, I hope this will not be long after those which go in the *Pique*, and you will long before have received two letters which I wrote, both going and returning, from New York.

The accounts of Mary Barrington[3] have filled us all with alarm

---

2 A reference to the Short Hills patriot raid in which seven Militia Lancers were taken prisoner, held for a short time, and then released. James Morreau was captured and hanged as the leader of the raid, but there is some evidence that he had resigned his leadership before the attack on the Lancers and had participated as a private. Bill Johnston was not involved in this incident.

3 Charles Grey's niece, the daughter of his sister Caroline. Mary Barrington had a bad case of whooping cough from which it was feared she might not recover.

such as I cannot describe and three weeks must probably elapse
before we can hear anything further. It is a comfort to think
that the latest account, the 1st June, was much more favourable,
but it was still far from encouraging. I cannot bear to think of
poor Caroline under such an affliction and I do pray most sincerely that it may be averted. Poor little Mary, she was looking
so well when I last saw her. I will not imagine the possibility
of her being otherwise now, and will look forward in the confident hope of finding her, and all those I love, quite well on my
return which I sincerely hope may not be delayed beyond next
spring. If in the meantime the winter should go over quietly,
I do not see what there can be to prevent it.

And I really hope, now that there seems some chance of a
bona fide co-operation on the part of the American Government,
that we shall not have any renewal of the disturbances. I confess, however, that such a hope is not in the slightest degree
founded on any opinion, such as that entertained by Lord
Gosford, either of the loyalty of the Canadian population in the
Lower Province, or of the good disposition of the frontier population of the United States. I am convinced that the former are
as disaffected as ever, and that the latter desire nothing more
fervently than any event which may bring about a war with
England, and that they are quite prepared to lend every assistance to any fresh attempts at insurrection on the part of the
Canadians. My hope of such wishes being frustrated rests
entirely on the knowledge which the disaffected have of our
strength, and the fear on the part of the American Government
that war may ensue if they do not exert themselves to control
the wild spirit of the frontier. I cannot possibly imagine from
what Lord Gosford derives his opinion that the Lower Canadians
are well disposed towards us and that they are actuated, on the
contrary, by feelings of the deepest hatred against the Americans. The very reverse I should say, from my own observation,
was the fact – that is, they hate us, and are at this moment well
disposed towards America inasmuch as they rest all their hopes

'John George Lambton, First Earl of Durham'
(Lord Durham was married to Charles Grey's sister, Louisa.)
From a lithograph in the Public Archives of Canada

'Some of the Grey Children on the sea-shore near Howick, 1813'
Charles, Henry, Balaam (the donkey), George, Louisa, William (died 1815)
Elizabeth   Frederick
In 'Lord Grey of the Reform Bill' by G. M. Trevelyan (London, 1920),
from the picture by Henry Thomson, R.A., at Howick

on the 'Sympathy' which they meet with in that Country. Not that they wish to become American a bit more than they wish to be English – their object is to be La Nation Canadienne – a French People with their own customs and Language – and it will not be easy to convince them that under any circumstances that must be impossible.

Great numbers of the Refugees are scattered about the frontier villages of Vermont and New York and talk pretty openly of fresh attempts. If they could organize anything, which I do not believe from the total want of Leaders, there is no doubt that the *whole* of that American population would join them. A very large proportion of the labouring population in Vermont is originally French Canadian and would of course join, and the Americans, without entering into the merits of the case, would assist them from the general principle that a distant country has no right to any dominion in Canada and from the bitter feelings, not at all yet subsided, created by the last war. It was impossible to come up, as I did, by the Canal boat from Albany to Whitehall and in the Steamer up and down the Lake Champlain without being convinced of this. There was but one language used and that most hostile to England. This feeling, however, certainly does not extend to the higher Classes and is otherwise confined to the frontier Provinces, but there it exists to a degree that, as the President himself told me, makes it impossible for them to call out the Militia with any security – and we know how little power the general Government possess of restraining their People.

I do not, however, anticipate anything in the Lower Province. Disaffected as I believe them to be, they are thoroughly frightened and their Leaders, who are now Refugees, are only anxious to make terms for themselves – Papineau, who is at Saratoga, among the first! I do not believe he has made any overture, but Mr. Fox told me at Washington that the President had more than once spoken to him about Papineau in a way to convince him that it was his wish, and on my way down the Lake Champlain

I met an intelligent American Lawyer, who has a great deal to do for LaFontaine, and others in the same situation, and he told me he *knew* that such was the wish of Papineau. LaFontaine was in the Steamboat with me and is coming back into the Country, and if he can do so with safety I do not think they will be in a hurry to attempt anything, at any rate for the present.

The English party has certainly been violent, but I do not see exactly how they can be compared to the Orangemen in Ireland. They were a Minority, but they had only the influence of a Minority and their grievances certainly were substantial particularly under the Administration of Lord Gosford, who was completely in the hands of the French Party. Now that they have got the upper hand they appear to me to show a great deal of moderation. I wish I had a newspaper here with the account of the proceedings of a meeting at Montreal to address Lambton to send you. I think you would be satisfied with the tone of the speeches made there. I confess, however, that I think the dangers from the English Inhabitants much greater than from the French. I do not think they will be satisfied with anything short of the Union of the Provinces and this I fear will not be conceded to them. Of course they have rather an exaggerated opinion of their own services during the insurrection. Their volunteers retain their Arms and bitter as is the feeling at this moment between them and the Americans, I do not think it at all impossible that if they are dissatisfied with our proceedings they may throw themselves into their Arms and then we may bid adieu to Canada. I have not the slightest idea what Lambton's views are. He tells me he has some plan, which he has shown to Sir John Colborne, who agrees with him most entirely in it. I hope he may succeed. I only fear lest the assiduity of all parties here in paying court to him should make him underrate the difficulties; and whatever he does, I hope the English Inhabitants will not get the idea that, having made use of them when their services were needed, they are now to be thrown over. For, as I said before, I am convinced the danger is not from the French, dis-affected as I believe them to be, but from the English.

Bill Johnston, the Pirate of the Thousand Isles, is still at work. We hear today that he has made an attack at Chippawa, and taken 10 Militia Lancers Prisoners, one of whom was killed and the others afterwards released. It is to be hoped that the joint operations of the two Governments in scouring the lakes and the River may have the effect of dispersing this band of robbers. At all events an avowed concert between the Governments in endeavouring to restore the peace of the frontier will have the best possible effect.

I cannot tell you much of what has been going on here. Lambton seems to have given great satisfaction so far and Colonel Couper is very sanguine in his expectations. It is for-tunate that he agrees most perfectly with Sir John Colborne and that they are on the most cordial terms. From all I hear he seems to have won everybody on board the *Hastings*, and the regret of the officers of that ship at going home was not to be told.

I return to Montreal with Caroline this evening. Every effort has been made to keep us and Lambton has spoken to me about being one of his Council. I have told him that if I can be of any use when he makes his tour through the Upper Province, I shall like to go with him, and when he establishes himself at Mont-real, to do whatever he may think best, but that at this moment I am most anxious to get back to my Regiment and to this he has agreed.

I have read the proceedings in Parliament with the greatest possible interest and they must so far be satisfactory to you, that a more perfect justification of your policy could not have been given than is contained in the speeches of Sir R[obert] Peel and Lord John Russell. The former being forced to support a measure similar, if not nearly the same, as that proposed by your Government in 1834, and thrown out by his Party in the House of Lords; and further to announce his acquiescence in the principle of Church Reform as always supported by you – in fact the principle of the Church Temporalities Bill passed in 1833; and Lord John being forced to confess that he forced upon you the consideration of the appropriation principle, which you had always stated he would find it impracticable to apply; to acknowledge the correctness of your opinion; and, after three years of agitation without a Government, to revert to the measure which they prevented from passing in 1834. I do not think he is quite correct, however, in stating so broadly that 'you agreed with him in principle'. What I always understood you to say was that if, on a redistribution of the Revenues of the Church, after all the demands of the Church itself had been fully provided for, there should be an actual surplus, you were not prepared to say that under no circumstances should it be applied by Parliament to other purposes.

But I hope now we may expect a settlement of these questions. It is for the members of the Government to reconcile themselves to the necessity, which I suppose they consider it, of retaining office under such circumstances, and for those who were the cause of the breaking up of your Government, by urging a principle which they are now forced to abandon, to excuse themselves if they can for what has since occurred.

I have seen extracts from Sydney Smith's last Pamphlet[4] in the *Times*. It amused me very much, but I had no idea he had become such a regular opponent of the present Government. He seems quite to have joined Dame Partington in endeavouring to resist the flood-tide of Reform.

I have been writing to you distracted by Duets practised over my head by Mary and Emily, and occasional most effectual

---

4 *The Times* of May 30, 1838, contained a critical editorial on Sydney Smith and his latest pamphlet, *Letter to Archdeacon Thomas Singleton*. Although a staunch Whig, Smith was opposed to levelling tendencies and radical reform. In his letters to Singleton, the first of which was published in 1837, Smith presented a strong case against the proposed levelling of incomes in the Church of England.

interruptions from Alice,[5] whom I constantly find established on my shoulders. They are all, I think, looking very well and are in very good spirits. The House is very comfortable – the library where they sit being really a beautiful room. I fear they like it so much that there is little chance of their settling at Montreal.

I do hope this letter may find you all well and quite happy about Mary. I will not anticipate the contrary, so pray give my best love to all, and believe me ever, My Dear Father,

Your most affectionate son,
C. Grey.

TUESDAY, JUNE 26

Take berths on board the *Canada* for this evening, but stopped by Lord Durham who wishes me to be one of the Special Council, to assemble on the return of Mr. Buller[6] from Montreal, for the purpose of disposing of the Prisoners who have pleaded guilty. Accompany Lord Durham etc. on board the *Cornwallis*, flag ship, where we lunch. Yards manned etc. Visit also the *Malabar* and *Inconstant*. Leaving the latter ship Lord Durham very nearly had a bad accident. His foot slipped as he came down the Accommodation ladder, and he fell head foremost into the Boat. Luckily his fall was broke [sic] by the Admiral and two of the Boat's crew who caught him. I forgot yesterday to mention that we visited the Ursuline Convent where an address was presented by the Pupils and a ceremony in honour of His Excellency and a little scene enacted, ending in the presentation of two Chaplets.

---

5 Lord Durham's daughters.

6 Charles Buller was first elected to parliament in 1830. His liberal views soon placed him on friendly terms with Durham and when Durham accepted the Canadian appointment, Buller accompanied him as his civil secretary.

THURSDAY, JUNE 28

A grand Review this morning on the plains of Abraham in celebration of the Coronation. Salutes by the Ships etc. A grand ball in the evening to the whole population, I should think, of Quebec. Unsatisfactory news this morning from Upper Canada, tho' I cannot exactly make it out. It appears that more men of Bill Johnston's stamp are in Arms than was supposed and the surprise of 10 Militia Lancers is confirmed. The 43rd is ordered up and we are to cross over [from] the Island. Sir John Colborne is also to proceed directly to the Upper Province. From all I can understand, however, the alarm is greater than is exactly warranted. Among the *loyal* Inhabitants the dissatisfaction with Government for releasing the Prisoners in Upper Canada is very great as appears by the proceedings at Sandwich.[7] In the Lower Province, they say that even the violent ones are satisfied at what is proposed. The Council met today at five and gave the authority of Law to Lord Durham's ordinance banishing eight of the leaders of the late Insurrection to Bermuda during Her Majesty's pleasure; declaring them, and 16 more, commencing with Papineau, guilty of high treason if they return to the Country without permission; and pardoning all others on giving sufficient security for future good conduct.[8]

An Act is also passed for establishing an efficient Police in Quebec and Montreal, and other Acts are announced as being in preparation for local improvement.

[7] At a public meeting held at Sandwich on June 9th, resolutions were passed censuring the authorities for the release of several prisoners and the failure to proceed with the trial of others, for the rejection of the Western District's application to raise a battalion of incorporated militia, and also for the commissariat's reluctance to pay for goods supplied during patriot attacks in the first three months of 1838.

[8] R. S. M. Bouchette, Wolfred Nelson, R. Desrivières, L. H. Masson, H. A. Gauvin, S. Marchessault, T. H. Goddu, and Bonaventure Viger were banished to Bermuda. L. J. Papineau, C. H. O. Côté, Julien Gagnon, Robert Nelson, E. B. O'Callaghan, E. E. Rodier, T. S. Brown, Ludger Duvernay, Etienne Chartier, G. E. Cartier, John Ryan, Sr., John Ryan, Jr., Louis Perrault, P. Demaray, J. F. Davignon, and Louis Gauthier were forbidden to return from the United States on penalty of being declared guilty of high treason.

Quebec,

June 29, 1838.

My Dear Father,

You will receive this letter at the same time with one which I wrote three or four days ago. I then wrote in a hurry thinking that the *Hercules* was to sail the next morning and that I was to return to Montreal that night. But here we both are still, the *Hercules* having been detained for Lambton's dispatches, and I having been ordered by him to wait till this morning, much against my will. He wished me to complete the Special Council, which met yesterday for the purpose of disposing of the Prisoners, as he was anxious that those who were pardoned should receive the grace on the day of the Queen's Coronation. Why anybody else would not have done as well or better I do not know, but he asked me to stay in a manner that I could not refuse.

He has got out of the embarrassment of the Prisoners very well and what he has done will, I believe, satisfy even the violent party in the Lower Province. The Prisoners all pleaded *guilty*, and yesterday, in consequence, an ordinance was passed banishing certain of the Leaders, names mentioned, to the Island of Bermuda, to be there kept under such restraint, during Her Majesty's pleasure, as may be sufficient to prevent their return to these provinces, and enacting that if without permission granted they or certain others who have withdrawn themselves from justice, such as Papineau, etc., names also mentioned, are found at large in Her Majesty's possessions in North America, they shall be deemed guilty of high treason and suffer death accordingly, the onus of proving that they have received such permission resting with them.

In all I do not think there are twenty names inserted. With regard to the rest of the Prisoners a proclamation orders their discharge, and also sanctions the return to their homes of all not mentioned in the ordinance on giving such security as may be deemed sufficient for future good conduct. The amount of security will be fixed in classes according to the nature of the offence charged against each. The Murderers of Mr. Weir[9] and somebody else are excepted, however, from everything.

From what I can hear the People of Lower Canada will be quite satisfied with this and the advantage it will give, by allowing a great number of Refugees to return home instead of agitating in the frontier villages of Vermont and New York, will be very great I think.

Many other acts for Local improvement are immediately to follow. We passed one yesterday for establishing an efficient police in Quebec and Montreal, the Act being the same as that for the London Police. Feudal tenures are immediately to be abolished, Registration established, and by an amicable arrangement with the Superior of the Seminary, the complaints of the Montreal people about the St. Sulpice seigniory will be removed.

I say I think this will all give satisfaction at least for the present in *Lower* Canada. In the Upper Province I fear things are not going on so well. I cannot exactly understand what has occurred. There are so many reports, but it seems certain that there are more people in Arms in connection with Johnston than was at first supposed, and though I still am of the same opinion that I gave in my last letter, that nothing serious can come of the attempts of such men, I fear the spirit of dissatisfaction, which exists to a very great extent – I believe I might say universally – against the Government, may make them more dangerous than they would otherwise be. There was a meeting at Sandwich, attended by all the leading men, and very violent

[9] Excluded from the general amnesty were François Jalbert, J. B. Lussier, Louis Lussier, François Mignault, François Talbot, Amable Daunais, François Nicolas, Etienne Langlois, Gédéon Pinsonnault, Joseph Pinsonnault and any other individuals accused of the murders of Lieutenant George Weir and Joseph Chartrand, or implicated in the escape of Louis Lussier. Weir was taken prisoner at St. Denis while carrying despatches and was subsequently killed by the rebels when he attempted to escape. Chartrand was suspected by the rebels of being an informer. He was captured by them at L'Acadie on November 27, 1837, and shot.

resolutions adopted, condemning the course taken by Sir George Arthur in liberating so many Prisoners unconditionally, and then finding out that those taken at point de Pelee are Prisoners of war and that there is no law by which they can be tried.

Sir John Colborne goes up to the Upper Province again this evening, and the *Malabar* sails for Halifax to bring the 93rd Regiment here. The 43rd goes at once to Upper Canada, making six Regiments which they will have there, and we cross over from our lovely Island to Montreal. Lambton is to be at Montreal on the 5th and thence goes to whatever Point Sir John Colborne thinks his presence will be most required at. I feel very sanguine as to the effect of his going. What makes the loyal People in Upper Canada so dissatisfied is their having no confidence that they will be protected, and I feel no doubt of Lambton's conciliating the violent men there, as he has done here, beyond what could possibly be expected.

There was a grand Review here yesterday to celebrate the Queen's Coronation. There were [*sic*] an immense number of people out and of course the Guards looked well – the ships all dressed, firing salutes – manning yards, etc. In the evening there was a Great Ball – as disagreeable as such balls generally are. It was provoking that it was a very wet night and we could not enjoy the illuminations. The ships with their yards manned, burning blue lights, with a light in each port, would have been very pretty if we could have seen them.

I do not think I ever saw Lambton looking better. Indeed they seem all remarkably well and I am glad to see Mary much improved, I think, in looks, and in very good spirits. I do hope the accounts that we next receive from home may be equally good and that we may be made happy about Mary Barrington. Give my love to my Mother and the rest of the family, and believe me ever, My Dear Father,

Your most affectionate son,
C. Grey.

I find the number of Prisoners to be sent to Bermuda is eight. The *Charybdis* is just coming in with Sir John Harvey[10] on board from New Brunswick.

FRIDAY, JUNE 29

Take places in the *Eagle* for this evening, but Sir James Macdonell and his relation, the Bishop of Kingston, have secured the only State Cabins, which is a bore. Go across to Point Levis in the Admiral's boat – hot and disagreeable. Go on board the moment after dinner, and sail at a quarter past eight. A slow boat and not expected to do the passage under 24 hours – very full. The above mentioned Macdonells, general and Bishop, Colonel Campbell, and Captain Bridges, Artillery, *Gibbon Wakefield*, of Miss Turner notoriety,[11] etc., etc. *The latter a very agreeable man.*

SATURDAY, JUNE 30

Get once more to my own quiet home at half past eight o'clock. Our passage on the whole was very pleasant – our fellow passengers being very agreeable. Go to General Clitherow and deliver my message, respecting the Prisoners. Denny, Dalrymple, the Adjutant, and [the] Paymaster call at my house.

[10] During the visit of Sir John Harvey, Lieutenant-Governor of New Brunswick, Durham discussed with him the possibility of implementing a federal union of British North America.

[11] Edward Gibbon Wakefield was a colonial theorist of some repute but scandals connected with his personal life had marked him as a social outcast. In his youth he eloped with a ward in Chancery, Eliza Prattle. After her death he persuaded Ellen Turner that she must leave her boarding school and contract a nominal marriage with him if she wished to save her father from financial ruin. The girl's father, a wealthy manufacturer, had Wakefield arrested and charged with abduction. He was sentenced to three years in prison and the marriage was annulled. Despite Wakefield's social reputation, Lord Durham was determined to make use of his knowledge of colonization and had him come to Canada with the intention of making him Commissioner of Crown Lands and Emigration.

SUNDAY, JULY 1

Parade at half past ten. Go with Caroline to Church. No sermon in consequence of being Sacrament Sunday. Call afterwards on the Bishop of the Seminary and arrange with him and the General that they shall come over tomorrow to the Island to dine at five o'clock. Go to the gaol, and make enquiry from the Governor etc. as to the escape of Lussier.[12] Very much disgusted at the language made use of by the English party respecting the measures adopted with the Prisoners. With no one single grievance, with every one hitherto insisted on in the course of removal, they are not satisfied because the Government is content to obviate the possibility of further agitation on the part of the Leaders of the French Canadians without Bloodshed. They seem to wish to do all they can to make the settlement of the question more difficult.

MONDAY, JULY 2

The Prisoners under sentence of transportation to Bermuda are sent down today at four o'clock in the *Canada* Steamer to be put at once on board the *Vestal* which is to convey them to their final destination. A great crowd was expected, but by embarking the escort at the usual place of embarkation and then sending the Steamer down to the wharf opposite the gaol, it was completely prevented. Sixty of my men under Sir H[ew] Dalrymple composed the escort. Letting off Girouard,[13] one of

12 Louis Lussier was accused of having participated in the murder of Lieutenant George Weir. He was imprisoned at Montreal, but escaped on June 23, 1838, and fled to the United States.

13 After his election to the legislative assembly in 1831 Jean Joseph Girouard soon became recognized as a leading French-Canadian reformer and played an important part in the drafting of the *Ninety-two Resolutions*. He was opposed to any compromise on constitutional issues but he was also anxious to prevent any resort to violence. None the less, when the rebellion broke out his name was included on the list of those for whom a reward was offered. After evading capture for a short time Girouard gave himself up and was imprisoned until July 16, 1838, when he was released under Durham's general amnesty.

the greatest agitators who was taken at St. Benoit, has caused great dissatisfaction and by all accounts it would have been better to include him and one or two more in the sentence. *The feeling here is certainly not near so good as it is in Quebec* and I think it important that Lord Durham should remain here if possible on his return from the Upper Province.

Sir James Macdonell and the Bishop of Kingston dine with us in the evening at St. Helen's. The latter is perfectly delighted with the Pipes and enjoys a Gaelic conversation with the Piper beyond measure.

TUESDAY, JULY 3

Lord Arthur Lennox and myself accompany the Superior of the Seminary, M. Quiblier, and Sir James Macdonell on a visit to the Congregation – an establishment of Sisters, not nuns, associated for the purposes of education. There are 78 in all, 30 of whom are constantly visiting in different parts of the Country and eight in town. They have altogether over 2,000 pupils of whom 800 are in town. Thence we drive round the mountain and, at twelve, dine with the Priests of the Seminary at their Country House. The Bishops of Kingston and Montreal, present. They come out here by way of relaxation every Tuesday, weather permitting, and have a very pleasant garden with plenty of shade. There is a school attached with about 150 boys which we also visited. They have a band which attends on these days. It was a long business for we did not get home till near four, but on the whole I passed a pleasant day.

WEDNESDAY, JULY 4

Sir John Colborne arrives this morning at seven. Awoke by the salute fired for him. Bad reports this morning from Upper Canada for tho' it appears that Morreau and the Band that attacked the Lancers are for the most part taken, yet it seems that Refugees and others have been crossing in considerable numbers farther west and the 34th and 43rd Regiments have both been moved in consequence. We are ordered to send a Captain with 100 men to Kingston tomorrow morning. In the afternoon, in consequence of reports from the Vermont frontier, we are all ordered to be within hail. Another attack is said to be intended from Missisquoi Bay. General parade at five to read the sentences upon four men convicted of desertion. Three transported for life, one for 14 years.

THURSDAY, JULY 5

Captain Speer, Lieutenant Wilkieson and Lord Aberdour march this morning with 100 men for Kingston. The *John Bull* arrives at six with Lord Durham etc. She anchors off the centre of the town. Go on board at ten. Lord Durham shows me the dispatches from Sir G[eorge] Arthur. The alarm is occasioned by reports from a confidential agent of the American Government who states that there are not less than 4,000 people along the line ready to invade the upper Province, and from Colonel Maitland, in command at London, who states that 1,500 men are moving on his post. The 34th Regiment had been sent up from Toronto to reinforce him and the 43rd moved up from Kingston. The *British America* arrives at seven with a Squadron of the King's Dragoon Guards also for Toronto. The alarm of an attack from Missisquoi Bay seems to have been without foundation. I cannot think there is likely to be anything in the lower Province. Land on the Island with my sister, etc. at twelve and caught in a thunder storm. Manage to get on board again tolerably dry, taking shelter in various places. The *Medea* arrives at one with the Admiral. Lord Durham's landing postponed till tomorrow in consequence of the rain. Dine with Caroline on board the Steamer at six. Row up the river in the evening and return home at eleven.

FRIDAY, JULY 6

Lord Durham lands today at twelve and is received most enthusiastically. He receives an address from the English Merchants etc. at three and gives an answer with which they are all satisfied. His coming has already had the effect I was sure it would produce and the feeling towards him in the high English party [has improved]. Dine again on board. Mr. Jones of the 43rd arrives with dispatches from Sir John Colborne. In consequence of what he says Lord Durham determines on taking the ladies with him. Mr. Jones says what we hear here is all humbug.

SATURDAY, JULY 7

Reviewed at four this afternoon on the old race course – tremendously hot and the worst ground for working anything but Light Infantry, I ever saw. However, it all looks very well. Dine again on board.

The heat wave continued on Sunday. Instead of going to church the Greys read prayers at home. In the evening they dined on board the 'John Bull' with Lord Durham's suite, but returned home early and Colonel Grey wrote again to his father.

> Montreal,
> July 8, 1838.

My Dear Father,

We have had no farther accounts from England since I last wrote, but we are now in daily expectation of hearing, and I need not say how more than anxiously we are looking for the next account. When I think of what news we may *possibly* receive I agree with Louisa in feeling a disinclination to write, but, as I will not anticipate any such misfortune, I think you would not wish me to lose the opportunity of telling you, as far as I can, what occurred since I last wrote.

My last letter was from Quebec and the State Prisoners had just been disposed of. At Quebec, as I told you, People were generally satisfied, but on my return here two or three days afterwards I found a widely different feeling existing. While the French party were very much downcast, particularly at the Act concerning Papineau and the other Refugees who had fled from justice, the high English party were discontented to the greatest degree and declared that they considered the Act equivalent to one of general amnesty, and saw in the proceeding a commencement of the same sort of 'conciliatory' policy which had been the fault of Lord Gosford's administration. To such an extent had this feeling spread, that on Lambton's arrival here last Thursday he asked me whether I thought there was any chance of his being insulted on landing, and it was only on being assured by others that no such thing was to be expected that he resolved to make a public entry. This he did on Friday, when he met with really a most enthusiastic reception and I am happy to say that his coming has been attended, as I was always sure it would, with the best possible effect. His answer to the address, both the formal one and the little speech he made after it, and still more, his civility to the leading men of the English party and his open manner with them have completely gained them, and they seem now disposed to place as much confidence in him as they before appeared to feel the contrary. I really hope that in this Lower Province he is taking a line which promises to be successful. The great cause of discontent here arose from Girouard, one of the Agitators of St. Benoit, and one or two others who had been active in the Insurrection, not having been included with the others who were either banished or whose return was made penal, and there seems to have been some mistake in not having mentioned them in some way, but Girouard did not plead guilty and therefore could not be dealt with like the rest, and People are now satisfied, since they know that he is to be reserved for the decision of the Government at home.

From the Upper Province we have been disturbed with all sorts of reports which have, at all events, had the effect of causing a considerable movement of troops. The 43rd was sent up to Kingston from hence at a few hours' notice and have since been pushed up to Niagara where they are now encamped with Sir John Colborne. The 34th have been sent on from Toronto to reinforce the 32nd at London in consequence of reports from Colonel Maitland. I have sent 100 effective men to Kingston and tomorrow send 90 more to Brockville, and 100 men of the King's Dragoon Guards are also gone to Toronto, which gives them now in Upper Canada six complete Regiments exclusive of Artillery and the detachments from my Regiment and the Dragoons – a Force, I believe, more than ample for any emergency. But there certainly has been some ground for alarm. The attack upon the Militia Lancers near Short Hills seemed serious at first, though the number of the Banditti who crossed over instead of being 1,200 does not appear to have exceeded 100, and though instead of the 1,500 men who alarmed Colonel Maitland so much at London I cannot make out that there were ever more than 300, and those I am told have dispersed. It is evident, however, that there is still a sufficient force of Refugees and Sympathizers in Arms along the frontier to keep us in hot water, and it must continue so till the American Government, now that they have got their Bill giving an increase to the Army through Congress, take more effectual measures for dispersing these pirates. I am happy to say that Lambton is convinced of the necessity of taking summary measures with whatever People may henceforward be taken in Arms and quite disapproves of Sir George Arthur's having handed over to the ordinary tribunals the men captured who were concerned in the attack on the Lancers.

He goes up with Louisa etc. the day after tomorrow to Niagara, where he is to meet Sir John Colborne and Sir G[eorge]

Arthur, and we accompany them. There was considerable doubt for some time how far it would be prudent to take the Ladies up for fear of an attack from Bill Johnston, but with the escort we take all the way and the patrols of Armed Steamers on the river on both sides there could be no danger, and so Sir John Colborne has written word. Besides nothing has been heard for some time of that worthy and I am inclined to believe, since the threatened crusade against him by both Governments, that he has left the Thousand Isles.

I do not think, however, we have yet done with Upper Canada and I fear the spirit there is far from good. The Volunteers I hear have positively refused to turn out again unless insured a service, with pay of course, of six months. This shows their principle of action.

I have written this in a great hurry since returning from dinner on board Lambton's Steamer and I must now break off as it is late and I must be up by six.

Give our best love to my Mother and the rest, and believe me ever, My Dear Father,

Your most affectionate son,
C. Grey.

MONDAY, JULY 9

Levee at two. Immensely full, and tremendously hot. Large dinners on board every day, but *very* bad. The Russian system does not suit without more servants, particularly Carvers, and more dishes of each sort than they can cook on board the Steamer, and everybody goes home complaining of being starved.

CHAPTER IV

Lord Durham's Visit to Upper Canada

The Greys rose early on Tuesday morning, July 10th. There was no time for breakfast as it had been arranged that they would join Lord Durham's party when it landed on the wharf.

As the boat carrying the Governor General and his family pulled towards the shore the 'John Bull' fired a farewell salute, in which the battery on St. Helen's Island joined. On shore, Charles Grey's thoughts may have turned to Upper Canada. He had readily accepted Lord Durham's invitation to accompany him, for he had become intrigued by the reports arriving from the upper province, and he was anxious to see if Durham's presence could quiet the unrest which appeared to be so prevalent.

TUESDAY, JULY 10

Start this morning at a quarter before seven for Lachine, en route for Niagara, etc. Lord Durham and family, Sir C[harles] Paget, Captain Pring, *Inconstant*, Lieutenants Otway, F. and Bagot, *Medea*, A.D.C.s, Colonel Couper, C[harles] Buller, and ourselves. Rendezvous appointed at the wharf opposite the Quebec Barrack Gate at half past six, and off at a quarter before seven. An escort from [the] Montreal Mounted Volunteers accompanies us. In addition to Lord Durham's own carriage, the General's, which takes Caroline and Mary Lambton, and a van with luggage, there are 10 stages (!) with the suite servants, etc. Reach Lachine, nine miles, at nine o'clock where we embark in the *Henry Brougham* Steamer for Cascades, taking on the riding horses, horses for Lord Durham's carriage and van, and six of the Montreal Cavalry as an escort. Breakfast on board and reach Cascades a little before twelve. We are here again transferred to stages – all who have horses, including the young ladies, riding – to go 16 miles to Coteau du Lac. I ride Colonel Couper's horse. Towards the end of the ride it comes on to rain furiously and all of those on horseback are wet through. Embark at Coteau a little before three in the *Neptune* Steamer for Cornwall, taking on board as before carriages, horses and Mounted Escort, in addition to a guard of 40 men of my Regiment under Lieutenant Stack, who are to see us in safety to Kingston. Get on dry things and dine on board at half past four. Reach Cornwall at half past seven where Lord Durham is received with a guard of honour – Colonel Turner, an old acquaintance of mine in Portugal, etc., etc. Lord Durham's reception very warm. An address is presented to him to which he returns rather a cold answer. My escort is sent on in waggons 12 miles, to Dickinson's Landing, to be ready for us tomorrow. Shortly after they start a most awful thunderstorm with the heaviest rain commences, to all of which they must have been exposed.

WEDNESDAY, JULY 11

Get up this morning at three in order to start at four for Dickinson's Landing. Such beds as we had last night! Straw mattresses, stinking to a degree and overrun with bugs and all kinds of horrible insects. Early as our hour for getting up was, I thought it would never arrive. A showery morning, but the young Ladies and A.D.C.s ride notwithstanding. An infamous

road, but very pretty, particularly when you reach the Long
Sault, about a mile from Dickinson's Landing. It goes all the
way along the St. Lawrence Canal, an immense undertaking
upon which upwards of £300,000 have already been spent, and
which they are petitioning for a grant from Government of
£50,000 more to complete. It is upwards of 50 feet wide and is
intended as a ship canal to connect Lake St. Louis with Ontario.
It was part of the subject of the Cornwall address, complaining
that in the Lower Province no steps had been taken to carry the
whole scheme into effect.

Embark in the *Brockville* as before about half past seven.
Find that my escort did not get in till half past one this morning –
drenched beyond description. Reach Prescott about half past
one. The passage up from Dickinson's Landing averages about
seven hours, while down it is only three. An excellent moderate
address is here presented to Lord Durham. If the same feeling
prevailed universally, there would be little difficulty in settling
matters. Remain at Prescott about an hour when we start for
Kingston. While we are at dinner pass Brockville. Lord Durham
does not mean to visit this place. It is considered the Head
Quarters of the Orangemen, or Ultra Loyalist party, and he
fears an address to which he would feel himself obliged to give
a sharp answer. I think he has decided wrong, and the strongest
reason for going there is to be found in the idea that prevails
that the feeling is not so good there as elsewhere. At the commencement of the Thousand Islands, shortly above Brockville,
we meet the *Experiment*, hired Steamer, with a guard of the
83rd on board. Captain Sandom comes on board us. No further
news. He has about 100 men in various boats about the Islands,
in search, in concert with the Americans, of Bill Johnston, but
I can hardly imagine the possibility of catching him if he is
determined not to be caught. It is impossible to conceive a place
more formed by nature for the resort of a buccaneer than these
Islands. Endless in number (being nearly 3,000) and ranging in
size from mere rocks to Islands of three and four miles in

length, they are mostly very steep and rocky, and densely covered with wood to the very water's edge. They abound in coves and creeks, and the channels between many of them, tho' very deep, are often barely wide enough for such boats as Johnston is said to have at his command. In short, both for concealment and escape if discovered, a better place for his purposes could not have been found. They say he is very popular even among those who do not belong to his band, and is connived at by many whom he assists by smuggling and this accounts for the large reward offered for him having failed in its effect. 'Johnston, or the Pirate of the Thousand Isles' is sure to be out, perhaps by this, at The Adelphi or some of the minor Theatres.

Colonel Maitland's alarm seems to have been without foundation. At least Captain Sandom says he has heard nothing more of it.

Reach Kingston at half past eleven. Lord Durham and family go on shore and sleep at Macdonald's Hotel. Caroline and myself change to the *Cobourg* Steamer, in which we are to go tomorrow up to Niagara, and get tolerably clean berths and have the good fortune to get the Steamer to ourselves.

THURSDAY, JULY 12

A great piece of work this morning in consequence of the neglect of Colonel Dundas, Commanding [the] 83rd here and the post, to come or to send a guard of honour. Clearly a mistake, however, and it is all put right. Visit the Dock Yard where the Admiral's flag had been hoisted, under a salute, on board the *Experiment*. With the exception of one good shore, which is to be converted into winter quarters for the Seamen employed on the lakes, it is in a terribly ruinous condition. Captain Sandom's pennant is hoisted in a vessel still only in frame (!) as she has been I believe for the last 20 years and probably may be 20 more. This phantom ship is dignified with the name of

Niagara.[1] A gun boat is building here and several have been fitted out and sent among the Islands.

While in the Dock Yard Captain Sandom receives a letter from Mr. Leary, commanding the *Bullfrog*, to say that a woman had given information that Johnston with two of his followers was at a house, which she pointed out, on Grindstone Island and that he was going in company with the Americans to make a thorough search. This is magnified by the Captain of the Steamer, who brought the letter, into an actual engagement with Johnston who only escaped as the Lieutenant of the Navy was in the act of cutting him down, by the former tumbling over his own Scabbard. One of his followers, however, was killed and a boatload of pistols was taken!! Mr. Leary writes word that nothing can be more cordial than the co-operation of the Americans and that he thinks they may be depended upon. From the Dock Yard we visit the fort above it where the detached Company of my Regiment is quartered. A very pretty work capable of containing 350 men in casemates. The detachment looks very well. Conroy and I eat a Beef Steak with the Officers.

At two there is a grand turn out for his Excellency's embarkation – Streets lined, guards of honour, etc., etc. An escort of Sappers relieves mine which is to return, or rather which has returned in the same Steamer to Brockville. In other respects we embark the same cortège as before in the *Cobourg* Steamer, Captain Harper, a Lieutenant R.N., for Niagara. The passage is usually made in 17 hours so we may expect to reach the river by seven tomorrow morning. It turns very cold in the afternoon, and the Admiral and myself are forced to cloak for our customary after dinner cigar.

---

[1] The name *Niagara* was not given to this vessel until 1838. She was originally named *Prince Regent* and participated in actions at Sackets Harbor in 1812 and 1813. She was renamed *General Beresford* in 1813, and *Netley* in 1814. In 1843 she was decommissioned and removed from the Navy List. See C. P. Stacey, 'The Ships of the British Squadron on Lake Ontario, 1812-1814,' *Canadian Historical Review*, Vol. XXXIV (1953), pp. 311-23. A previous *Niagara* (originally *Royal George*) was sold 'in frame on slip' for £7:10:0 in 1837.

FRIDAY, JULY 13

At seven this morning, as we expected, we make the entrance of the Niagara River, between Fort Niagara, U.S., and Fort George, U.C. Stop at the wharf under a salute from Mississagua, a bad fort about a mile down which is being put into a defensible condition, and where the escort of Sappers we have now on board is to be quartered for the present. Mr. Cavendish sent on shore to enquire after Sir John Colborne and we proceed seven miles up the river to Queenston. The sail up the river so far is beautiful and the view looking up towards General Brock's monument very fine. Breakfast on board while we are waiting for Sir John Colborne whom we find that we missed at Fort George. He arrives about half past nine and the whole party, with the exception of my sister and Caroline, ride to the Falls. The Clifton House is taken here for Lord Durham at $150 [?] a day. . . .

Lord Durham is, as usual, engaged seeing quantities of people. I go out with Captain Pring after luncheon. Visit the table rock, etc., and walk round by the Hill where the 43rd are encamped. A very large dinner and the day concluded by a cigar under the Verandah with the Admiral.

SATURDAY, JULY 14

A start made today at ten o'clock by [the] Governor General, Sir G[eorge] Arthur and Sir J[ohn] Colborne, etc. to visit Fort Erie opposite Navy Island. I desert the party, preferring a visit to Mackenzie's camp[2] to going 14 miles over a bad road to Fort Erie. I had enough of the North American roads and stages in

2 After the failure of the rebellion, Mackenzie fled to the United States and endeavoured to raise a force to invade Upper Canada. He established his headquarters on Navy Island in the Niagara River about two miles above the falls, and set up a provisional government. A large body of Canadian militia was assembled at Chippawa but, because Sir Francis Bond Head was unwilling to take the military and diplomatic risks involved, it was not permitted to attack the island. Mackenzie evacuated Navy Island on January 14, 1838, and it was occupied by the Canadian militia the next day.

my journey from Whitehall to Albany. Manley Power of the
85th accompanies me, and we walk round the Island. Mackenzie's Batteries, Sundry places, and head Quarters are pointed
out to us. They had, towards the termination of their occupation of the Island, cut down trees all round with their branches
pointed outwards to form an abatis to prevent troops from
Landing. But it was all nothing and one good company ought
at any moment to have been sufficient to root out these robbers.
An excellent landing Place at the upper end of the Island – not
the slightest risk from the current, which on the contrary
would have assisted the operation much – three armed Schooners
and 150 boats prepared – with from four to five thousand
Militiamen assembled and kept for six weeks watching without
daring to attack an accessible Island, garrisoned, *at most*, by
500 Raggamuffins!! It is an eternal disgrace to Colonel MacNab[3]
and Sir F[rancis] Head, and such is the opinion of every Volunteer I have spoken to, officer and man, in the neighbourhood.

                                                    Niagara,
                                                    July 15, 1838.

My Dear Father,

    I have nothing new to tell you as to the state of the Country.
As I expected we have found that all the reports we had heard
of rebel and Patriot movements in the west were immensely
exaggerated, where they were not actual inventions. Instead of
1,200 men who were said to have been engaged in the surprise
of the Lancers at Short Hills, I cannot make out that there were
ever more than 60, most of whom have been taken, and of the
1,500 men that Colonel Maitland mentioned in his dispatch as
marching against his post, it is not *clearly* ascertained that even
42, the number they have now dwindled to, were ever actually

---

[3] Sir Allan Napier MacNab commanded the Gore militia during the rebellion.
   In 1838 he was the commanding officer of the Canadian militia on the
   Niagara frontier and was knighted for his services.

assembled. In short, though it is said, and one cannot help believing those who state it, that there is a great deal of disaffection in this Province, the Country is at this moment in perfect tranquillity. And, as the American Government does appear now to be exerting itself in earnest to prevent aggression from the other side of the lines, I hope there is little chance of a renewal of disturbances. Bill Johnston still holds out somewhere in the Thousand Islands and in spite of the united exertions of the English and American Boats, who are cruising in concert and acting, I hear, most cordially together, I do not think he will be caught. . . . It seems too absurd that one man should keep a whole Country in hot water, but so it is, and till he is caught there is no doubt that the navigation of the river in this neighbourhood is unsafe.

It is satisfactory to think that my journey to Washington is considered to have been most useful. Sir George Arthur says there is a most marked difference in the conduct of the American authorities since that time and on all hands I hear that they have never, till now, been sincere in their exertions to preserve the peace of the frontier. On this side People are getting much more confidence and the feeling generally seems much better between the opposite sides of the river.

After a brief description of the trip from Montreal to Cornwall the letter continues:

We got to Cornwall, where we slept, at half past seven, where Lambton received an address to which he gave rather a cross answer, in the course of which he found great fault with Sir F[rancis] Head for sending away the troops. I agree with him perfectly in this, but that was not the fault of the Volunteers and it is rather hard to snub them for being proud of the services which they certainly did render. It is the only answer of Lambton's with which I have not been quite pleased. In general they have been excellent and the other parts of this one were very good.

Tuesday, July 17.

The bag is to be closed this evening, and I must therefore finish the letter which I began on Sunday. Contrary to my hopes there is not yet any further arrival from England, and we are still doomed to suspense.

I have not told you anything of our journey, or given you any description of the Country we have passed through, or the 'Grand falls'. . . . I will only say that *at first* I was disappointed, but that every time you look at them you are more and more struck with the Falls. Of course we have been to all the proper points of view. . . . I went this morning under the fall, as everybody either does it, or says so. It is a disagreeable, nervous undertaking and you get a tremendous ducking without being able to see anything. The effect of Lambton's reception was very fine – a Guard of honour from the 43rd, and a salute fired by the Artillery over the river, with an immense crowd of People from both sides, added much to the beauty of the scenery. . . .

We go tomorrow to Toronto and I believe we shall be back at Montreal by Monday.

I forgot to tell you that they got yesterday the news of the Capture of one of Johnston's boats and two of his Crew and that they had information which was hoped might lead to his own Capture. . . .

Give my best love to all, and believe me ever, My Dear Father,

Your most affectionate son,
C. Grey.

FRIDAY, JULY 27

My journal has been neglected for the last ten days, and I must trust to memory to bring it up.

On Sunday, the 15th, we all went over after dinner, in full

uniform, to the American side, crossed to Goat Island, ascended the tower, etc., visiting all the regular views of the Falls. The best point of view I still think that from the Pavilion on the top of the Hill. You see the whole of the American fall, Goat Island, the rapids on both sides, and get a finer idea of the Magnitude of the Horseshoe Fall, by seeing the waters drawn together, and thunder as it were in immense masses over the rock into an abyss the bottom of which you cannot see, and which is lost in one mass of vapour. Everybody was very civil to us on the other side, and we met few people who did not take off their hats to Lord Durham.

On Monday, the 16th, I went with the Admiral, Captain Pring, and Sir J[ohn] Colborne and staff to Allanburgh Mills, midway on the Welland Canal between Lakes Erie and Ontario, from whence we rode two miles to Port Robinson and thence proceeded in a track-boat twelve miles to Port Colborne, late Gravelly Bay, on Lake Erie. Lord Durham was to have gone to judge of the necessity of improving the water communication between the lakes, but was prevented by illness. At Port Colborne we find the *Brock* Schooner, purchased and armed by our Government, but are disappointed to find that Captain Sandom is gone in the Steamer, in which we had hoped to return to Chippawa, to the Grand River. We consequently return to Port Robinson as we came and very slow work it was in consequence of the tow rope breaking every minute. Major Young, commanding the U.S. troops at Niagara, and another American dine with Lord Durham. The former a gentlemanlike man.

TUESDAY, JULY 17

The 43rd, half a troop of the King's Dragoon Guards, and two guns are reviewed this morning at eleven o'clock – an immense quantity of Americans from the opposite side, Buffalo, etc., as well as a great number of our People from all parts. The day is too hot, but the sight is beautiful and the Field Day, as one of Booth's is always sure to be, excessively pretty, tho' the number of spectators spoils the effect. After it is over Caroline and myself and the young Ladies drive to the Whirlpool, about three miles. One of the things best worth seeing at Niagara. The river is here compressed into a very narrow space between two high hills and is consequently of immense depth and great rapidity, and the channel thro' the hills turning at the same time nearly at right angles, an extraordinary Whirlpool is formed in a sort of basin at the turn. The banks are nearly perpendicular and covered with wood and retain the same character nearly all the way to Queenston. . . .

At four o'clock Lord Durham gives a sort of cold dinner to about 200 People from both sides of the river and after dinner the room is cleared for dancing, which is kept up by the English till ten o'clock. The Yankees clear out about eight. Very well done considering the want of means.

WEDNESDAY, JULY 18

Leave Niagara this morning at seven o'clock in stages for Queenston, a riding party going on at half past six to meet us at Fort George. The Admiral remains behind ill. At Queenston embark once more in the *Cobourg* for Toronto. Put in on the way at Port Dalhousie, the Ontario end of the Welland Canal. Reach Toronto about four where a grand procession and reception [has] been prepared by Sir G[eorge] Arthur – Trades with their banners, Firemen Companies (These beautifully turned out), Triumphal Arches, etc., etc. Go first to the Council Chamber, where Lord Durham receives and answers an address and makes a short speech to the People. Thence proceed round the town to Government House where Sir George puts up everybody but the A.D.C.s very comfortably. A large dinner in the evening to near 60 people. Intensely hot.

Toronto is the best built town I have seen in Canada. The principal street is really a very fine one.

THURSDAY, JULY 19

Leave Toronto today at two o'clock. Processions arranged as on landing, but unfortunately as Lord Durham was on the way to the Steamer, the heaviest storm I ever saw in my life came on – Thunder and lightning with rain more like a water spout than anything else. It is impossible to conceive People more drenched than they were. I escaped by walking down quickly beforehand. A succession of storms in the course of the night and a strong head wind which prevents our reaching Kingston before eleven o'clock.

FRIDAY, JULY 20

Streets lined and guard of honour on the Quay. After receiving an address at the Hotel, Lord Durham again embarks about one in the *Cobourg* which is to take us on to Prescott where we are to change into the *Brockville* to sleep. Meet Mr. Leary of the *Bullfrog* here who tells us that Johnston had had a very narrow escape. The concentrated search of Grindstone Island, which we heard of as being intended on our way up, had taken place. It was so far successful that he was surprised, but made his escape by speed and knowledge of the woods, losing his boat and Arms, and leaving two of his crew behind, Prisoners. If the American Party had been at its appointed post in time, they would all have been taken.

Reach Prescott about half past seven. The *Brockville*, however, does not arrive till near eleven, for which Captain Brush gets well rowed. A deputation arrives in her from Brockville with a moderate address to Lord Durham. I am sorry he did not go there. I believe the fear of an intemperate address was perfectly visionary.

SATURDAY, JULY 21

Start at four this morning, taking in tow the Bateau in which we are to go down the Rapids to Cornwall. Get the baggage trans-shipped and embark ourselves about five miles above Dickinson's Landing. The Escort (of my Regiment under Lord Aberdour from Kingston) and servants go by land in stages. Disappointed in these Rapids, having heard so much of the long Sault, but by going down the Channel on the American side we avoid every[thing] in the shape of danger. It is in fact nothing. Reach Cornwall in about an hour and three quarters! about ten minutes before the land Party. Colonel Turner receives us here with his guard of honour of Cornwall Volunteers. Embark in the *Neptune* without landing and proceed at once for Coteau du Lac where we again take Bateaux to shoot the Rapids for Beauharnois. We go in one with part of the Escort while the rest of it and the servants go in another. These Rapids are much more deserving the name than those we shot in the morning. At Coteau it is nervous enough, having been prevented taking the best channel by the violence of the wind, and we only just miss a dangerous rock. The Cedars is also a fine and rather nervous rapid. The lower part of it, where the different streams meet, being very rough and we manage to get into the rough water. The Split rock rapid is the next, also rather a nervous one, and here again we are driven by the wind so far into the stream that we cannot make the boat channel and are forced to go down the rougher one meant for rafts only. However, we shoot them all in perfect safety, without even getting the least wet. The Cascades rapid we shoot delightfully under sail and the wind thence being fair for Beauharnois we reach that place exactly in three hours from Coteau. Mr. Ellice comes out to meet us in a bark canoe, belonging to the Hudson's Bay Company, manned by Indians who come paddling up at a great rate singing the whole time. It has the most extraordinary effect possible to see a canoe of this sort coming up to you. The short red bladed paddles flashing in and out of the water incessantly in time to the music. It is like an animal with so many legs on each side.

The Ellices turn out of their own house to make room for us.

The Escort is lodged in a barn and we are all made tolerably comfortable.

SUNDAY, JULY 22

Attend the Presbyterian Church, the only English one here, most of the settlers being Scotch or descendants of Scotchmen.

MONDAY, JULY 23

Lord Durham receives addresses from different bodies. Too unwell to go today. In the evening we drive twelve miles along the river and on our way back stop at the Point de Bouillon to see Sturgeon speared, or rather hooked. One man holds a torch made of long thin laths while the spearer, with a sort of gaff, hooks the Sturgeon out of the Stream. He gets five. We began too soon, there being still a little daylight in the west. Had it been quite dark, he said he might have got as many as fifteen or twenty.

TUESDAY, JULY 24

Captain Pring and myself leave Beauharnois at 11.30 in the Hudson's Bay Canoe and reach Mr. Keith's[4] House (the Agent for the Company) at Lachine at half past one. A very heavy shower during the passage. The Steamer arrives with the rest of the Party in half an hour and I ride with the young ladies and A.D.C.s into Montreal. The most drenching rain I ever remember nearly the whole day. Dine on board the *John Bull*.

WEDNESDAY, JULY 25

Lord Durham, etc. go to the Seminary for the distribution of prizes to the Scholars. Take the Regiment out to practice Field Day for tomorrow. Dine on board as usual.

4 James Keith.

THURSDAY, JULY 26

Brigade Field Day at eight A.M. I command the troops. Well devised Field Day, but badly executed. Commanding Officers slow and General interfering. Dine on board the *John Bull* at four. Bid the Durhams goodbye at five and they sail for Quebec a few minutes afterwards. Walk out with Caroline in the evening. Call on the Arthur Lennoxes, etc.

FRIDAY, JULY 27

Having now brought up my journal to this day I will try and keep it regularly. The Estcourts, A[rthur] Lennoxes, Sir H[ew] Dalrymple, and Lord Aberdour dine with us.

Montreal,
Tuesday Evening, July 24.

My Dear Father,

There are letters in town to the 15th June, but by some mistake in the manner of sending them we have none, with the exception of one from Lady Farquhar[5] to Caroline dated the 6th, later than the 1st,—and by *we* I mean all the Durham Family as well as ourselves. I have no doubt *particular* care has been taken of our letters which is the reason that we are the only People who have not received them; for there are bags and bags of letters to other People under cover to Lambton. The one letter received by Caroline has, however, been a great comfort, as it announces that on the 5th, four days later than the former accounts, little Mary continued to improve. It has put me, what I was not before, quite in spirits about her, and I now look forward with confidence to the letters which we hope to receive, being sure they will contain continued good accounts.

We returned here this afternoon, having since we left Niagara spent a day at Toronto, three hours at Kingston, and near three

5 Charles Grey's mother-in-law.

days at Beauharnois with Edward Ellice. At every place Lambton received addresses in much the same style and to all he gave much the same, and I think very good, answers. And it is so far most satisfactory to think that, as well as one can judge, his professions have been well and cordially received, and that he is certainly popular with all parties.

The Country remains perfectly quiet and I do not think there is the least chance of any further outbreaks for the present. In the Thousand Islands Johnston has had a narrow escape owing to the Americans being behind their time, though they say it was owing to us being *before* ours. He was surprised with his crew, two of whom were taken, as was his boat, with sundry Arms, etc. Johnston himself and the others only getting off by speed of foot and knowledge of the country, in a chase in which both pursuers and pursued threw away their Arms for the sake of speed. Our seamen were so near Johnston that he could not stop for a shoe he lost in running. It was on an American Island. Prisoners and Spoil were, therefore, according to agreement, given up to them, and there is little doubt, even if there was more evidence against them than there appears to be, that the two Prisoners will be acquitted.

I wrote you a long rigmarole from Niagara about our movements. I believe I quite forgot to mention in it that I had paid a visit to Navy Island, walked round it, and had the situation of Mackenzie's Camp, of his guns, etc., etc., accurately pointed out to me. I have also had a great deal of conversation with both Officers and Men of the Volunteers who, under the command of the doughty MacNab, *watched* the Island for near six weeks, and I must say that the *universal* complaint of these Volunteers agrees entirely with the opinion I formed at once on seeing the Island and its situation – that anything more disgraceful to the Authorities in this Province than the occupation of that Island by Mackenzie for six weeks could not possibly have happened. I will be bound to say *one Company* of any Regiment in this Country would at any moment have been sufficient. There is the finest landing place in the world at the head of the Island – *not the slightest danger* from the neighbourhood of the Falls – the best possible place of embarkation three quarters of a mile above it – and there were 800 volunteers for the service with three Armed Schooners and 150 boats prepared for their transport! And yet we are to allow these Rebels to derive all the moral advantage to be gained by bearing the whole British force in the Upper Province for six weeks!

We have had most changeable weather during our trip – both cold and very hot. On the whole I have enjoyed it, but I cannot say I am sorry to be back in my own house, and I shall not now leave it again, with my own consent, for some time. There is a chance, however, of the Regiment being ordered up the Country as I hear the 73rd are arrived from Halifax and I do not know where they can find room for them in this garrison, where I hear they are to be quartered, without moving us. If it was not for being near Louisa, etc., I should not care about this, as, from what little I have seen, I think I should prefer the upper Province. Toronto is infinitely the best town I have seen in Canada, and the Country generally looks much more civilized.

Lambton has been very unwell, and consequently very irritable for the last three days. Having nothing to do with him he is always good natured to us, but I daily thank my stars that I *have* nothing to do with him. It is astonishing, taking everything of importance as coolly as he does, to observe how trifles upset him. With it all, however, he is very good natured to those about him, and I think is liked by them all, in spite of his *occasional* bursts. Louisa and the rest, and also Caroline, are all quite well.

I will write more comfortably in a day or two, at present in addition to being hurried I am both sleepy and tired. I must therefore end, and with best love to all, am ever, My Dear Father,

Your most affectionate son,
C. Grey.

CHAPTER V

_____

A Lull Before the Storm

With the departure of Lord Durham for Quebec, the Greys dropped into a more quiet way of life. Colonel Grey was able to devote himself to his regimental duties and much of his time was spent in routine military administration, inspections, parades, and manoeuvres. Cricket matches, pigeon shoots, and hunting trips provided occasional diversions, and during the latter part of August a horse-racing meet was held, the feature of which was the race for the Governor General's Cup presented by Lord Durham.

Some evenings Grey and his wife dined out or had guests in to dinner, but they spent many quietly at home together, Charles reading to Caroline. Their reading reflected a wide range of interests extending all the way from Sir Walter Scott's 'Rokeby' to Russell's 'Modern Europe', and theological discourses. For his own instruction Grey read the 'Duke of Wellington's Dispatches'. In late summer touring theatrical companies offered additional evening entertainment at the Theatre Royal.

As Grey had anticipated, his father did not entirely approve of either his mission to Washington or his membership in Durham's Special Council. Lord Grey recognized that his son-in-law was a man of exceptional ability, but on numerous occasions he had been made acutely aware of his impetuous, explosive temperament. In the critical Canadian situation he was very much afraid that a close identification with Lord

Durham would jeopardize both his son's military career and his position at court. 'I foresaw from the beginning', he reminded Charles, 'the probability of much difficulty in the new arrangements and therefore was anxious that you should stick to your Regiment, your proper place, the duties of which would furnish a sufficient excuse for declining any employment Lambton might propose to you.'[1] In Lord Grey's opinion Durham should have communicated with the American Government through the regular channels rather than sending his own special emissary to Washington. He regretted that Charles had served as a member of the Special Council, which passed the ordinances relating to the rebellion prisoners, because 'however right and expedient the thing done might be, the manner of doing it could not fail to produce the effect here which we have witnessed'. Concern for his son's future led Lord Grey constantly to urge him to 'keep as clear as possible of all political employment and confine yourself as much as you can to the command of your Regiment'.[2]

In answer to his father's warnings Grey provided a detailed analysis of the American problem and the benefits which had been derived from his mission.[3] He also endeavoured to explain the circumstances which had made it impossible for him to refuse to serve in the Special Council or to retire from it despite his wish to do so.

During August and the first part of September, rumours of planned uprisings are recorded in Grey's journal and letters with increasing frequency, but these he consistently discounted. He

[1] The 2nd Earl Grey to Charles Grey, July 4, 1838.
[2] The 2nd Earl Grey to Charles Grey, August 19, 1838.
[3] After receiving Charles' explanation Lord Grey agreed that 'all's well that ends well'. He was pleased that Charles had had an opportunity to see so much of the country and to meet the leading political figures in the United States. Although he was certain that the manner in which Charles had performed his mission 'cannot fail to meet with approbation,' Lord Grey still adhered to his original opinion that Durham would have been more prudent to have used the regular channels of communication. See the 2nd Earl Grey to Charles Grey, July 12, 1838.

anticipated nothing more than 'isolated outrages in different
parts against those who are obnoxious to either *party'.*

SATURDAY, JULY 28

Inspected today by General Clitherow. Sees us at half past
nine A.M. by Companies, in heavy marching order, in the
Barrack Square. He then inspects the Books and this first operation lasts till one o'clock. In the afternoon he sees us in the
Champ de Mars where we perform a few manoeuvres, quick
and tolerably well. Weather intensely hot. Dine with the 24th
in the evening. While on Parade in the morning, hear of the
arrival of the *Royal William*, which sailed from Liverpool on
the 5th, bringing the news of the Coronation. The brevets much
smaller than expected – very few Peers made or promoted.
Among the latter Lord Mulgrave to be Marquis of Normanby! The
Royal William was 19 days on her passage having had very heavy
weather and foul winds.

SUNDAY, JULY 29

A fine breeze, but still intensely hot. Read prayers at home and
go in the afternoon to Church with the Regiment. The Admiral
calls, having just arrived with his son from Niagara. General
Patterson of the Pennsylvanian Militia brings me a letter of introduction from Mr. Poinsett, Secretary at War. He is come to
Canada for the sake of seeing the troops.

MONDAY, JULY 30

Walk to the Exchange Coffee house to call on General Patterson and caught in a most tremendous shower. Take him round
the dinners at half past one. He dines with us at the Mess in the
evening and seems on the whole much pleased. The *Gazette* contains a debate from the London Papers on the appointment of

Mr. Turton[4] which will not please Lord Durham. Lord Melbourne had stated that he was gone to Canada without an appointment and without the slightest intention on the part of Lord Durham to appoint him to anything, and now, in answer to Lord Wharncliffe, he states that he had so expected and that he has since heard of his appointment with 'equal surprise and concern'. Lord Brougham, with the professed intention of doing *justice* (!) to Mr. Turton, gives a whole history of the transaction, with which probably few people were acquainted, but which must now be pretty well known.

There will be an explosion at Quebec when this debate arrives there.

TUESDAY, JULY 31

Muster on the Champ de Mars at six A.M. and afterwards perform a few manoeuvres for General Patterson. Sufficiently ill done, tho' probably well enough to please a Militia General. Drove with Major Denny in his car round the mountain. Dine with the 7th Hussars.

Montreal,

July 31, 1838.

My Dear Father,

Papers brought by the *Royal William* arrived in Town the day before yesterday, as late as the 3rd July from London, but we are still without any letters later than the 6th June, to which

---

[4] Thomas Turton, a lifelong friend of Lord Durham, became a social outcast when his wife successfully sued him for divorce and named her sister as co-respondent. Although Turton had lived an exemplary life for more than fifteen years since the divorce scandal, Lord Melbourne raised strong objections when Durham made known his intention of appointing him a legal adviser on his staff. Durham remained firm, however, and a compromise was reached whereby Turton was not to receive any appointment from the British government, but Durham could use his services in Canada either unofficially or by appointing him to office on his own responsibility.

date Caroline has one from Lady Farquhar, all our others being no later than the 31st May.

Though Lady Farquhar's letter gave a much improved account of Mary to the 5th June, there was still enough to make us very anxious for further accounts and it is too provoking to be kept in this manner without the letters, which I am convinced are on their way to us. If they went to Quebec they may be back tomorrow, but I fear it will be too late to acknowledge them by the *Royal William* which is to sail on the 4th.

Having been busy there two days with my inspection, I have barely had time to look at the account of the Coronation and the Brevet, and have not been able to read any of the debates, except that on Mr. Turton which was copied at length into the Montreal Papers. Lambton will be very angry, though, if there was any assurance from him to Lord Melbourne as Lord Brougham insinuates, he has behaved very ill, I think, in appointing him. Mr. Turton will be as little pleased, I should think, with Lord Brougham's defence of him and his discussion with the Bishop of London as to the nature of his crime. I think no man ever had more cause to pray to be delivered from his Friends.

I am told there is also some debate on the formation of the Special Council, but I have not seen it. As far as I am concerned, I was put in for a special purpose, which being executed, I have successfully resisted being taken back to Quebec, and shall endeavour to resist in future.

I only consented to be put in at Lambton's earnest request, as he said he had no other means of making it up in time to settle the Prisoners on the day of the Queen's Coronation, and agreeing perfectly in what he proposed to do, I had the less objection. But I never expected to be again called upon to act, and I explained to Sir John Colborne, when I met him in the Upper Province, that I had only come out here to command the 71st and beyond that in its destination he would not consider me in any other light.

The Brevet seems to me a very shabby one, particularly in the Navy. There is no opening made by it in any of the staff situations, by which I could have profited, and perhaps it is just as well. A winter spent here with my Regiment will not diminish my claim at some future time, and if everything goes on quietly there can be no possible reason why I should not return home in March. I should come home on leave, and towards the expiration of it I should be able to judge whether I should come out again or not. If still an Equerry, and everything remained quiet, my wish would be to go on half-pay, but at present I need only say that I think I shall certainly return to England next March.

Lambton went back to Quebec on Thursday evening and we are now comfortably settled once more in our own home. Having been constantly on the move since I started for Washington on the 4th June, I am not at all sorry to be quiet now, and I trust we may be now left here undisturbed.

Lambton returns for the races the 20th of August, and stays a few days, after which I believe he will go to visit the Eastern Townships, and will come to reside here about the end of September.

All the accounts from the Country continue perfectly satisfactory, and I do not in the least apprehend any renewal of disturbances. The United States Government is certainly exerting itself more effectually, and I hope and believe that all the proceedings at Niagara have produced a much better feeling on the other side of the line. Certainly nothing could exceed the civility which was shown to Major Young and all the Americans who came over to the Review; and the Buffalonians most assuredly did not deserve it.

The weather has been intensely hot for the last few days, in spite of a very high wind. The rain at times has been heavier than I ever saw before, even at Gibraltar. Yesterday as I was in the street I heard a sudden rushing sound, and turning round saw a regular deluge splashing off the roofs of the houses close behind me. It had the most extraordinary appearance I ever saw, and I had barely time to jump into a shop when it came down in a heavy splash. The thunder and lightning has been incessant almost ever since we left Toronto, and on Lake Ontario I think it was the most awful thing I ever beheld. Today there is a sudden change, and the weather is almost cold.

Give my best love and Caroline's to all the Family, and believe me ever, My Dear Father,

Your most affectionate son,
C. Grey.

WEDNESDAY, AUG. I

A bag for the *Royal William* announced to start tomorrow morning by Express. Get letters to the 29th June – i.e. I receive *one* from Frederick,[5] and Caroline one from Georgiana.[6] Mr. Turton's appointment has made a great sensation in England. The Creations and promotions in the Peerage also considered very bad. No other news. Everything taken up with the Coronation. General Clitherow parades the Regiment to ask if there were any complaints and says it is the only one he has inspected which had none. Go over to the Island with Caroline. Work at the Cricket ground and dine in a Marquee. Return home at eight and make up a Packet, under cover to the Adjutant-General, for the Post.

THURSDAY, AUG. 2

The Chambly Cricket Club, composed of officers 7th Hussars and 15th Regiment, come over to play the Montreal Club at St. Helen's. Montreal Club beat, but no very good play on either side. Dine with the 24th.

5 Admiral Frederick William Grey, Lord Grey's third son.
6 Georgiana Grey, the fourth daughter of Lord Grey.

FRIDAY, AUG. 3

Shoot a pigeon match at the Island with Captain Williams. Win it. Cole, Lennoxes, etc., dine with me in the evening.

SATURDAY, AUG. 4

General inspects the 24th. Dine at their Mess in evening. Not well.

SUNDAY, AUG. 5

Had to send for the Doctor at half past two this morning. Ill with Cholera – bled, etc. In bed all today.

MONDAY, AUG. 6

Better today, and could have been quite well, if I had not been bled. Too weak to go to shoot at Isle aux Noix tomorrow as had been arranged with Williams, and Colonel Whyte of the 7th Hussars.

TUESDAY, AUG. 7

Well again, but still weak as ditchwater. Dine at five [and] go to the Island with Caroline afterwards. Read Cooper's *Charity* and return home. . . .

WEDNESDAY, AUG. 8

Great Western mail arrived, bringing papers from London of 20th July. She was twelve and a half days going home and fourteen and a half coming out. Arthur Lennox promoted Major by purchase vice Levinge who retires 6th July. This has been caused by an accumulation of misfortunes in the Levinge Family such as have rarely occurred before. Last autumn at Kilkenny he lost three children. His wife is just dead in Dublin after a most protracted illness and he himself, I hear, is now so ill he is not expected to live! Add to this his Brother, Sir R. Levinge, lost two sons – one, of the 71st, at Kilkenny. Arthur Lennox will go home in consequence to command the Depôt. Read the Papers at the Royal Mess – not much news in them. In the House of Lords rather awkward discussions had taken place on the appointment of Mr. Turton, etc., in which Lord Durham seems to have been somewhat thrown over by Lord Melbourne. There are also discussions on the subject of the Executive and Special Council appointments and the tone taken by Lords Brougham, Lyndhurst, and Ellenborough, seems one assumed for mischief and nothing else. This apparent want of confidence at home, will not make Lord Durham's mission less difficult. Major Warde, who was killed in a duel on our first arrival here, was gazetted Lieutenant-Colonel by Brevet on the 15th June.

Read first Canto of *Rokeby* to Caroline and begin the *King's Own* by Marryat for evening reading. Much interested myself in Duke of Wellington's dispatches – Advance to Poonah. By the bye, I see Colonel Gawler who compiled them is appointed Governor of Van Dieman's land. He might have left out a great many letters, where those to Colonel Close, Sir J. Stuart, and the Governor General are, in fact, copies of each other.

THURSDAY, AUG. 9

Have not got my letters yet which are probably gone to Quebec. Captain Williams has got leave to go home on a year's leave! He will take our letters. . . . Dine early and go over to the Island afterwards where I read the second and third Cantos of *Rokeby* to Caroline. Return home and read *King's Own* till half past ten.

FRIDAY, AUG. 10

Cricket at the Island where I idle away the day. Dine at Mr. McGill's[7] – Lennoxes, Colonel Wetherall, Whyte, Colonel and Mrs. Gascoigne, Mr. James Stuart,[8] etc., etc. . . . . A sort of dance in the evening, but we return home early.

SATURDAY, AUG. 11

Receive our letters from Quebec this morning from my Father and Mother, Howick, Frederick, etc. All preparing to leave town. The Session being expected to close about the 10th. George[9] expected home about the end of September with a freight which will put near £3,000 in his pocket! Write letters all day and read *King's Own* in evening till half past ten.

Montreal,

August 11, 1838.

My Dear Father,

The *Great Western* has made her third voyage out, in fourteen and a half days, and brought us Papers to the 20th of July. These we have had these two days, and today's post has brought us back from Quebec letters from you and My Mother, Caroline, Henry and Frederick of the 14th and 19th. Caroline has also received long dispatches from her mother, so that this has proved a most satisfactory post.

The accounts of Mary, Frederick's letter of the 19th continuing to give a good account, have made us very happy, and I confidently hope now that her recovery may be sure, if it is not

---

[7] Peter McGill, an influential Montreal merchant and president of the Bank of Montreal.

[8] James Stuart was appointed Chief Justice of Lower Canada by Lord Durham in 1838. He had presented the argument in favour of a legislative union of Upper and Lower Canada in 1822 and remained a staunch supporter of such a union.

[9] Admiral George Grey, the fourth son of Lord Grey.

rapid, and that there may be no remaining cause of uneasiness to prevent your going to Howick as soon as you wish. You are probably, I think, settled there at the moment that I am writing this, and I cannot say how I wish I was there with you.

I have not stirred from Montreal since my return with Lambton from Niagara, etc., and with the exception of two short notes from Mary to Caroline, we have heard nothing from them. Colonel Couper, however, wrote me word that the Turton debate had made much less sensation than he expected. But I heard yesterday that he (Mr. Turton) had resigned, and that a Mr. Thom,[10] formerly Editor of the *Herald*, a very violent ultra-English Paper, has been appointed in his place. I know not how far this is true and merely give it [to] you as a report which was current yesterday. I confess the whole business puzzles me. Either Lambton has behaved ill in giving Mr. Turton an appointment in the face of an assurance to the contrary given by him to Lord Melbourne, or the latter has behaved as ill in throwing Lambton over as he did in the House of Lords. Either way I am surprised to hear from Colonel Couper that it has been taken quietly.

I had quite the same opinion that you express of what should be the channel through which Lambton ought to make any representations he might think necessary to the U.S. Government, and when I went to Washington I was determined, unless such an opportunity as was afforded to me offered, to sink merely into the Bearer of the dispatches to Mr. Fox. Any conversation I had with the President and Mr. Poinsett was in fact sought by them and it is satisfactory to know that my mission did prove useful. Everything Mr. Poinsett told me should be done, was done. A communication with General Macomb at Sackets Harbor was opened by the officers in command of the Land and Sea forces respectively at Kingston. The promised instructions

10 Adam Thom, a former schoolmaster of Scottish origin, had been the outspoken champion of the English minority in Lower Canada for several years. The rumour that Turton had resigned was incorrect but Thom was appointed to the Commission on Municipal Government.

were sent to that officer and all the movements of the two Governments since, for the security of the navigation of the River and Lakes, have been made in concert. As Sir George Arthur says, the American Government has for the first time exerted itself with apparent sincerity to preserve the peace of the frontier and this, together with the improvement which has certainly taken place in the feelings of the People on the other side towards us, leads me to think there is little further danger to be apprehended at present from the Sympathizers in the States.

But there is, no doubt, a strong republican feeling in Upper Canada among certain Classes of the population and if any unfortunate event should lead to their getting the upper hand, there is no doubt that the whole population of the Border provinces would turn active sympathizers. The danger to us then, as in the case of a war with the United States, would be in the Militia – not the regular Army. Even with this addition of 4,000 men, divided as it is over the whole union, it can never be of much consequence as an offensive force. From all I hear it is in a miserable state and the desertions from it are very much greater in proportion than those from our troops. But every man belongs to the Militia and the Militia force is Formidable. Mr. Fox told me he had little doubt that in the event of a war 250,000 American Militiamen might be poured into Canada and such a force would certainly be sufficient, in the first instance at least, to overrun the two Provinces. But fortunately, though there is a strong Republican party, they are still a minority in Upper Canada, and *we* have also strong adherents in the States themselves among the Irish settlers. Sir John Colborne told me there was not a single instance of an Irishman being even suspected during the late disturbances. Protestant and Catholic were equally loyal and there are great numbers of them in the district on both sides of the Welland Canal and along Lake Erie. Captain Sandom also, who commands the flotilla on the lakes, told me he would engage in a very short time to raise 1,000 seamen, chiefly Irishmen employed in the American Craft on the lakes.

The chief Malcontents are the descendants of American settlers, who emigrated into Canada on the separation of the States from England – great numbers of settlers from Pennsylvania who were located about 20 years ago in the London district – a large proportion of the recent Scotch settlers, and a small number of English. Being a very decided minority, however, with the lesson late events have given them, I cannot think there is much danger of any fresh outbreak at present. But we ought never to forget that they, as well as the Sympathizers on the other side, are only 'biding their time'.

In this province it is very different, and though here the disaffected are a decided majority, inasmuch as I firmly believe *every* Frenchman to be disaffected, I think the danger to be apprehended is much less. Here though the Americans 'sympathize' with them on the vague principle that every people who resist legitimate authority must be right, they can have nothing really in common. The French Canadians have no more desire to become American than they have to remain English. Their object is to be the independent 'Nation Canadienne' with their own language and customs – an object which the United States Government would be much too wise to allow them to attain. But in Upper Canada the Malcontents are those whose object is to be added to the Union and, though they may be put down for the present, it is an object which it is not to be supposed that either they or the sympathizers on the other side will lose sight of. We have done, therefore, very little in my opinion till we have settled the Government of this country upon a basis which shall make the future attempts of these People less likely and less dangerous, and the Question is – how is that to be done?

I am a bad person at finding out what is the general feeling or opinion upon any subjects. I stay a great deal too much at home and make too few acquaintances, but I sat by Mr. Stuart yesterday at dinner, formerly Attorney General, of whom I had

often heard, from Colonel Couper and others, as the Cleverest
Man in this Country. He talked a good deal of the prospects of
the Provinces and considered the union of the Canadas as the
one thing necessary for their preservation. He told me he was
afraid any federal Union, such as was hinted at, of the five North
American Colonies would not answer, but repeated again and
again that the union of the two provinces under a constitutional
government, with the internal concerns of which England
should interfere as little as possible, was indispensable, not only
for Lower Canada, to neutralize in the only way in which it
could fairly be done, the French influence; but for Upper Canada, as the most effectual means of weakening the desire to be
united to the States, and this he considered much the most
important object. A Federal Union, leaving local concerns to
provincial assemblies, would do little good he said, as the French
influence in these local matters was the chief English grievance
here. I must say I have never yet met an Englishman in this
province who gave a different opinion. Mr. S[tuart] made very
light of the opposition to the union in the upper Province which
he affirms to be confined to Toronto where they are afraid of
losing the seat of Government. Mr. Robinson,[11] Chief Justice of
Upper Canada, who resides at Toronto, is the chief opponent
of such a measure and is considered the Cleverest Man, except
Mr. Stuart, in the Country.

I have inflicted a long twaddle upon you, which I am almost
ashamed to send, but you are always good-natured enough to
say you wish to hear my speculations and I will therefore let
them go.

I cannot judge of course, having heard nothing, what
Lambton's proposition is likely to be, but I judge it will *not* be
for a union of the Provinces – first because in reading a Pamphlet

---

[11] When Durham visited Upper Canada, Chief Justice John Beverley Robinson
accompanied the Governor's party from Toronto to Prescott in the steamer
Cobourg. It was probably during this journey that Robinson pencilled his
criticisms on Durham's plan for a federal union of British North America.
Public Archives of Canada, *Durham Papers*, Section VI, Vol. 3, pp. 647-73.

the other day, I found a passage recommending it, noted in his writing as 'fudge', secondly because I believe those whom he sees mostly at Quebec are opposed to it, and thirdly because he has some grand idea of a union of the whole of the Provinces into one important Government.

I have heard nothing of what has been going on since I last wrote. Sir John Colborne passed through two days ago from Upper Canada and is to be here again in a day or two. I am in hopes, as everything is perfectly quiet, that my detachments at Kingston and Brockville which cut up my Regiment sadly will be brought back to me. At Brockville some Americans tried to entice my men to desert. They appeared to listen to them, but instead of deserting, when they had concerted their measures, seized the People and their boats. Other Regiments here lost a good many, but so far I have been fortunate. In three months only seven have attempted it – all bad characters and men who have deserted before in England. Five were caught and transported, two got off.

They all come back here from Quebec I believe this day week for our Montreal races, but I don't believe they remain long. It is possible, but I do not think probable, that I may go back with them for the Quebec races. Much as I like being with Louisa, I dislike the constant worry of it, and always long for my own quiet evenings at home. After September I take for granted they will be settled here for good. . . .

I will now end this most unmerciful letter. As I could add nothing, I will not inflict one upon my Mother in answer to hers. I hope, however, that will not prevent her writing to me again. Give my best love to her and all the rest of the Family, and believe me ever, My Dear Father,

Your most affectionate son,
C. Grey.

We have still had very hot weather up [to] today. It is now pouring, and has been all the morning, and is grown quite cool.

In about a fortnight I am told we shall be very glad of fires. It is wonderful to see how short a time the foliage lasts, not a leaf was out when we came here three short months ago, and they are already brown and withering fast.

SUNDAY, AUG. 12

Go to English Church with Caroline and to Scotch Church afterwards with Regiment. Finish my letters which I put under cover to Sir J. Macdonald and give in charge to Captain Williams who starts tomorrow morning. Read Blunt on the *Articles of Religion*[12] and after dinner Whewell's *Natural Theology*.[13]

Applied yesterday for leave of absence for Lord Aberdour, who has been very ill and is only now recovering slowly, to go home for six months. I am sorry to say he means to leave the Regiment. Also apply for A[rthur] Lennox to be sent home to the Depôt.

MONDAY, AUG. 13

Edward Ellice calls on his way down to Quebec. Reports a good deal of excitement on the frontier of Beauharnois in consequence of a Captain Davidson having been arrested in the States on a civil suit for damages for some American detained on our side during the disturbances.[14]

12 Henry Blunt, *Discourse upon some of the Doctrinal Articles of the Church of England.*
13 William Whewell, *Astronomy and General Physics considered with Reference to Natural Theology.*
14 During the winter of 1837-8 Hiram Paddock, an American customs officer, was seized on suspicion of spying at Huntingdon. Captain James Davidson of the Huntingdon Volunteers, who was officer of the guard, detained Paddock over night. In the summer of 1838 when Davidson visited the United States, Paddock had him arrested on charges of false arrest, assault, and battery. Davidson protested that he had been acting under the orders of a senior officer and had not committed assault and battery. At first he refused to post bail, but on the advice given to his brother by Charles Buller he did so and returned to Canada.

Read fourth and fifth Cantos of *Rokeby* to Caroline. Duke of Wellington's dispatches – state of things leading to the Marhatta war. Dine at Mess. Lord Cochrane, 66th etc., etc. Sit till half past ten listening to the Bugles.

TUESDAY, AUG. 14

March out with the Regiment at six A.M. Skirmish across the Priest's Field. At four P.M. start with A[rthur] Lennox in the *Britannia* Steamer for Sorel, and thence to go up the Richelieu river to Chambly. Touch at a great many places on the way and reach Sorel at half past ten. Sleep on board in the Ladies' Cabin. Very cold indeed all night. The Commissioners for settling the claims for indemnification for losses sustained at St. Denis and St. Charles during the winter disturbances [are] also on board.[15]

WEDNESDAY, AUG. 15

Leave Sorel at six. Touch at St. Ours, a pretty village half way between Sorel and St. Denis, the report of which being occupied prevented Colonel Gore[16] taking the direct road and was the probable cause of the failure of his expedition. We did not land at St. Denis, owing to the lowness of the river (it was so low in fact that we had some difficulty in getting up the Shallows opposite that place), but we could see the nature of the place

15 Under an ordinance passed by the Special Council (I Vic., Cap. VII) P. E. Leclerc, E. A. Clark, and Charles Tait were appointed on May 19, 1838, to investigate claims for losses sustained by loyal inhabitants during the rebellion in Lower Canada. They began taking evidence on August 15, 1838, but had not finished their work when the second insurrection occurred. After order was again restored they resumed their investigation. Five reports submitted by the commission were published in Appendix LL of the *Journal of the Legislative Assembly* for 1846.

16 When the rebellion broke out in Lower Canada, Sir John Colborne ordered Colonel Gore and Colonel Wetherall to proceed simultaneously from Sorel and Chambly and to join forces at St. Charles. Gore was repulsed by the rebels at St. Denis on November 23, 1837, and was forced to retreat.

pretty well. The end which Colonel Gore attacked was certainly strong, owing to the strong stone house which was occupied by the Rebels, but there did not appear, as far as we could judge, any difficulty in turning the village and coming in at the other end where there were no strong buildings. Anything I should think would have been better than firing away for near six hours, without making an impression on the house – only one shot out of near sixty that were fired at it having gone thro' the wall. But the whole business seems to have been most grossly mismanaged. The *St. George* Steamer might have brought up the detachment to St. Ours in spite of any annoyance from the banks. If that place had been occupied it would not have been difficult with fresh troops to dislodge the Rebels and thence they might again have proceeded in the Steamer and landed within a mile of St. Denis and come fresh to the attack.

At St. Charles we landed and walked to the position occupied by the Rebels which was, in fact, nothing at all and it was evidently impossible for them to make a stand. A little to the rear they might have made more of a fight from a stone church and stone house on either side of the road, but even then it would have been impossible for them to resist the troops any time.

The Captain of the Steamer tells me that the spirit among the People is every bit as bad as it was last year, if not worse, and that it has been kept alive by the traitors who were released from Prison. He ought to know for he sees a great deal of them taking up the Market People to Montreal every Friday. At the same time he thinks they are too much frightened to try anything this winter. Mr. Debartzch came on board at St. Ours. His house at St. Charles was considerably damaged and a grove of trees cut down to form Abatis by the Rebels for which he claims £6,000 compensation. I trust the Commissioners will give him nothing as there is no doubt that he is worse than any man in the country. He was the original instigator of all the agitation which led ultimately to Rebellion, tho' his cowardice made him desert his party and give information before it broke out. He is considered a very clever, tho' most unprincipled man. The Commissioners who are on board seem to know him thoroughly and I do not think they will give him anything if they can possibly help it.[17] Our next stopping place was St. Hilaire where we went into a very pretty garden belonging to a Colonel Rouville,[18] who is besides the Proprietor of the Beloeil Mountain, a beautiful hill about a mile in rear of his house. This might be made the prettiest thing I have seen in Canada. As it is, it is wretched, and Colonel R[ouville] himself, a little mean-looking old man dressed like a labourer. About a mile above St. Hilaire there is a rapid where the stream comes round a point and, the tide catching us on the bow, we are shoved right round out of the Channel before she can be met with the helm and we get ashore. Stick for an hour when we get off again and reach Chambly without further disaster or adventure at half past two. Get some luncheon at the 15th Mess after which I lie down in the room Cole of the Hussars has got for me. It belongs to one of the 7th Officers who is gone in for a field day to Montreal. He is very fond of driving and the ornaments to the walls consist of a set of four-in-hand harness, a Pair harness with bits, whips, and saddles innumerable. The furniture, one barrack table and chair, a large rough deal box turned up for another table, the same for a washing stand, and the bed, what they call a canteen bed, about the width of a hammock! Try to sleep, but

[17] Pierre Dominique Debartzch was the owner and editor of the *Echo du Pays* and, in November 1833, published inflammatory editorials in an attempt to incite the French-Canadian population to armed revolt. In 1837 Debartzch made a *volte face*, accepted an executive council appointment from Lord Gosford, and opposed Papineau and his followers. The commissioners estimated that Debartzch's property had suffered damages to the value of £3,581:2:10 but questioned whether, in view of his career up to 1837, he could be awarded compensation under the terms of the ordinance. None the less, £2,581:2:10 compensation was paid on July 24, 1839. The government had previously made Debartzch a loan of £1,000 against his claim. Public Archives of Canada, *Rebellion Losses Records*, Record Group 19, A2, Vol. 26A, Claim No. 11.

[18] Jean Baptiste René Hertel de Rouville served with the Voltigeurs at Châteauguay in the War of 1812. He was commissioned Lieutenant-Colonel of the 1st Rouville Militia, May 7, 1830.

the flies will not let me and therefore read Kincaid's random shots[19] which amuse me much. The story of the man who got his head shot crooked at Badajoz from a ball in his right ear and got it shot straight again at Waterloo from a ball in his left is rather too good. Dine at the 15th Mess. Smoke a cigar in Mr. Ashhurst's [15th Regiment] room and go to bed at ten.

THURSDAY, AUG. 16

Hire a two-horse waggon for $3 to take us to Longueuil and start at half past nine. Dreadfully rough, but not so bad as the stage from Whitehall to Comstock's landing. Good land apparently, but *wretched* cultivation. Even the gardens round the houses are shamefully neglected. The land is cleared the whole way across, so much so that firewood is becoming dear. Just as we arrive at Longueuil it commences raining heavily and continues to do so till late at night. Cross in the ferry boat, which is worked by fourteen horses in a Mill, the boat being constructed of two boats at a considerable distance apart, planked over, with a wheel worked by the horses between them. It can bring over at one time from 20 to 30 of the Country Carts. Get home at one o'clock completely drenched. Dine at the Mess and return home at ten. Receive letters from England from my Father, etc. No further news, being older dates than those received by [the] *Great Western*. Also a letter from Lord Durham telling me that the Government approved of the 'discretion with which I had executed the important commission entrusted to me'. Read sixth Canto of *Rokeby* to Caroline.

FRIDAY, AUG. 17

General parade at half past ten A.M. to read Court Martial. Afterwards overlook the Mess concerns. At three P.M. parade on the Champ de Mars for Mr. Forsyth, U.S. Minister for Foreign

19 Sir John Kincaid, *Random Shots of a Rifleman*.

Affairs. Dine with the General who has an evening party for
Mr. F[orsyth].

SATURDAY, AUG. 18

Parade of 7th Hussars and Artillery in Champ de Mars for
Mr. Forsyth. Nothing can look better than the former, or work
better considering that upwards of one half of their horses have
been bought since they came to the Country. In the Evening
Mr. Forsyth, the General, and all Heads of Regiments and
Departments dine at our Mess. Ellices arrive from Beauharnois
for the races.

SUNDAY, AUG. 19

Go to English Church with Caroline. Ellices, etc. lunch. Take
the Regiment to St. Andrew's. Arthur Lennoxes, who start tomorrow for Niagara, and the Ellices dine with us. Read in afternoon – Blunt on 39 *Articles* – with Caroline.

MONDAY, AUG. 20

Royal Regiment and 24th reviewed by General for Mr. Forsyth. Governor General arrives at eleven. Go on board. Lord
Durham lands at twelve and comes to my house. Go to the races
at one. Bad sport and intensely hot in stand. Return and dine
on board at six. At eight whole party go to the play – hot beyond
endurance. Sir C[olin] Campbell, Governor of Nova Scotia, Sir
C[harles] Fitzroy, Governor of Prince Edward Island, The
Admiral, Captains Pring and Baynes, of H.M.S.s *Inconstant* and
Andromache, accompany Lord Durham. Mr. Forsyth and party
dine on board. Lord Durham drinks health of President after
a very neat speech. Mr. F[orsyth] acknowledges it most
awkwardly.

Montreal,

August 20, 1838.

My Dear Father,

Since the Ordinances disposing of the Prisoners I have had nothing to do as a Member of the Special Council, nor do I mean again to attend, and I shall ask Lambton, who is arrived this morning for our Montreal races, to allow me to resign it. So far I must say the only ground I can see that he has given for attack is the unlimited expense to which he goes in everything. His trip to Niagara cost £7,000! and this visit to the races here is estimated at £1,500, though he only means to remain three days. I am told the state liveries are something more magnificent than ever were seen. Edward Ellice has wisely withdrawn himself entirely from any management of these matters. He considers that the expense of the Mission, exclusive of the cost of Buildings etc., will not be less than £60,000. I do not think it will be thrown away if he settles the Country and, hitherto, he has given unmixed satisfaction to all parties. The Proclamation which he issued on the spur of the moment when the *Sir Robert Peel* was burnt, and which has been so violently attacked in England was, I should say, of all his Acts, that which gave the most satisfaction. It gave confidence to the People and I really believe prevented retaliation from our side which might have led unavoidably to war with the U.S.

I have my doubts, however, of his settling the question. As I have told Henry, I firmly believe that any such scheme as is hinted at, of a Federative Union of all the North American Provinces, will prove a complete failure and will give no satisfaction *anywhere*. I also fear that he is not aware of how very general the wish is in this Province for a union of the two Canadas or of the difficulty, I believe I might say the impossibility, of devising any plan which can give British influence and interests the predominance which they *must* have in a local legislature if we are to retain the Colony. But I have no time to write upon this subject, and I do not know that I ought to give an opinion upon it.

Mr. Forsyth, the U.S. Minister for Foreign Affairs, is here at present and we have all been paraded in turn for him. On Friday he dined at our mess and was rather astonished at our turn-out of Plate, China, etc. I suppose he is come to see what we are about, but I do not see what he can discover except that the different Regiments are in a state of discipline that must rather astonish an American.

Lambton is come up alone, but I believe they are anxious to get to Montreal as soon as possible, being heartily sick of Quebec.

The Bugle is sounding and I must go. Caroline sends her best love with mine to all the Family, and I am ever, My Dear Father,

Your most affectionate son,
C. Grey.

TUESDAY, AUG. 21

Lord Durham comes on shore at half past twelve. Go to the races in same order as yesterday – better sport. The race for the Cup[20] very pretty – 13 horses starting. Dine on board. All the party except [the] Admiral and Lord Durham go to theatre. I remain and smoke a cigar with the Admiral after which I go to the theatre in time to take Caroline home. The *John Bull* is to sail tomorrow morning at daylight.

WEDNESDAY, AUG. 22

No races today. A Cricket match at the Island between Garrison and others resident at Montreal and Visitors. Latter win, after a good match, with two wickets to go down. Dine at

[20] The Governor General's Cup, presented by Lord Durham, was won by G. W. Yarker's *Midas* in a close race.

home, but too sleepy to read much in evening. Very hot today. In the evening the Aurora Borealis was extremely bright.

THURSDAY, AUG. 23

Take the Regiment to Champ de Mars at six A.M. Read Duke of Wellington's dispatches which have been getting on slowly for the last few days – Advance to Ahmednuggar and lengthened negotiations, preparatory to war with the Marhattas. Read half a chapter of Russell's *Modern Europe* to Caroline – Civil war in France between Huguenots and Catholics – Presbyterian Intolerance in Scotland – Catholic Bigotry of Philip II in Spain – Religious wars and controversies everywhere without one speck of Christian feeling on any side. Denny and Aberdour dine and go to the Play – Lady of Lyons – Miss Tree[21] – not well got up and Pauline a part that does not suit Miss Tree. Captain C. comes into our box to drink [and] I take Caroline home. Denny, Dalrymple, Foy and Aberdour sup – *very badly*.

FRIDAY, AUG. 24

Major Denny taken ill this morning in consequence of a mistake about some medicine sent him by the Doctor. Very nearly poisoned. He has been in very low spirits lately, having taken it into his head that the officers and garrison generally looked cold upon him. Walk on the Champ de Mars to hear the Band,

---

[21] The highlight of the dramatic season was the engagement of the company featuring Miss Ellen Tree. Commenting on the engagement the Montreal *Gazette* stated, 'the acting of Miss Tree was superior to anything we have ever witnessed.' Among Miss Trees' admirers was John Quincy Adams, who addressed the following lines to her during her visit to Washington in 1838:

> 'Tis nature's witchery attracts thy smile;
> 'Tis her soft sorrows that our tears beguile;
> Nature to thee her fairest gifts imparts
> She bids thee fascinate to win all hearts –
> The wife, the queen, the wayward child we see,
> And fair perfection all abide in thee.

etc., etc. Read in the evening Duke of Wellington's dispatches –
Commencement of hostilities with Marhattas. A chapter of
Russell's *Modern Europe* to Caroline – to the Flight of Mary
queen of Scots into England.

Montreal,
August 24, 1838.

My Dear Father,

Lord Aberdour sails from New York for Liverpool on the
1st September, and, I believe, starts from hence on Monday
next, and he will take our letters home in a parcel which he
will drop at Alnwick as he goes through. He has been very ill,
which is partly the cause of his going home, but I am sorry to
say it is not his intention to rejoin us as his Father means him
to leave the service. He hopes to be in time for his sister's
marriage with Lord Milton.

Since I wrote last, Lambton has been here for the Montreal
races. Louisa and the children remained at Quebec as Louisa
was not allowed to leave her sofa, and Lambton only remained
Monday and Tuesday, returning on Wednesday morning at
daylight. I had not much conversation [with him]. He was so
constantly occupied with deputations and other people coming
to see him. But he seems much less annoyed than I expected
about the discussions in Parliament on the Turton business. He
means to uphold him unless absolutely ordered to rescind his
appointment by the Home Government. But Edward Ellice tells
me that so far from having given Lord Melbourne any assurance
that he did not mean to appoint him to any situation, which
alone, I think, could warrant Lord Melbourne in making his first
answer when questioned on the subject, it was distinctly understood that he was to be employed. He has received the most
unqualified approbation from the Government of his constitution of the Executive Council, of his proclamations on assuming

the government, and on the burning of the *Sir Robert Peel*, and of his communications with the Government of the United States. He had not yet heard what was said to his Special Council, and the Ordinances, but I should think there is no doubt these acts will also be approved. And if so, even orders to rescind the appointment of Mr. Turton, who, by the bye, has given the greatest satisfaction in the Province, would not cause him to resign. But he would mask his opinion by asking Mr. Turton to remain with him as his friend. I spoke to him about my unwillingness to have anything to do with the Special Council, but he at once stopped it by saying that if I or any other member of it, General Macdonell or Clitherow, were now to withdraw, it would make it very difficult for him to go on. He certainly put it in a way that makes it impossible for me to resign and, as at the same time he told me there was no great likelihood of there being anything for it to do for some time, I do not so much mind. I told Colonel Couper, however, that I should certainly not be satisfied to be called upon as a Member of the Special Council to sanction an Act which I might only hear for the first time when assembled to pass it, and begged him to manage that if I was to be called upon again, I might know beforehand what was proposed to be done. Couper spoke very highly of Turton, but said Buller was the worst man of business possible, so extremely undecided and so vacillating in his opinions.

Sir C[olin] Campbell, the Governor of Nova Scotia, and Sir C[harles] Fitzroy, Governor of Prince Edward Island, came up here with Lambton, having arrived from their respective Governments the day before. I hear the Governor of Newfoundland is also expected, so I conclude the grand scheme for uniting the Provinces goes on. But, as Lambton does not mention the subject to me, I do not like to ask Couper or others about it; and I cannot speak to other People much without being supposed, from my connexion with Lambton and being a Member of the Special Council, to know more than I do, so that it is difficult for me to ascertain anything. If, however, as I gather from what I heard on board the *John Bull*, it is proposed in this Scheme to have no Legislative Council, it makes it still more objectionable than I before thought it.

Sir Colin Campbell does not apprehend anything serious from the present state of the Maine question. I cannot but think he may find himself deceived.

In my letter to Henry, which I wrote some days ago by Mr. Purvis, I told him that it struck me on seeing the position, that Colonel Gore had nothing to do but to turn the village of St. Denis by his left instead of knocking his head for three hours against a strong stone house at the entrance of the village. This opinion is confirmed by what I heard from a gentleman, whose name I don't know, but whom I sat next at dinner on board Lambton's Steamer. He is a French Canadian, which I did not at first ascertain, from his speaking English so perfectly, and I only discovered it by his warmth when, in mentioning my trip up the Richelieu, I alluded to the spirit among the People as being as bad and hostile to us as ever. He did not attempt to deny that it was so, but said it was only the natural consequence of what had occurred last winter, and then he went on to say that a great deal too much had been made of it. He criticized the whole of the movements, made the same remarks which I have done about Colonel Gore, and then asked a question which had before occurred to me. If the Country was *really* in the state in which Sir John Colborne believed it to be, or in which it was represented to be, viz: that the whole population was in arms, was it prudent in him (Sir J[ohn] Colborne) to make such a division of the very inadequate force at his disposal, and to act, which is generally contrary to principle, on a double line of operations? I take the answer to be, Sir John did *not* believe the state of the Country to be so bad, or I cannot but think he was wrong in not uniting the force under Colonels Gore and Wetherall.

I believe everything to be going on as quietly as possible, both in the Provinces and on the frontier, at least I have heard nothing to the contrary this long while. There has been a dearth even of reports.

We have had an immense number of American visitors here lately, and they are mostly gone on to Quebec for the races there. Mr. Forsyth went straight back as he said his presence was required at Washington. I believe he had intended to go to Quebec and to return through Maine, but he heard such bad accounts of the road that he did not attempt it.

I think I shall very likely go down to Quebec for ten days about the middle of September. Louisa and Mary were so very pressing for us to come down now that it was with difficulty I could refuse and, as it is, I fear we may be pressed further in a manner that it will make it impossible for us to refuse.

We are looking out anxiously for the arrival of the next Steamer. Unless there were more of them I do not think I like it. Formerly Sailing Packets were constantly arriving – each bringing a few days later intelligence than its predecessor. Now we get late news by a Steamer, and then for a whole month the Sailing Packets come dropping in, bringing nothing but stale news. I believe the *Tiger* is to be the next Steamer and that she was to sail from England somewhere about the 14th. The *Great Western* is still our latest arrival.

Give our best love to my Mother and all the family with you at Howick. I hope that next year at this time we may be added to your party there. In the meantime, I am ever, My Dear Father,

> Your most affectionate son,
> C. Grey.

SATURDAY, AUG. 25

Call on Denny who is much better, tho' weak and still in low spirits. Ride out to Mr. Aubrey's where there is a Cricket match – a pretty place, infamously kept and wretched ground for

Cricket. Return before luncheon. Dinner at half past six to Colonel Dundas, Captain L'Estrange and his wife and all the officers of my Regiment present except three whom my table would not hold. All go to the play which is under our patronage. The Fox Chase – Constance by Miss E. Tree – much amused.

In the morning Captain Armstrong of the *British America* came to me – anxious to make a proposal to [the] Governor about establishing a Steamboat between Quebec and Halifax. I write to Colonel Couper on the subject. As I am riding out, meet Mr. McGill, who, declaring at the same time that he is no alarmist, says that he is *convinced* there will be further disturbances 'this fall' and that the People are better prepared. I believe he is right as to the *inclination* of the People, but *we* are also better prepared.

Get on a good deal with the Duke of Wellington's dispatches – opening of the Campaign and capture of Ahmednuggar – excessively interested – Full of instruction – particularly for a Military man.

SUNDAY, AUG. 26

Go to Church with Caroline. Read Blunt on 39 *Articles* – Whewell. Write a letter to Georgiana.

MONDAY, AUG. 27

My trip with Colonel Whyte, 7th Hussars, to Isle aux Noix, which had been fixed for today, put off till tomorrow. Field Day of Garrison in field near Lachine Canal. Dine at Mess. Two officers of *Malabar* present.

TUESDAY, AUG. 28

Start at nine in *Princess Victoria* for Laprairie. Thence by railroad to St. Johns and on by *Winooski* Steamer to Isle aux Noix which we reach at half past two. . . . Go out after woodcocks in the Island opposite Isle aux Noix and kill between us seven and a half couple in two hours. With our woodcock this would be good sport, but these are tame brutes and would not be worth shooting if it was not for the difficulty caused by the thickness of the cover. Put up at a house kept by a man of the name of Bates. Barrack bedding, etc. – hard and uncomfortable. Whyte and I sleep in the same room. Cold enough for a fire which we can only light in our bedroom where we consequently dine. The Commander of the Garrison, Captain Gratton, comes in the Evening and smokes a cigar with us.

WEDNESDAY, AUG. 29

Little sleep last night. My bed was so hard and uncomfortable. Delighted to get up at six. Breakfast and start out Snipe Shooting a little before eight. Find scarcely any in the bog, killing only four couple. Return home before eleven when Whyte and I separate, he going down and I up the river after Ducks. Both equally unsuccessful and return home disgusted and determined to start tomorrow. Walk up to the Fort before dinner and round it accompanied by Captain Gratton. A prettily laid out work, but the scarp and counter scarp, having only been faced with pickets, falling in in every direction. When the disturbances broke out last year the present fort Major, an old man of 88, was Commandant and he had only 10 men! His account of what he did is very amusing. At present there is a garrison of 170 effective men from the different Regiments in the Montreal district and four guns are mounted on each bastion.

Reports here, as elsewhere, that the 'Rebellion' is to break out again in the winter. Our resident officers at St. Johns, etc. appear to listen a great deal too much to all the stories they hear, at least to attach too much importance to them, but there is no doubt the *inclination* to rise is as strong as ever it was.

The Rideau Canal, Bytown

(Charles Grey considered the canal 'the thing . . . best worth seeing' in the Canadas.)

From a drawing in 'Canadian Scenery' by N. P. Willis, Vol. 2 (London, 1842) – Public Archives of Canada

Looking east on King Street, Toronto, in the 1830s
('Toronto is infinitely the best town I have seen in Canada.' – Charles Grey)
From a lithograph by T. Young in the Public Archives of Canada

THURSDAY, AUG. 30

Get up at four o'clock to be ready for the *Winooski* Steamer on her way back to St. Johns. . . . The rain came through and wet my bed through last night. Wait an hour and a half nearly, sitting in a Sentry box on the wharf. Get to St. Johns a little after seven, breakfast, and take the railroad for Laprairie at nine and get home a little after eleven. Remain at home all day. . . .

FRIDAY, AUG. 31

Not very well this morning. Muster and drill on Champ de Mars. . . . Walk with Caroline in Champ de Mars to hear the band. Dine at Mess.

SATURDAY, SEPT. 1

Write to Captain Hanson about an application of his forwarded by me to Lord Durham. Read Duke of Wellington's dispatches – operations subsequent to Battle of Assaye. Ride out to drill fields. Sign the returns. Dine with the General and lose three rubbers of whist. Heard today that two of my men have deserted from Kingston. The first we have lost there in two months. News from London to the 23rd July. A large batch of Commanders and Companions of the Bath created and a few grand Crosses, among them Lord Gosford. Nothing interesting. Debates on Irish tithes in Committee. Questions from Bishop of Exeter about the Protestant Church in Canada – Not calculated to do any *good*.[22] Sir Pulteney Malcom is dead.

SUNDAY, SEPT. 2

Go to Church with Caroline and take the Sacrament. Read as usual – Cowper's *Truth*, etc.

---

[22] The Bishop of Exeter was critical of the government's failure to provide adequate assistance for the 'established church' in Canada and its tendency to consider the Roman Catholic Church as being co-established.

MONDAY, SEPT. 3

Field Day of Garrison at eight A.M. General too fussy and too anxious to command every Regiment himself. . . . Walk out with Caroline and call on Mrs. Love, 73rd, a pretty person. Colonel Love, an old 52nd man, now commanding 73rd. Commanded the 2nd Brigade nominally this morning. But the General allowed him to have as little to do with the Brigade as he allowed Commanding Officers to have with their Regiments. Commence the *Fortunes of Nigel* to Caroline in the evening.

TUESDAY, SEPT. 4

Morning employed as usual, in Orderly room, and reading Duke of Wellington's dispatches – Peace with Scindiah. Cross to the Island with Caroline after luncheon and sit there for two hours reading *Fortunes of Nigel*. A most delicious day after a series of very cold weather. Still a fire, which I have now begun some days, is very grateful in the evening. The Sergeant Major tells me that one year at Toronto it was nearly as warm on Xmas day! That the whole week till after New Year's day was the same – the ground perfectly clear of snow which only lay six weeks during the year! Receive and answer a letter from Captain Impett for an extension of leave. . . .

WEDNESDAY, SEPT. 5

Woke at half past twelve last night by the Alarm Bell for a fire. See it at some distance down the Quebec Suburb. It appears to be got under [control] and, as I hear no bugle or drum, I turn in again. A most lovely night – bright moon – nearly as light as day. Receive a letter from Captain Speer from Kingston reporting the desertion of two men – the first he has lost from his post, tho' the 83rd Regiment quartered there are said to have lost an immense number. Some Americans had been put into prison for tampering with the men to induce them to desert. The *Morning*

Courier states that the Short Hills Convicts, who were ordered for execution on the 31st, have been respited! Surely it cannot be intended to let them off after the example we have had of the effect of Clemency. At this moment the people in this province who are the most active in keeping up irritation and discontent are the released Prisoners. Orderly room. Read an hour with Caroline – Menzel's *Geschichte der Deutschen*. Cross to the Island with Caroline and read *Fortunes of Nigel*. Dine at home and read again in evening.

THURSDAY, SEPT. 6

. . . Hear that Sir J[ohn] Colborne is to be here on Monday and to see the Garrison on Tuesday. Put off going to Quebec in consequence. General went yesterday morning to Niagara.

FRIDAY, SEPT. 7

Cricket on the Island. Lunch there and return half intending to go to Quebec. Walk with Caroline on Champ de Mars to hear the Band play. Hear that Sir J[ohn] Colborne does not come till Thursday. Return home intending to go at once to Quebec in consequence and again change our intention. Hear that the Murderers of Chartrand[23] have been acquitted. . . .

SATURDAY, SEPT. 8

Field Day in the morning from which we do not get home till twelve. . . . Bitterly cold and have a fire all day. In the evening just as I am comfortably settled to read to Caroline, the Arthur Lennoxes return from Niagara. Very glad to see them, but also very fond of a quiet evening. This we cannot again have till Wednesday next when they start for England. I fear I am a very

---

23 *supra*, p. 60, n. 9.

unsociable person and very easily put out. Go with Arthur to the Mess. Find Colonel Williams there, formerly of 85th, now one of Missionaries [?] and stationed at Missisquoi Bay. He says everything is now quiet on the frontier and that what reports are going come from the interior. Colonel Taylor, however, who is at Odelltown, is more easily caught by the different reports he hears.

Montreal,
September 9, 1838.

My Dear Father,

Since I wrote last everything has been going on in perfect tranquillity. There have been reports at different times, from the frontier of Vermont and other places, of intended disturbances during this month, but none I believe deserving of the least attention. They had, however, at one time become so frequent that General Clitherow thought it necessary to go to Isle aux Noix to endeavour to ascertain their truth, and I believe, for he is very mysterious that he came back perfectly satisfied they were, at any rate, greatly exaggerated. What was ascertained as certain is that Messrs. Côté and Nelson are on the frontier and that they are daily receiving visits from numbers of the Habitans who cross over the line and, after examination, are introduced to them individually, People say for the purpose of administering oaths. I am convinced it is with no good purpose, but though, as I have before said, I believe the disposition of the People to be as bad as possible, I do not apprehend anything beyond isolated outrages in different parts against those who are obnoxious to *either* party. Of this I fear we shall have a good deal. From the French Canadians I always expected it, but the unfortunate acquittal of the murderers of Chartrand the day before yesterday by a Canadian Jury has excited the other party to the greatest degree. They are almost as violent in the abuse of the Government as Lord Brougham or Lord Lyndhurst [and] declare openly there is no law in the Land, and that they will now show that they know how [to] defend themselves, and that they are independent both of the Government and England. These men being left to the ordinary tribunals I never had the slightest doubt as to the results, and it would have been the same with the subjects of Lambton's Ordinances if they had stood their trial.

Between the English party here, who regard the Ordinances in the light of a general Amnesty, and the trio at home, Lords Brougham, Lyndhurst and Ellenborough, who consider them a disgrace to Central Africa, Lambton has certainly a difficult task and I confess I am not now very sanguine as to his success. . . .

I see Caroline's name in the Papers as attending the Queen so I hope confidently that little Mary continues to do well. Give our best love to my Mother, etc., and believe me ever,

Your most affectionate son,
C. Grey.

I am come back to fires. Yesterday was one of the coldest days I ever felt, sharp, searching, easterly wind, and though it was hot all this day, it had turned very chilly again this evening. The Quebec Papers mention sharp frost and ice already.

MONDAY, SEPT. 10

Idle all day. Read the *Deutsche Geschichte* and *Fortunes of Nigel* to Caroline. Denny and Dalrymple dine.

TUESDAY, SEPT. 11

Go to the Island and play Cricket. Brickenden, Blennerhasset, and Cole dine.

WEDNESDAY, SEPT. 12

Arthur Lennoxes start for the States en route for England. Brigade Field Day. Read *Deutsche Geschichte* to Caroline. Dine with the 73rd on the Island.

THURSDAY, SEPT. 13

Very wet and cold morning. Wind changes and becomes fine in the afternoon. Walk out with Caroline. Read Menzel. Dine at Mess.

CHAPTER VI

Lord Durham's Departure

On September 15th the Greys went down to Quebec for a short visit before Lord Durham moved to Montreal for the winter. A few days after their arrival they decided to accompany the Durham family on a cruise down the St. Lawrence and possibly up the Saguenay River.

In the hope of enjoying some shooting at Château Richer, Charles Grey left Quebec on September 19th, a day ahead of the rest of the party. He was to join them the next day at Ste. Anne de Beaupré. After Grey's departure an American newspaper arrived in Quebec containing news which caused Lord Durham to change all of his plans. His ordinance banishing eight rebels to Bermuda had come under attack in the House of Lords and the Whig government had withheld its full support in the ensuing crisis. The banishment was declared to be illegal by the law officers, but an attempt could have been made to uphold Durham's action by means of supplementary legislation. Melbourne recognized that to pursue such a course would be courting almost certain defeat in the House of Commons, and he was unwilling to sacrifice his government for such a purpose. The ordinance was disallowed, and an Act was passed to indemnify, against prosecution, those who had advised and acted under the Bermuda ordinance.

Durham was both furious and dejected. He decided that he would resign and return home as soon as he was officially noti-

fied of the government's action. The projected cruise no longer appealed to him and it was curtailed to a single day's excursion to the falls at Ste. Anne.

Charles Grey's journal and letters record his own amazement upon learning the news, and the general reaction in Lower Canada when it became known that Lord Durham intended to resign.

L'ACADIE, DEC. 19, 1838

Exactly when events began to occur which were worth recording, I became too idle to go on with my journal. It is now three months since it ceased and how much has happened in the meantime! I have nothing to do here at present and I will endeavour to recapitulate.

On the 15th September Caroline and I went down in the *St. George* to Quebec, meaning to stay there till Lord Durham should move his establishment to Montreal for the winter. Two or three days after we got there a party was arranged to visit the falls of Ste. Anne, about 25 miles below Quebec. Villiers and I started in a market boat the preceding day [19th Sept.], hoping to get a day's snipe shooting at Château Richer. In this we completely failed, having only arrived an hour before sunset and the marsh being covered by the tide, and we passed a very uncomfortable night at a farm house kept by one Mme. Thibaut [sic]. The next morning we went on to Ste. Anne's to meet Lord Durham etc. who were to come in H.M.S. *Medea*. About twelve they arrived. Crossed the mud from the boats in Carrioles and cars which we had sent to meet them and the first word I heard from my sister, on reaching dry ground, was that it was all over. The ordinances disposing of the Prisoners had been disallowed by the Government at home and nothing was left for Lord Durham but to return home! A packet had arrived at New York from England by which Lord Durham had received the unqualified approbation of the Government to these very ordinances publicly and privately expressed in letters both from Lord Melbourne[1] and Lord Glenelg.[2] Lord Glenelg concludes his letter with the words, 'Go on and Prosper' with a passing intimation that there was some difficulty *in form* as to sending them to Bermuda, but which, it was added, '*would be easily put to rights*'. Not one word as to the probable necessity of disallowing them which, however, it appeared too certain, from the later intelligence contained in the New York Papers, Lord Melbourne had yielded to within a day or two of the writing of these letters.

Till the *official* news should arrive, shortly expected by the *Great Western*, it seemed premature to decide upon any plan tho' Lord Durham said at once there *could* be no alternative left him. Still we were all in hopes it might appear in a more favourable light when we knew exactly *what* had been done, and we enjoyed our excursion almost as much as we should otherwise have done. These falls are beautiful and I am told are yet finer three miles higher up, but we had not time to visit them as we were to return to Quebec that night and the tide would not serve if we did not re-embark before half past three. Dined on board the *Medea* and got back about half past seven.

The next morning Lord Durham's intention of throwing up the Government seemed pretty well known. Between 300 and 400 of the principal British Inhabitants came to write their names; and a few days afterwards, when the arrival of the *Great Western* brought out the official intelligence, without such explanation as could make it possible for Lord Durham to change his intention, and when he had unequivocally announced that intention in an answer to an address from the Deputies who had been sent from New Brunswick, Nova Scotia, and Prince

---

[1] On July 28th the Prime Minister wrote to Durham regarding the ordinance, 'I have nothing to express but the most entire approval and concurrence. I am happy to hear that you have settled the difficult affair of the prisoners and settled it so well.' Cited in Chester W. New, *Lord Durham* (Oxford, 1929), pp. 438-9.

[2] Charles Grant, Baron Glenelg, was Colonial Secretary from 1835 to 1839. His letter to Durham was dated July 31st.

Edward Island, to confer on the subject of a general Union of
the Provinces, there was but one expression of indignation
against the authors of the mischief, of confidence in Lord
Durham's administration, and of regret and dismay at his departure from the whole British population of both Provinces.
Addresses and deputations came pouring in from every town
and village in the Canadas and so much unanimity had, I believe,
never before existed. Lords Brougham³ and Melbourne were
burnt in Effigy in Montreal, Quebec and other places. At the
same time the French population seemed to exult and a meeting
was called at Quebec in the suburb of St. Roque for the purpose
of voting thanks to Lord Brougham and Mr. Leader.⁴ This meeting was a failure – One man, a Mr. Charles Drolet,⁵ having been
chairman, Secretary, Mover and Seconder of every resolution –
but the mischief had been equally done. From this moment, all
hope of reconciling the two races, slight as it had ever been, was
completely lost in the proceedings which were forced on by this
act of folly and cowardice on the part of the Home Government.
Every day now made the breach between them wider. Some
objection to the wording of the resolutions, or other pretext
equally frivolous, was made use of by the French Canadians to
account for their declining, almost to a man, to unite in any
address to Lord Durham and they began openly to show their
disposition. On one occasion objecting to the use of the expression 'British Interests' by Lord Durham, at another complaining
of distinctions being made between the English and French
Inhabitants in the civilities shown (most impartially to all) at

³ Lord Durham and Lord Brougham had been close friends early in their
   careers but they had quarrelled and had become antagonistic to each other.
   Brougham led the attack on Durham's ordinance.
⁴ John Temple Leader was a prominent Radical who acted with Brougham in
   an effort to embarrass Melbourne's government.
⁵ Charles Drolet was a Quebec lawyer and a supporter of the *patriote* cause.
   He was subsequently arrested for assisting the imprisoned patriots, Theller
   and Dodge, to escape from the Quebec citadel but eluded his captors and
   fled to the United States.

the Château, and a French Judge, Bédard[6] (of whom more afterwards), was even encouraged to pronounce the ordinance of
the Governor in Council, establishing a Police for Montreal and
Quebec on the same footing as the Metropolitan Police of England, illegal!

But in another way the mischief appears to me to have been
still greater. Tho' the effects are yet to be seen, I am convinced
that nothing ever tended so much to weaken the connexion
between England and the Canadas, as a Colony, as this unfortunate act of the Home Government. Before this, People had
begun to say that if the only consequence of preserving the
connexion was to have constant interference from home when it
was not wanted, the sooner they looked out for themselves the
better, and that language has now increased to a great extent
and will, no doubt, at last produce its effect.

Lord Durham will go home as a most popular Governor with
all the British Party, tho' the great majority of them were
strongly opposed to the plan, to which he was supposed favourable, for a general federal Union of all the North American
Provinces. Nothing could be more clearly proved than this was
at the meeting called at Montreal to address him on the subject,
where at the same time that resolutions were passed expressive
of regret at his proposed departure, and of hope that his determination might yet be changed, another resolution was all but
unanimously adopted, deprecating the proposed plan and recommending as the only means of preserving British Connexion, an
immediate Legislative Union of the two Canadas.

Early in October Lord Durham issued a long proclamation,
explaining the motives which actuated him in resigning and the
Principles on which he had wished to conduct the Government

6 Elzéar Bédard, the son of Pierre Bédard, was a supporter of Papineau in the
legislative assembly and moved the *Ninety-two Resolutions* in 1834. As
Papineau became more extreme Bédard split with him and in 1836 accepted
an appointment as judge of the Court of King's Bench. He was suspended
in 1838 for ruling against the legality of Sir John Colborne's ordinance
suspending *habeas corpus*, but he was reinstated on August 8, 1840.

of the Province. It was too long and one part, in which he announced to the Exiles and Refugees affected by the disallowed ordinance that there was nothing now to prevent their return to Canada, was, in my opinion, extremely objectionable. It will give his enemies some ground for saying that his wish was to resign in such a manner as to make the embarrassment of the Government and of his Successor as great as possible, and besides I doubt the Law of it. Mr. Hagerman,[7] Attorney General for Upper Canada, who was at Quebec at the time, was distinctly of opinion that the disallowance of the Ordinance merely put these men back in their former position and that the amnesty extended to all others could in no case be taken to include them.

The various addresses, etc. made no change in Lord Durham's intention of returning. At one time he thought of going thro' the States and embarking from New York, after visiting Washington, etc. the first week in December, the *Inconstant* being sent round to meet him there. But, before the time proposed for his departure arrived, such alarming accounts had arrived from both Provinces of organization on the Lines and in the States that it was thought better that he should start direct from the River, and accordingly the *Inconstant* was ordered to be in readiness for the first of November. Cavendish, one of his Aides-de-Camp, had been sent home by the *Great Western* to announce his intended return.

I saw some of the letters giving information of the designs and plans of the Patriots and sympathizers. The accounts of the organization in the west about Detroit and on the Ohio, were certainly formidable – 80,000! men being said to be sworn and to have paid a dollar each for the Laudable purpose of invading Canada, and establishing a republic. One division of the Liberating Army was to act simultaneously from Vermont upon Lower Canada and success was certain!

Lord Durham appeared to me wrong in attributing this entirely to the news of his going home. Tho' greatly exaggerated,

---

[7] Christopher Hagerman was an Upper Canadian high Tory and an uncompromising opponent of any plan to unite the two Canadas.

it was quite clear that some organization had been going on all the summer with a view to troubles in the winter and his remaining would not, I am convinced, have prevented them. The danger might probably be (and I think it was) increased by the distrust this act of the home Government created among the Loyal Inhabitants and by the increased courage it gave the Rebels.

Sir John Colborne had already consented to remain for the winter at all events. Lord Durham gave him Carte Blanche as to the measures necessary to be adopted, and before he sailed the 93rd Regiment had been brought up from Halifax and another Regiment was sent for to New Brunswick and an immense number of Volunteers were authorized to be raised in both Provinces.

In the meantime a great sensation had been created in Quebec by the wonderful escape of the Political Prisoners, Theller,[8] Dodge,[9] etc. from the Citadel at Quebec. The accompanying account by Theller I believe to be substantially correct, having seen a letter, after their escape, from Sutherland[10]–who had been confined with them, tho' previously separated from them, and declining to join in the attempt – giving a nearly similar account of the manner in which they *intended* to effect it. There is no doubt of the connivance of the Sergeant who had charge of them and I have since heard that he and one of the Sentries have been sentenced to be shot. This turns out not to be true. The Sergeant is reduced – two of the Sentries sentenced to imprisonment, and two are acquitted.

[8] Edward Theller, an adventurous Irish-born American and a patriot general, was captured while leading a raid on Amherstburg in January 1838. After being held in the Toronto jail under sentence of death, he was moved to the Quebec citadel from whence he escaped and returned to the United States. Theller published an account of his experiences in his *Canada, 1837-8*.

[9] 'Colonel' W. W. Dodge was among the patriots captured with Edward Theller on board the schooner *Anne*.

[10] Thomas Jefferson Sutherland had been a solicitor and the editor of several New York newspapers before joining the patriot movement. In January 1838, he led the force which briefly occupied Bois Blanc Island about 500 yards from Amherstburg. He was arrested by Colonel John Prince on the ice between Detroit and Windsor in March 1838 and was sentenced to transportation, but after spending several months in the citadel at Quebec he was deported to the United States.

A few days before his departure, the Brigade of Guards invited Lord Durham to a great farewell dinner which was given at the Château. Nothing could be more flattering than his reception. The more so that nearly the whole of the officers are of high Tory Families. Sir John Colborne comes down to take over the Administration of the Government and to see Lord Durham off. On the 1st November, as had been settled, at two o'clock he embarks on board the *Inconstant*, and at four o'clock, the wind being foul, the *Canada* Steamer tows her down the river. The streets were lined by the Guards. The Trades walked in procession and every possible compliment was paid by the British Inhabitants. Sir J[ohn] Colborne and Sir J[ames] Macdonell accompanied them on board. Captain Pring had arranged the Cabins as comfortably as possible considering the small space and the number of Passengers he has. Caroline and I bid them good-bye soon after three and returned to the *desolate* house of Assembly where we eat a melancholy dinner. At four o'clock Sir John was sworn in as Administrator of the Government and the salute customary on the occasion was fired at the moment the *Inconstant* got under way, serving thus both as a farewell to the Old and a welcome to the new Governor!

Montreal,

September 30, 1838.

My Dear Father,

I must refer you to a long letter which I have written to Henry, partly on board the Steamer and partly since my arrival here, for most of what I have got to say on what I must call this most distressing news. I have directed it to Howick, and if Henry is not there, pray open it. It is the letter with my initials in the corner. I fear it is a long twaddle, but I do feel so very strongly: First, that the Ordinance itself was the only course to be adopted under the circumstances; Secondly, that Lambton has been so

infamously treated from the moment he left England, both by
the opposition and the Government; and thirdly, that the consequences to this Country are likely to be so very disastrous that
I have written much more than I intended. I would give anything
to know what you would have done in his situation. I think it
impossible for him to stay, and yet I wish I was more clear in
my opinion. He has been infamously treated and owes no consideration for the situation in which his return may place the
Government. This Country and his own character are what he
must consider, and I wish I could be more sure of the manner in
which his return will affect both. He thinks his authority will
be so much weakened by what has taken place, that anybody
else, particularly Sir John Colborne, will now have more chance
of doing good than he has. And there is no doubt that Sir John
Colborne's Acts would not be questioned as his have been. But
he had acquired the confidence of all those who have a stake
in the Country. They had hopes of a satisfactory settlement of
all the long existing causes of dispute, and there is no doubt
that his return under these circumstances will produce a most
discouraging effect, if it does not altogether destroy these hopes.
I say nothing of the increased irritation between the two races
which is the result of this unfortunate business, and which will
probably end in bloodshed. His continued presence might, I
cannot but think, at any rate lessen some of these evils. Hope
would not be quite destroyed and hope, at present, is everything.

For himself I could not advise him to stay – I really think it
would kill him. I never knew a man so affected by the attacks
upon him both in Parliament and the Newspapers, and his mind
works upon his body to a degree that is quite fearful. Colonel
Couper and Charles Buller both told me they were at one time
really frightened about him. Whether having had so much to do
with Newspapers makes him more irritable under their attacks,
I do not know. But I am more than ever convinced that no public
man can steer too clear of any connexion or communication
whatever with the Press.

The feeling in this Country, as far as he is concerned, is certainly most satisfactory and flattering to him. I do not believe there is a man in the Country who has British Interests at heart whose confidence he has not gained, and the whole Press now, without exception of Parties, joins in the anxious expression of their wish that he may be induced to stay and in their indignation against the author of all the mischief and the Government which has been weak enough to sacrifice him.

There is to be a meeting here tomorrow, called by all the People of most influence in the Place, to address him on the subject and he will return home with the unanimous expression of the confidence of the British Inhabitants of both Provinces. Meetings having also been convened at Quebec, Toronto and other Places of which the results are not doubtful. I think too he richly deserves any expression of confidence that may be given him. No Governor ever came to this Country more bent upon ascertaining its real state, more free from Party bias or predilection, or more anxious to propose such measures as should really be for the benefit of the Colony.

I wish you could see his dispatch of the 9th August to Lord Glenelg. It is a confidential one on the state of the Country generally and so clear and correct a statement I think I never read. I had no idea he had formed so correct an estimate of the state of the Parties in this Country, as far as I can judge from what I have heard on all occasions and in all places, on board the different Steamers and elsewhere. I really believe that if he had not been thus interfered with he was in the fair road towards effecting, or at all events towards laying the foundation of a satisfactory and permanent settlement. It really is too provoking to think that the Duke of Wellington[11] and the Government

---

[11] In the debate on Durham's ordinance, the Duke of Wellington asserted that it was illegal to banish men without trial and to threaten them with death if they should return. He placed the blame on the Melbourne government for failing to issue any instructions regarding the composition of the Special Council which was intended to advise Durham on the use of his extraordinary powers.

should have assisted Lord Brougham in destroying all these prospects.

The winter is coming fast on now – the leaves are quite dead, and a few days' frost, and a high wind will leave them as bare as they were when we came here four months ago. I do not know how winter would agree with Louisa and her Children, but I do not think I ever saw any of them looking half so well as they were when I left Quebec the night before last. Louisa herself was not looking well, being very much out of spirits at all that has occurred. Before that she was very unhappy about Lambton's low spirits and was only just getting comfortable again when this unexpected blow came. I have written a great deal about it and still it is impossible that I should give you any adequate idea of the effect it has produced in this Country. It is not too much to say that Brougham is universally *executed*, and that the whole Imperial Legislature, Government and Parliament, come in for their share.

I shall go back to Quebec on Thursday next, being merely come up here for the returns. Caroline is still there, and we shall remain now, in all probability, till they go. I certainly now shall not be anxious to remain one day longer than I can help, and hope that by March next I may be able to turn once more towards home. I need not say I wish the time was come, and that in the meantime I am, My Dear Father,

Ever your most affectionate son,
C. Grey.

Quebec,
October 10, 1838.

My Dear Father,

Since I wrote to you by the *Great Western* I have received your letters of the 19th and 29th of August. It is most satisfactory to me to think that though, as I did myself, you disliked

my being a member of the Special Council at all, you approved
of the Act for the purpose of passing which I was appointed,
and that you condemn as strongly as we do here the conduct
of the Government in disallowing it.

My last letters to you and Henry, with the correspondence
you will no doubt see in the Newspapers, will acquaint you in
some degree with the consequences of this Act of the Government. But it will still give you an inadequate idea of the reality.
I really do not think I ever knew dismay so general, not so
much from the mere fact of Lambton's going home, as from
the loss of all hope of *any* permanent settlement of Canadian
affairs being effected.

He certainly had obtained their confidence, as the unanimous
addresses from all Parts of both Provinces prove to an extent,
I believe, never before reached by any Governor, and confident
hopes had begun to be entertained of a successful result to his
Mission. Who, they now say, will even attempt to succeed in
what, from the want of support at home, he has failed? And
what hopes are there, while the Provinces are merely used at
home as a means of Party warfare, of *any* Government considering the question with a view to Canadian interests? Whether
Lambton *would* have succeeded or not, I can hardly judge.
There is no doubt – as the result of the Meeting at Montreal
proves, where a resolution was carried all but unanimously,
that a Legislative Union between the two Provinces was the
only remedy for existing evils, and that any plan of a general
Confederation would only increase these evils – that there was
a formidable opposition to overcome, before he could have
obtained such an acquiescence in his plan as would have enabled
him to carry it. But there were almost the same objections to
every plan. The Upper Canadians, though to what extent is
much disputed, are said to be as much opposed to the plan of
a Legislative Union between the Provinces. Whether or not they
are more favourable to the general Plan I know not, but I should
doubt it. At all events Mr. Hagerman, the Attorney General of

the Upper Province, with whom I came down a few days ago in the Steamboat from Montreal, is decidedly opposed to it, as leading inevitably to separation from England within ten years. This is the great objection made by all the opponents of the Plan, and this, notwithstanding that the original proposition of doing away with the Legislative Councils has been abandoned.

But this difference of opinion, or rather this belief that Lambton was favourable to a plan for the future Government of the Country to which the great majority is opposed, has in no degree affected the confidence they are universally disposed to place in him. They are all convinced that his sole object is to do that which is found, on consideration, to be best for the interests of the Provinces themselves, and the fair way in which he discusses everything, and the readiness with which he listens to any objections, and yields to them when convinced of their propriety, wins everybody. I hardly expected this from him, but Couper tells me that he never knew anybody who took any remarks in better grace than he does. Then he certainly had been very diligent in endeavouring to obtain every possible information respecting the Country. In short, I think *he* *deserved*, to the fullest extent, the confidence he had acquired.

I wish I could say that I think he has done equally well since the arrival of the news of the disallowance. I do not like any of the three long dispatches he wrote announcing his intention to return home, and arguing the legal question. And I disapprove most strongly of the answers given yesterday to the addresses presented from Toronto and this place. I speak entirely now from the impression they made upon me when he read them, for I have not yet seen them in print. In the former he took such a view of what he had actually done in this Country as made me hot to a degree I can hardly describe – and very incorrect as far as I can make out, as to facts. In the latter he makes what struck me as a most improper attack upon the House of Lords. His object seems to have been, both in these answers and his proclamation, which I enclose, to make it as difficult as

possible for Government to settle the question. I am inclined
to think he was right not to acquiesce in the suggestion of Lord
Glenelg to pass other Ordinances, sentencing the banished People
to any punishment short of death if they should return, and
continuing the suspension of the Habeas Corpus Act. Even if
he had agreed in the propriety of doing so, he could have no
assurance that they would not have been disallowed, in the
same manner as those he did pass, under similar pressure in the
House of Lords. But I think he has acted very wrong in declaring in his proclamation that there is nothing to prevent these
men returning when they please.[12] Of course, after such a
declaration it would be impossible to interfere with them, and
yet the opinion of all Lawyers here that I have seen, with the
exception of C[harles] Buller, is that they are merely placed in
the same situation as they were in before the passing of the
Ordinance. It seems to me clear that they are still excepted from
the Amnesty, though the manner in which they were to be
disposed of under the Ordinance has been disallowed. I cannot
understand Buller's law, that the punishment awarded being
disallowed, the exception of these men which is mentioned in
the Proclamation of Amnesty is also necessarily disallowed.

I regret it all very much. I had approved so entirely of his
Government of the Provinces that I am grieved beyond measure
for his sake that he has not taken higher ground on resigning.
I fear that by his Acts since the disallowance of his Ordinances
he has laid himself open to just censure and attacks and has
weakened beyond measure, in his anxiety to make things as
difficult as possible for the Government, the very triumphant
case he would otherwise have had.

I hear the three dispatches I allude to are to be copied to send
to you. I think you will agree with me that even if he had been
inclined to retract his resignation, the Government could not

---

12 Durham's proclamation, issued on October 9, 1838, contained his defence of
   the policy he had followed and censured the Melbourne government for not
   supporting him.

have allowed him to remain after these dispatches, unless they are even meaner than I take them to be. He had before written a dispatch on the Turton affair which I can scarcely imagine being submitted to and I almost expected to hear of his recall at any rate.

I have not heard how his answer was liked yesterday. Certainly the meeting was most enthusiastic. There could not have been fewer than 2,500 People present, all respectably dressed, and far superior to any similar Assemblage I ever saw in England, and the cheering both when he appeared and when he read his answer was tremendous. There were 4,279 signatures to the Quebec Address including a good number of Canadians.

The expectation seems now very general that we shall have a disturbed winter and the 23rd Regiment has been sent for to Halifax. I believe they will go at once to the Upper Province and in that case we shall certainly remain at Montreal. I cannot myself believe in our having anything serious, though I think isolated cases of outrage very probable, and that we shall have endless reports for the purpose of harrassing the troops as much as possible. It is very fortunate that Sir John Colborne remains, who understands these reports, and will not suffer us to be disturbed more than is necessary.

I will keep my letter open and add anything I think may interest you, but it has already grown to an unconscionable length.

SATURDAY, OCTOBER 13.

There are no tidings yet of the *Royal William*, but the bag is to be made up tonight, therefore I will close my letter. There is nothing new of any sort. Preparations are making for departure, the *Inconstant* getting bulkheads up and arranging the cabins as fast as possible, in order to start for New York or the Chesapeake, wherever it may be settled that they shall embark. The last dinner is given here today, and I believe they will certainly leave this for Montreal on the 27th. They propose remaining there four days, and then we shall bid them good-bye. We shall spend the winter very differently from what we expected, but though we shall miss them so much ourselves, I cannot but rejoice on their account that they will not pass a winter here, if the circumstances under which they go home had only been more comfortable.

I hear nothing more from the Country to induce me to believe in our having really anything to do. Attempts will no doubt be made to harrass us, but Sir John Colborne understands it so well that I hope we shall get through pretty quietly.

I hope this will find you all quite well at Howick. I do not say much when I say I would willingly exchange Niagara, and everything else that we either have seen or may see in North America, to be with you there.

Give my best love to my Mother, Georgiana, etc., and believe me ever, My Dear Father,

> Your most affectionate son,
> C. Grey.

I hear Lord John Russell has written advising Lambton to come home if he thinks his authority so much weakened as to deprive him of the hope of doing any good by staying.

> Quebec,
> October 20, 1838.

My Dear Father,

Mr. Dillon goes home with dispatches this afternoon at three o'clock which I was not aware of till after breakfast, or I would have had my letters ready. Not that I have a great deal to add to what I have before written to you on the subject of the disallowance of the Ordinances and Lambton's resignation. What I then said about his proclamation has since been more than confirmed by the tone of nearly all the Papers. It was the doing, I believe, entirely of Mr. Wakefield and Charles Buller, of the latter of whom particularly I have not the slightest opinion. He is clever certainly, but he is weak and vacillating to a degree, and, like all of his class of Politicians, unpractical and tricky. When I talked to Lambton on the subject before he had issued his proclamation, I thought he was of [the] opinion that though the Ordinances were disallowed as to the manner in which the Prisoners were to be disposed of, they were still good as explaining *who* were intended to be excepted from the Amnesty. However, Buller and Wakefield appear to have convinced Lambton that the Ordinance being annulled, there were no longer any exceptions to the Amnesty, and he has overlooked the obvious construction which was to be put upon his announcing that there was nothing to prevent the return of the Refugees. I fear too the construction is not altogether wrong, and that he has not been able to avoid spiting the Government by making the embarrassment caused by their Act as great as possible – forgetting that he was the person who would be most affected by it. I hear Sir John Colborne's first Act will be the suspension of the Habeas Corpus Act, and other measures to which Lambton has declared he would not have resource, and I think he will be quite right. In the present state of the Country it is evident we can only be considered as in Military occupation of it. The accounts from the frontier leave no doubt of an organization to an *immense* extent in the United States which has been preparing all summer for an invasion of Canada during the winter, and this, added to the equal certainty of active agitation having been resumed since the late events in the Lower Province, makes it indispensable, I think, at once to prepare by calling out and Arming the Volunteers. But this is a state of things which cannot continue. Parliament must at once interfere to settle something, though what that something is to be puzzles me. I doubt it being possible in any manner to preserve the Colony – as a Colony.

Lambton's plans are changed and instead of going through the States he sails on the 1st November in the *Inconstant* direct for England so that in all probability you will not receive this till after his arrival.

There is another circumstance connected with his resignation which has annoyed me, if I am correct in my suspicions, but which I have not mentioned to anybody and should not like to mention to anybody but you as it seems to me that it must be wrong. Several Copies were made of his dispatches of which one was sent to you. There were two similar packets, which were not put in the bag, but which Conroy had to forward otherwise, directed to the King of the Belgians and to *Count Nesselrode*, and marked confidential. If these were Copies of his dispatches, it seems to me it must be very wrong to communicate them to the Russian Minister at Petersburg and I cannot conceive what else they could be.

I have no more time nor have I anything more worth writing about. The escape of the Prisoners you will see ample details of in all the Papers. There is no doubt in my mind of the connivance of the Sergeant in charge of them. I will write again by the *Inconstant*, and we shall be better able to judge then, in all probability, as to our prospects for the winter.

Our best love to my Mother, etc., and believe me ever, My Dear Father,

Your most affectionate son,

C. Grey.

I find I have forgotten to mention that Mr. Turton protested against the part of the Proclamation to which I have alluded, not giving any decided opinion as to the Law, but a very decided one, in any case, as to its impolity. He is out of sight the best man Lambton has about him. Colonel Couper also agreed with him about it. Mr. Turton was unfortunately absent when the Proclamation was issued.

Quebec,
October 31, 1838.

My Dear Father,

Lambton sails in the *Inconstant* direct for England tomorrow, and though of course you will receive from him much more information than I can pretend to give you, I will not neglect the opportunity of writing by them.

I do not know what the last accounts from the Country are, but I know that all the Authorities, even those who have hitherto been least disposed to attach credit to the constant reports which have been poured in upon us, are now convinced that unless we are well prepared, serious attempts will be made both from without and within in the course of the next few months. The 93rd Regiment has in consequence been already brought up from the Lower Provinces and the *Athol* and *Andromache* sail tomorrow to bring up another. The Volunteers are also in the course of being very generally called out.

I cannot doubt these precautions being necessary. For Sir John Colborne is certainly very far from being an alarmist, but I cannot imagine with the force we shall thus have at our disposal that, mad as the People are, they will be mad enough to incur the certain consequences of an open outbreak. In Upper Canada they expect an invasion conducted on similar principles to that which has obtained possession of Texas and I certainly believe that, if we are not prepared for it, something of the sort is likely, and in this Country it is equally clear that the disaffection among the French population has gained strength, from whatever cause, and is now much more general than it was last year. But in Upper Canada we have the bulk of the Population with us, and in this Province, though the great majority are against us, we have so strong a force of regulars and volunteers in the very midst of them that I cannot conceive any movement being attempted with the slightest chance of success. Then I cannot quite understand the winter being the

best season for such attempts. It is quite clear if we have anything serious to do in this Province, that our system must be to
burn the houses on each side of the roads as we go along and,
with the thermometer 20 degrees below zero, what will become
of the poor misguided wretches? And yet I see nothing else for
it if, unfortunately, the disturbances recommence in Lower
Canada. We should be mad, with the whole of the Country
population against us, not to take the only means of preventing
successful resistance to the troops.

In Upper Canada it is clear, whatever is in contemplation is
in connexion with a systematic plan organized in the States
for the Conquest of the Country, and it does seem to me that it
will be the very extreme of weakness and cowardice if we do
not make the general Government answerable for any invasion
of our territory conducted by American Citizens with means
furnished entirely in their Country. It is not quite enough to
say that it is against their wishes.

It is said that 80,000 men are sworn in Ohio, Michigan and
the west of the State of New York for the invasion of Upper
Canada. And that nine Steamers have already been secured by
them on Lake Erie. The number, of course, is an exaggeration,
but there is sufficient ground for alarm, and in consequence, in
my opinion, for serious remonstrance with the United States
Government.

I do hope Parliament will be called together with as little
delay as possible and that some steps will be taken to get out of
the embarrassment the state of this Country occasions. I believe
the only way will be to establish an independent Country on
any terms. I must say I shall be very glad when I am able to get
out of it all, for the service we shall have is not likely to be of
the most agreeable nature most certainly.

I was very glad to see in the papers this morning an account
of the arrival of the *Cleopatra*. I suppose she will be at once
paid off and that George will lose no time in joining you at
Howick. This is an additional reason for regretting being in this

Country. I can only hope that the state of things may be such in spring as to enable me to return home, though I cannot say I feel very confident on the subject at present.

I do not expect to be moved from Montreal. I fancy Sir John is anxious to keep a strong force concentrated there in reserve, ready to move on any point. There will be four complete Regiments of Infantry there, with two on the Richelieu, besides Artillery and the two Cavalry regiments and, as the Brigade of Guards will also be brought higher up in all probability on the arrival of the Regiment at Quebec, which has now been sent for, there will be a force of 5,000 regular troops ready at very short notice to repel any attack from the side of Vermont.

I fear some of my letters, if put under cover to Lambton, may find their way back to England which will be very provoking. It is now some time since I heard from you, and I need not say I am anxious to get a letter.

Give our best love to my Mother, and all my brothers and sisters who may be with you, and believe me ever, My Dear Father,

Your most affectionate son,
C. Grey.

CHAPTER VII

The Second Insurrection

Two days after Lord Durham's departure the Greys left for Montreal. At Sorel they heard rumours of a new uprising which were confirmed when they reached Montreal early Sunday morning, November 4th. Three days later Colonel Grey's regiment was ordered to St. Johns where a force was being assembled to attack the rebel headquarters at Napierville. The summary entry made in his journal on December 19th provides a first-hand account of the suppression of the second outbreak of rebellion in Lower Canada.

L'ACADIE, DEC. 19, 1838 (cont.).

Friday, 2nd November, take our places to return to Montreal in the *John Bull* Steamer. Sir J[ohn] Colborne and suite, Colonel Couper, etc. also go in her. I dine with the Grenadier Guards and embark at twelve. Owing to the state of the tide, we do not sail till four A.M. and having a Schooner and heavy barge in tow make but slow progress, and do not reach Sorel till half past six o'clock. All sorts of reports reach us here. People have come in from the neighbourhood of St. Charles and St. Ours with the news that the People are up on the whole line of the Richelieu, and that an attack is meditated on Sorel in the course of the evening. It is clear that something has happened, tho' to what extent we are, of course, quite in the dark. Sir John Colborne, in consequence of the intelligence received, determines to go on to Montreal and we sail again after remaining about two hours. We get to Montreal early on Sunday morning about half past eight. Just as I was dressed a messenger arrives from Beauharnois with the intelligence that the People had risen, had made Mr. Ellice and the other 'Old Country' People Prisoners, and were in occupation of the place to the number of 400 or 500 men. On going with this news to Sir John Colborne, I heard that similar intelligence had been received from Châteauguay, that at La Tortue, six miles from Laprairie, similar occurrences had taken place, and that two Farmers had been murdered.[1] On the road to Quebec the mail had been stopped, tho' afterwards allowed to proceed. On the Richelieu the People were out in great force and 'Traitor' Debartzch had escaped from St. Ours with great difficulty. In short a combined movement of Rebels had taken place to a great extent. It was said Montreal was to be attacked and the troops were ordered to be kept in readiness and at three o'clock the different Regiments assembled at their different alarm Posts and remained under Arms till seven. The Volunteers also mustered in great force. In short there was all the excitement of a besieged town.

In the meantime Martial Law had been proclaimed for the district of Montreal and all suspected Persons were arrested in the course of the day – among whom the most prominent were M. LaFontaine, formerly a fellow Labourer of Papineau's, and against whom there was a warrant last year, Viger,[2] President of the Banque du Peuple, and his Brother, etc., etc. The Governor had previously received such reports that it was thought right to take the precaution of sending the 73rd Regiment to

[1] On November 3, 1838, a band of *patriotes* began seizing arms owned by the loyal population at Rivière à la Tortue. David Vitty, with whom several of his neighbours had taken refuge, refused to open the door to the rebels. Shots were exchanged and Aaron Walker was killed and Vitty seriously wounded.

[2] Louis Michel Viger. The 'brother' referred to was Denis Benjamin Viger. Both men were cousins of Louis Joseph Papineau but they were not brothers.

St. Johns and 100 men of the 24th to Laprairie where it was said the Barracks were to be burned. Intelligence was received by Sir John Colborne in the course of the day that the Head Quarters of the Rebels were fixed at Napierville where Côté and Nelson were with some French officers. Reports varied as to their numbers, some making them as many as 4,000 with seven guns. The *Canada* was dispatched to Quebec to bring up a Battalion of Guards and preparations were commenced for attacking them with a force which it would be impossible for them to resist. On Monday [November 5th] the 24th Regiment was crossed over to Laprairie. On Wednesday [November 7th], on the arrival of two Companies of the Grenadier Guards, we also crossed and went by railroad to St. Johns where we joined the 73rd under Colonel Love. The next day [November 8th] we marched to L'Acadie where we joined Sir James Macdonell's Brigade consisting of the Guards, 71st and 7th Hussars, and where the Force for the attack on Napierville was concentrated. The next day [November 9th] we advanced within three miles of the Place where we halted for the night and went on the next morning [November 10th] to find the birds all flown. About 1,500 of them had dispersed just before we came up. A great many Arms were found and about 100 stragglers taken Prisoners. Colonel Love with the 73rd and King's Dragoon Guards came up at the same time. The whole Force halted at Napierville with the exception of the Cavalry sent different ways in pursuit.

This may be considered as the end of the rebellion, as in a very few days afterwards we heard that the People on the Richelieu had also dispersed and on the same day the Glengarry Volunteers from Upper Canada with a Company of my Regiment entered Beauharnois and liberated the Prisoners. Those at Châteauguay also dispersing on hearing the news of our arrival at Napierville. The only show of fighting was at the river Lacolle where the Volunteers were attacked on the 7th, repulsing the rebels with some loss, and at Odelltown on the 9th where the Rebels were again the Assailants being again repulsed with a heavy loss – the Volunteers losing a Captain and four men killed and nine wounded. At Beauharnois, also, the rebels fired one volley before they ran, which killed one and wounded three of the 71st. Since that time the troops have been marched about in different directions, making arrests and disarming the Inhabitants and, with the exception of the reports still current as to the designs of the Refugees on the other side of the Lines, the rebellion in Lower Canada may be considered at an end. It is remarkable that none of the Districts engaged in last year's Rebellion did anything this year. The People assembled certainly at St. Charles, but dispersed without doing anything, and to the North of Montreal all remained perfectly quiet. Colonel Wetherall told me on the 3rd, when we were under Arms in Montreal, that he heard Girouard, a notorious Rebel pardoned for last year's offenses, had sent word that it was a failure and that they had better remain quiet. It is clear from what I heard afterwards that the rising was premature, but what caused it to be so does not appear. It could not have been the arrest of several Persons by Colonel Taylor from St. Johns, on Friday night the 2nd, for this could not have been known the next day at Châteauguay and Beauharnois.

I should have mentioned that on Saturday the rebels left Châteauguay with their Prisoners, Mr. Ellice, etc. and dispersed that night at La Pigeonnière, near St. Edouard.

To return to our own movements, on the 11th we received orders to march from Napierville on St. Edouard's. Sir John at first intended to burn the rebel homes at Napierville and we were ordered to select Non-Commissioned Officers for the purpose. It was countermanded, however, but too late to prevent several homes being burnt, among them Dr. Côté's which we saw in full blaze after we left the place.

My People got a good deal of money here which was the occasion of a good deal of irregularity afterwards. On arriving at Napierville on Saturday [November 10th], 50 of my men had

been sent round the back in rear of it in search of straggling
rebels who were said to be concealed there. They came up with
a Charrette which had upset in attempting to escape and a box,
which appears to have belonged to Dr. Côté, coming open in
the fall, a great number of half dollars were scattered about
with other property of which the Soldiers became possessed.
There could not have been less than £150 – money that had been
taken by the Rebels from the Curé. I was not aware of the circumstance in time to get it from the men who considered it as
lawful plunder as, to a certain extent, it was. The officer in
charge of the Party gave me a large bundle of letters which
were from Dr. Côté to his wife, beginning before their marriage. There being nothing material in them as to the Rebellion,
I took care of them for the purpose of having them restored to
Mrs. Côté. One or two that I looked at were amusing from the
manner in which he mentions Lord Aylmer,[3] whom he always
calls 'Old Matthew', and Lord Gosford, whom he describes as
having the confidence of *no* Party. Tho' the money obtained by
my men on this occasion may be considered as fair plunder, I
am afraid there was a great deal committed by the troops generally which did [not] admit of such justification. I can only
say I did my best to prevent my People sharing in it and succeeded so far that we had less than our neighbours. But for the
first three days, having no Commissariat, the different Regiments had to supply themselves and it was difficult to prevent
the men confining themselves to Poultry and Provisions. The
indiscriminate slaughter of the former by the Hussars, Guards
and Artillery in particular, I never saw equalled, and the example was too seducing not to be followed, tho' I did endeavour to
check it by ordering officers commanding Companies, where
they did not receive rations, to supply their men and by pun-
ishing severely all such men as I found helping themselves. Still
I could not prevent [it] entirely till, after our arrival at Beauharnois, five men were tried for plundering and sentenced to a

[3] Matthew, 5th Baron Aylmer, Governor of Lower Canada from 1831 to 1835.

'Howick, the Grey Family Estate, in 1832'

In 'Lord Grey of the Reform Bill' by G. M. Trevelyan (London, 1920)

Montreal from St. Helen's Island   (A view that became quite familiar to Charles Grey)

From an aquatint by J Gray in the Public Archives of Canada

twelve months' imprisonment. Since that time, with the exception of isolated cases, all severely punished, I have had no complaint against the Regiment.

At St. Edouard's I was lodged with Major Denny and the Adjutant, Robertson, in the house of a M. Robitaille,[4] a cousin of Papineau's, who had been a Rebel last year, but who talked so candidly, apparently, of the fault he had then committed and his anxiety to avoid it for the future that I was surprised to hear he had been arrested some time afterwards as one of the prime movers of the Revolt in that neighbourhood. While halted here one of my men, Sentry over the General's quarters, shot a Canadian who attempted to rescue a Prisoner in his charge and then to make his own escape across the River. It appears that the man was quite justified, but I regret it nevertheless. Going into Napierville the light Company of the Guards shot three People, one a woman, under no such justification.

On the 12th the Brigade moved to St. Rémi in consequence of a Report that the Rebels had fortified themselves there in the Church. This, however, turns out to be unfounded and the next day we return to St. Edouard's. The road between these two places is execrable, leading thro' a black swamp in a wood which is found to be impassable for the Artillery, the frost having given, and is only made practicable for our light baggage cars by cutting down quantities of small trees to lay across the road.

On the 14th, in consequence of news received that an American force had landed below Prescott in Upper Canada, we are ordered to Beauharnois which forces us again to pass this road. I leave the Battalion with Denny and get Sir James Macdonell's leave to go round by Montreal. Ride to Laprairie where I am detained two hours waiting for a Steamer and do not reach Montreal till three o'clock. Every house as I passed had a small red handkerchief or rag stuck out of the thatch or window with 'Loyal' chalked in large letters on the door. Not one in 100 of

---

[4] Robert Robitaille was a cousin of Papineau's wife but was not directly related to the French-Canadian leader.

the men belonging to them had not joined the Rebels, but on
the failure of the revolt they had returned home and were now
in the greatest fright expecting their property would be burned.
I should have mentioned that on our first arrival at St. Rémi
we met the Glengarrys from Beauharnois and the expression
the Commanding Officer of them made use of to me was that,
'They had left a trail six miles wide'. His excuse was that this
was the second time they had been brought from their homes
and 'a Third time it would be worse'. Mr. Roebuck,[5] brother of
the Canadian Advocate and Agitator at home, accompanied this
party and distinguished himself beyond every one else as a
Plunderer and Robber. It was a common expression of the
Glengarrys that it was no use entering a house for 'Roebuck's
been there'. I heard afterwards at Beauharnois that he returned
to Coteau du Lac, where he resides, with two Bateaux loads of
Plunder, besides horses. These seem to have been the chief object
of the Glengarrys and the extent to which they carried the
system of appropriating them, whenever they found them, to
their own use, may be imagined from the fact of only 50 out of
their whole number – amounting to near 600 – who left
Beauharnois, returning on foot!

At Montreal I saw Sir John Colborne and received orders from
him not to move from Beauharnois without hearing from Head
Quarters as he considered the force which would have assembled
at Prescott, in addition to two companies of the Royals sent up
with Colonel Wetherall, as being amply sufficient.

Return to Beauharnois on the 16th in the *Henry Brougham*
Steamer which was making her first voyage since her capture
by the Rebels. Find the officers all crowded into the seigniory
House and the village completely gutted – one half of it at least
being burnt. Receive a note here which had been left by Colonel
Wetherall, desiring me to follow him with the 71st, which of
course, under the orders received from Sir John Colborne him-

---

[5] Henry William Roebuck, a stepson of John Simpson, the customs collector
at Coteau du Lac.

self, I pay no attention to. He had taken back the company of
the Regiment which came down from Kingston. The Regiment
remains at Beauharnois till the 26th November during which
time we are employed disarming the Inhabitants of the neighbourhood and collect from St. Timothée and Ste. Martine about
150 ball fowling Pieces which are destroyed. We also make
several arrests of Persons said to have been active during the
late disturbances.

A Board sits daily at the Mill, Major Denny President, to
enquire into the cases of the Prisoners brought in by the Volunteers. The result of which is that about 70 are sent in to
Montreal to stand their trial while about as many more are
discharged. They all appear to have turned out, but most plead
compulsion which, whether true or not, is allowed as a pallia-
tion in the cases of those not proved to have been particularly
active and, therefore, all those whom we do not consider it
worth while to detain are released. Many of the arrests made by
the Volunteers may be traced to local quarrels. These men have
certainly had a great deal of provocation, but now that they
have again got the upper hand they are disposed to exact too
severe a retribution and require to be kept in order. At the
same time it must be done with prudence as it would not do to
indispose those upon whom we must entirely depend for the
preservation of the Colony. Four companies, to consist each of
100 men, are ordered to be raised for the Beauharnois District
giving, with the Sedentary companies assembled for drill once
a week, a Volunteer force of near 1,100 men divided into two
Battalions. Head Quarters of one at Huntingdon – the other at
Beauharnois.

The Prescott attack having been completely defeated before
the arrival of Colonel Wetherall, my company here rejoins the
Head Quarters of the Regiment. The whole of the Invaders had
been either killed or taken Prisoners and it is satisfactory to
know that there were only *eight* British Subjects among them
and that they were not joined in Canada by a single man.

The Leader Von Schoultz,[6] a Pole, and I think 11 others of
the principal men among them have since been hanged in pur-
suance of the sentence of a Militia General Court Martial
assembled for their trial at Kingston.

On the 26th the Regiment marches to St. Pierre, or St. Constant as the village in the Parish of the above name is called,
where it remains till the [–] December. Here as at Beauharnois
we are employed disarming the People, making them take the
oath of allegiance and making arrests. One Company is detached to La Tortue where several men implicated in the murder of Walker[7] – a Farmer in the neighbourhood, on the night of
the 3rd November – are taken up. (Since tried and hanged at
Montreal on the 18th January. Their names were Ambroise and
Charles *Sanguinet*, François *Hamelin*, and Joseph *Robert*).[8] The
whole of the People of this district turned out on the night of
Saturday the 3rd November and on Sunday morning. According
to the account given by the Curé of the Place, M. Tessier, in
whose house I am lodged, about 1,000 men were assembled in
the large open space forming the centre of the Village. Towards
the evening of that day they dispersed, with the exception of a
few who went to Napierville on being told by Hébert,[9] who was
to have commanded the attack on Laprairie, and Camyré,[10] one
of their Leaders since arrested, that it was a failure; and since
that time they have professed unbounded loyalty. M. Tessier,
the Curé, is said to have [been] implicated and if not, it seems

6 Nils Szolteocky Von Schoultz was a Polish-born patriot who was captured
  on November 16, 1838, after the Battle of the Windmill near Prescott,
  Upper Canada. He was tried by court martial and was defended by John A.
  Macdonald.

7 Aaron Walker. See *supra*, p. 145, n. 1.

8 This comment on the hanging was inserted in the journal by Grey at a later
  date. In the original the journal is entered on right-hand pages only and the
  left-hand pages are generally left blank. This comment appears on a left-
  hand page.

9 Médard Hébert, one of the leaders of the second insurrection.

10 François Camyré, a St. Constant innkeeper. Although he actually took little
   part in the rebellion, the court martial which tried Camyré sentenced him
   to death with a recommendation for clemency. The sentence was shortly
   set aside and he was released from prison.

extraordinary how little these Priests seem to have known of what was going on. They all deny all expectation of anything till it actually broke out which appears hardly credible. As to the plea of compulsion, a man named Louis Decoigne, himself very active as a leader at Châteauguay, says it was not the case, that they began swearing in as early as June last, that he himself swore in 250 on the 1st of August, that they had not the slightest idea of failing, they had been led to expect great assistance from the Americans, and that 7,000 stand of Arms had already been brought in and that more were expected with 42 pieces of cannon! If the Americans have assisted them at all to the extent the language of the sympathizers would lead us to suppose, it seems odd that in the 400 stand of Arms more or less, which we have collected and destroyed, I should not have seen a single American piece.

Charles Grey's letters to his father provide additional details concerning the events of November and December, 1838.

Montreal,
November 5, 1838.

My Dear Father,

On Saturday night all my anticipations of again writing were upset by a simultaneous rising of the People in different places. We had heard at Sorel as we came up in the Steamer on Saturday night that several hundred People were in arms on the Richelieu, about St. Denis, St. Charles, etc., and Sir John Colborne, who was on his way up to Montreal in the same vessel, received also letters from General Clitherow from this place, written in great alarm. Still Sir John thought little of it, and he was with difficulty prevented from remaining at Sorel, where he has a house and where part of his Family were, in order to pass a quiet Sunday. I was rather surprised therefore when we received such a confirmation of all these reports on Sunday morning.

I had hardly got up here from the Steamer, on board of which we slept, when a boy arrived from Beauharnois to say it had been attacked and taken possession of by about 400 Rebels at two o'clock that morning, and that Mr. Ellice, his Agent, and all the 'Old Country People', as they call them, had been taken Prisoners. No lives had been lost, or indeed anyone hurt, with the exception of one Canadian, and he made me comparatively easy by saying that the rebels had said they had no wish to interfere with the Ladies in any way, and that they had shown no further intention than that of detaining those they had taken as Prisoners. We hear today that Mrs. Ellice and her sister are in safety in the Priest's house, but that Edward, though without further ill usage than having his hands tied behind his back, has been taken with the others to the Village of Châteauguay about nine miles off, on this side. This is the last we have heard of them. I trust there is no doubt the Ladies are safe, and I think they would hardly venture to offer any violence to Edward. But hitherto it has been impossible to do anything for them. Of course I went the moment I heard of this to the Government House to inform Sir John Colborne. I found there Messengers from various parts of the Country, announcing similar events in the course of the night. From St. Denis and St. Charles on the Richelieu four Magistrates had made their escape with difficulty. At La Tortue, a place about six miles from Laprairie on the other side of the River, two English Farmers had been murdered and all the English inhabitants disarmed. Further towards the frontier the same things had occurred, and towards Quebec the Mail had been stopped, clearly showing combination, and a well laid scheme. There is besides every reason to believe that similar events may have occurred in Upper Canada, but the Mail Steamer[11] having been seized on Lake St. Louis by the rebels at Beauharnois, we are without intelligence from that province.

After all, however, I am inclined to believe it to be a failure,

[11] The steamer *Henry Brougham* was captured by the rebels at Beauharnois and the engine disabled to prevent her being used to transport troops.

and that the movement, well concerted as it evidently is, is premature. All so far is quiet to the northward about St. Eustache, etc., and though we are told that the People are all prepared, they have not ventured to do anything on this side, and it is still confined to the south shore of the St. Lawrence. In the meantime we have gained time, and Sir John has thrown off with great vigour. Martial Law has been at once proclaimed, all suspected Persons arrested, and the Volunteers called out. We got 2,000 of these People under arms yesterday and I have no doubt there are more today. Then a Steamer went down yesterday to Quebec to bring up the Guards. Two Regiments have already been sent to different points on the other side. We are ordered to hold ourselves in readiness, and on Wednesday next Sir John hopes to be able to strike a decisive blow upon them at Napierville where they are said to have their Head Quarters. I have little doubt, unless we hear worse accounts from Upper Canada, that in this Province it will at once be put down, and that after the excitement of these few days, we shall have a quiet winter.

Yesterday we were all out in this town to show the troops their different alarm Posts in case of attack which has been threatened, and to cover a search for Arms by the Police and Volunteers. About 40 or 50 stand were found, but the remarkable thing is that few or no men were in the houses searched. I want them to adopt a hint from the Irish Insurrection Act, and to insist upon a list of all the Inhabitants of every house being placed on every door, and everyone forced to be at home in his own house after eight o'clock, but the suggestion does not appear to meet with favour.

I send you a slip I have cut out from the *Morning Courier* of today, giving a very fair account of what happened yesterday. The Indian achievement is quite true.[12] I saw the Prisoners come in, 64 in number, having been captured as stated by 28 unarmed

---

12 On Sunday, November 4th, while the Caughnawaga Indians were at worship, a band of *patriotes* surrounded the church. Led by their chief the Indians rushed out shouting war cries. The chief wrested a musket from the first rebel he encountered and the rest of the party hastily surrendered.

Indians! An Officer has been sent today to their Village to organize them.

I feel so sure the insurrection will be speedily put down as far as Lower Canada is concerned that I should be perfectly happy but for the Ellices, and I hope the discomfort and fright, both bad enough Heaven knows, will be all they may have to suffer.

I shall probably be able to write again by the *Liverpool* Steamer, which is advertised to sail on the 12th, and every home mail gives us additional information.

With my best love to my Mother and all with you, believe me ever, My Dear Father,

Your most affectionate son,
C. Grey.

Tuesday evening, November 6th

The Rebels are assembled, it is said, in considerable numbers at Napierville, a place not marked in the map but situated, as far as I can make out, about 14 miles from St. Johns, and six from Isle aux Noix, to the west of the Richelieu River. The Guards have been sent for and Sir John intends to strike a blow on Thursday or Friday if they only wait long enough to give him an opportunity. I march with my Regiment tomorrow morning at seven o'clock to join the 24th and 73rd already assembled there, and I fancy we shall push on by Steam to Isle aux Noix, whence we shall cross on a pontoon bridge as soon as the General joins us. At the same time the Glengarrys to the number of about 1,800 men raised about Cornwall in Upper Canada, with 140 of mine on their way back to join their Regiment from Kingston, etc. and the 93rd Regiment, if the messenger overtakes them in time, have received orders to come from the other side upon Beauharnois so that we shall have them completely hemmed in.

I hear that the Rebels at Beauharnois have been in a constant state of drunkenness ever since and that 50 men might have taken them all prisoners. I heard today of Edward Ellice, that he was detained a prisoner at Châteauguay, 7 miles on this side of Beauharnois, but that no violence had been used towards him. The Ladies continue at the Priest's house. Sir John thinks, when they find themselves pressed, that the Rebels will at once release him.

The Mail came in today from Upper Canada and so far all was quiet. This is also the case, as far as we can learn, to the Northward here, and should this continue long enough to allow us to disperse those already assembled to the south, I do not think we need be under any apprehensions as to the result of this outbreak.

In all probability you may receive other letters from me before you get this as I will take any opportunity of writing from St. Johns or Isle aux Noix, but I prefer writing as things occur and I wish to leave this to accompany the first dispatches which Sir John Colborne may send home.

I am sure I need say nothing to convince you how constantly I think of you all when I go upon anything that even has the appearance of service.

Give my very best love to my Mother and all with you, and believe me, My Dear Father,

Your most affectionate son,
C. Grey.

St. Edwards,
November 11, 1838,
Sunday.

My Dear Father,

Since we left Montreal on Wednesday morning last, I have not been able to sit down to write. Indeed till today I have never been in a billet where it was possible to do so.

I wrote to you before I left Montreal, and left the letter to be forwarded, giving you some account of the very sudden outbreak which took place on Saturday night last, in various parts of the Country, and sending you an extract from one of the Montreal Papers giving a tolerably correct account of everything as far as we then knew. Other Papers, which I have not yet seen myself, will, in all probability, have given subsequent details of the general state of things, but I know nothing beyond the proceedings of the Brigade to which my Regiment belongs, and these I will now tell you.

It appears that Napierville, a small village, but the principal place in the district of which Dr. Côté had been Member in the Provincial House of Assembly, had been fixed upon as the Head Quarters of this most insane attempt, both as being at a convenient distance from the States, and in the centre of a district where the Population was almost entirely French and much disaffected. Also because all the roads leading to it were as bad as possible and at this time of year almost impassable. On Monday and Tuesday they had assembled in great numbers, variously stated at from 5,000 to 3,000. The latter number is certainly not over the mark. They were said to be generally well armed, to have seven pieces of cannon, and to be commanded by French officers and Drs. Nelson and Côté. Fortunately the rising appears to have been again premature. The North, where they were so bad the year before, remaining quiet and allowing Sir John Colborne to turn his whole attention to the rising in the South.

The Grenadier Guards were at once sent for from Quebec. And, on Wednesday morning when they arrived, my **Regiment** was sent out to join the 73rd at St. Johns, with the intention of sending us round by Isle aux Noix to get between these Rebels and the States, while other Troops were moved upon them by the direct roads. Bad weather and an accident on the railroad made some change necessary, and postponed the operations one day, and instead of moving on by Isle aux Noix we were marched on Thursday in the severest rain and snow storm, and through the deepest muddy roads I ever saw, to L'Acadie, a village on the direct road about 10 miles from Napierville, where we were brigaded with the Guards and 7th Hussars. The next day we moved on within two miles of the place and yesterday morning, at half past seven, advanced again and found the place deserted! They had begun scattering the night before on hearing of our approach and the last of them, about 500 in number, left it just before we came in, setting fire to a house full of Arms. It does not appear that they had received any assistance from the States beyond Arms, or that more than one half of them were ever armed at all. Two Regiments would have been ample. But considering the account he had received, I think Sir John Colborne was quite right to risk nothing, and the imposing appearance of upwards of 3,000 men coming almost simultaneously into Napierville from different quarters will no doubt have a great effect. We had yesterday assembled there the Grenadier Guards and 71st Regiment and 7th Hussars under Sir James Macdonell, the 15th and 24th under General Clitherow, the 73rd and Dragoon Guards under Colonel[s] Cathcart and Love. Sir John Colborne was also there, so that we had a Lieutenant-General, Two Major-Generals, Heaven knows how many Colonels and Lieutenant-Colonels, etc., etc. all to defeat an enemy that a division of the Metropolitan Police would have been sufficient to defeat. We have now been sent on in different directions to search for arms and the Leaders and I hope that in a very few more days we may be back in Montreal having concluded, as far as we are concerned, a bloodless campaign; and if the news from Upper Canada, of which I know nothing since I left Montreal, only continues satisfactory, I do not think there is a chance of our being again disturbed this winter. It has been to me a most painful duty. I cannot bear to see the poor wretches of women and children when their husbands, etc., etc. are dragged away by the Volunteers, and in many cases their houses burnt over their heads. It is to a certain degree unavoidable for you certainly cannot allow people to give you all this trouble and to act as they have done towards the loyal part of the popula-

tion, and then to go to their homes without receiving any punishment. Thank Heaven I have had nothing to do with any burning,
nor do I believe have any of the regular troops, and I have not
suffered, as far as I could prevent it, my men to pillage – but I
believe I am the only person who has tried to prevent it, and the
sort of plunderers that the Guards, Artillery and the 7th Hussars
are, I think I never saw.... And this was not the worst – I know
the Guards shot two men and a woman in cold blood in going
into Napierville, and I believe the Dragoons slashed away at the
defenceless wretches at the first moment. In short it is a service
for which I have no relish, and if I can get home in the Spring,
I shall not think it the least necessary to return for the chance
of another outbreak next winter.

Further towards the frontier the Volunteers had two smartish
skirmishes on Thursday and Friday last, in the latter of which
they had a Captain and four men killed, and several wounded.
They beat the rebels completely, and I hear a great many Prisoners, and some important ones, have been taken, among them
a French General. There are also two Rebel Colonels (French)
taken at Napierville, and I should hope, from the way in which
the Volunteers are now spread all along the frontier, more will
be taken. Among them I hope Dr. Nelson and Dr. Côté may be
caught and that then Sir John will not hesitate long as to their
disposal.

Edward Ellice was brought away by the Party which had
captured him and had kept him at Châteauguay, but was released
yesterday, and slept here last night. As the Beauharnois People
must also have been dispersed before this by the Glengarrys
from the upper country, I hope Mrs. Ellice and her sister are by
this time comfortable with him at Montreal. I do not think they
will be long leaving the Country for England.

As this cannot go till after my return to Montreal, I will keep
it open. At present I am so sleepy and tired I must finish.

St. Edwards,
Tuesday,
November 13.

We are just returned to the same place from which I began this letter. Yesterday morning, hearing that about 500 of the Rebels had barricaded the Church at the Village of St. Rémi, about seven miles from hence on the road to Beauharnois, we started off for it, but as before found it deserted and our only duty was to take up a few men who were represented as having been very active. The houses of these unfortunate People were also generally burnt by the Volunteers whom it is quite impossible to prevent retaliating in this manner for the fright they have been in. This morning an order came for us to return here and just before we started the Glengarrys arrived having come through from Beauharnois where they had dispersed the rebels leaving a trail, to use their own expression, of six miles wide as they came along – burning and pillaging. I heard nothing but dropping shots the whole day which is said to be the Volunteers shooting Poultry, etc. I hope, but would not answer for it, that they are not shooting Canadians as well. Colonel Fraser, who commands the Glengarrys, says they are looked upon as savages, to which I could not help answering that I thought by his own account they rather deserved it. . . .

I had a Company with the Glengarrys when they entered Beauharnois and it lost one man killed and four wounded by a volley which the Rebels fired from behind the Church before they ran off, which they did without further resistance. I am told that Company of mine has not been very regular and that it aided efficiently in burning houses, etc. I can easily believe it for I know what those with myself would be, with the example that is set them on all hands, if they were not kept very tight, and the Captain of that Company is at no time a very efficient officer. Colonel Fraser tells me they consulted whether or not they should not put the Prisoners to death and that they were only saved by one man. Mrs. Ellice and her sister were still there when they arrived at the Place. Colonel Fraser also tells me that all was still quiet in Upper Canada, but that threatening Reports were still Prevalent. But of all this you will in all probability get earlier intelligence than I can give you, for, though I go on writing, I am in utter ignorance as to when I may have an opportunity of sending my letters.

I was quartered last night in the house of a most respectable Canadian of the better class, of the name of Lapierre. He told me of one among many cases of the extreme misery caused by this outbreak. At Napierville we had all been much shocked by the appearance of a madman, almost completely naked, that our Sentries could not keep from thumping at the Prison door. At other times he would be dancing among the ashes of a burnt house and putting burning coals in his mouth and he never ceased crying 'Vive Papineau' and other things I could not make out. He had been put in prison to keep him quiet if possible, but had been again turned out to make way for our Prisoners and he was in the streets in the state I describe, with the thermometer at 20. It appears that on Sunday week he was taken out of his house by the Rebels, forced to cry 'Vive Papineau' several times, and put by them in Prison as a Loyalist till he went mad, which he did entirely through fright. He was [a] nephew of our host, and his mother, a very nice old woman, was in the house with us. I think I never saw a family more distressed. Mr. Lapierre told me that this was by no means a solitary instance.

I am sorry to say that on Sunday night, while we were here, one of my sentries shot a man. He endeavoured to rescue a Prisoner, and, though it does not appear that he did more than his duty, I would give a good deal [if] it had not happened.

I shall probably have again to add to this letter before I have an opportunity of sending it. Not having a book it is my only occupation and I think you will like to hear from me all we have been about.

Montreal,
November 15, 1838.

I am almost ashamed of sending the first part of this letter,
written at different times during our march, it has got so dirty
in my Portmanteau.

I came in here yesterday, having got leave from our Brigadier,
Sir James Macdonell, to come round by Montreal and to over-
take the Regiment tomorrow at Beauharnois. We got an order
yesterday morning, just as we were leaving St. Edwards, to
return by St. Rémi to that place in consequence of the Glengarrys having been ordered back with all haste to oppose a body
of some four or five hundred men who had effected a landing
about two miles below Prescott in Upper Canada. We are to
remain there till further orders. With the force they have got in
Upper Canada I cannot think it likely that we shall be wanted
and, if not, I am still in hopes we may be settled quietly in Montreal once more before many days are passed.

The Ellices start on Saturday for England and will not, I think,
be sorry to get out of the Country. They look surprisingly well
considering. Two of my men were killed at Beauharnois – both,
fortunately, very bad characters.

I have so much to do that I have not another moment to
write. I will write again from Beauharnois. Give my love to my
Mother, etc.,

Ever your most affectionate son,
C. Grey.

Montreal,
November 25, 1838.

My Dear Father,

Since a letter which I wrote at different intervals on the line
of march, I have had no opportunity of writing. Crowded, a
dozen officers into a small house at Beauharnois, a perfect bear

garden, there is no possibility of doing anything. I have regretted it the less as I could have told you nothing which you will not see detailed much better and more fully in the Newspapers.

My Regiment is for the present at Beauharnois, where I have the charge of getting the Volunteers – who are to be retained at present for the defence of that district – organized, and disarming the Inhabitants. Whenever I shall have effected this, I am given to understand we shall be brought back into Montreal and kept there for the winter. Organizing the Volunteers is the difficulty. I believe we have already got most of the Arms the People were in possession of. They are now the most loyal People in the world, and in the different villages where I have had them assembled to give up their Arms they have been quite ready to give three cheers for the Queen. We have arrested out of them those who have been pointed out as having been particularly active, who will, in all probability, be transported, and to the rest I have promised protection, on their remaining peaceably at home for the future. In the three Parishes which come more immediately under my charge they were all to take the oath of Allegiance to the Queen today after Mass.

Ignorant as these People are to a degree which I could scarcely have believed, I cannot quite understand how the conspiracy could have been organized so perfectly and with so much secrecy. The Curés of all these parishes assure me they had not the least suspicion of what was going on till it actually broke out. None of the Leaders we have yet got appear to me at all capable of the direction of such an affair, and yet, there is no doubt it had been going on for *months*. Lambton will not believe this. He will assert that the whole thing has been caused by the proceeding at home. I do not mean to say that it had not some effect in increasing the evil, but I cannot believe it produced it. The Plot was preparing for months before it broke out, as is, I think, proved by its being so well organized, though it again, I believe, broke out prematurely. And I think it would equally have happened if Lambton had been here.

Lower Canada I take to be quieted for the winter. The rest of the troops are doing on the Richelieu and elsewhere what I am doing at Beauharnois, and, as the People are thoroughly frightened and generally disarmed, I do not the least apprehend any further trouble from them. I am in hopes too that the signal failure of the Sympathizers in their attempt on Prescott may make them shy of attempting anything in other parts of Upper Canada, though it is certain numbers of Persons are sworn, and prepared to collect in various parts for the invasion of the Country. But we have a large force of Volunteers, daily getting more efficient, and I can hardly think they can get a sufficient number together on any point to encourage them to come in.

They have been rather alarmed at Quebec. Information, which has been believed, has been received of 3,000 People being sworn there and of an attempt being in contemplation to seize the Citadel. The gates of the town have, in consequence, been kept shut day and night.

Another instance has occurred there too, which further proves the mischief done by the interference of the Lords, which, though I do not think it has been the cause of the present outbreak, I do think has been most injurious.

Just before Lambton went away one of the judges, Bédard, declared the Ordinance establishing the Police to be illegal on the ground that it interfered with some Act of the Imperial Parliament which was declared, in the Act conferring the extraordinary Powers, to be beyond the power of the Governor and Council.

Now the same Judge, with his French Colleague, Panet[13] – in the absence of the Chief Justice and the other English judge – have declared the Ordinance of Sir John Colborne, suspending the Habeas Corpus Act, illegal; and the Prisoners having been previously removed from the Civil Prison to the Citadel, and Colonel Bowles having refused to deliver up the Prisoner in whose favour the writ had been granted by the Judges, they have

13 Philippe Panet, one of the puisne judges at Quebec.

had the impudence to issue a warrant against him, and he only avoids the execution of it by keeping the Sheriff out of the Citadel. The Judges have been written to for their reasons and I trust Sir John Colborne will not hesitate to suspend them. I should have mentioned that the Prisoner in question was arrested on a charge of high treason.

I came in here last night and return tomorrow morning, that is if I can get back, but there appears every chance of the lake being frozen up, in which case I shall find some difficulty in getting across. The frost these two days has been intense. Yesterday it was three degrees below zero, and it cannot be much higher today. They say it is not usually so severe so early in the year and that in all probability it will open again.

I leave this letter to go by the first opportunity in Sir John Colborne's bag, though it is hardly worth sending. If I had had more time I would have written to thank Georgiana for a long and most agreeable and satisfactory letter. I will endeavour to do so from Beauharnois.

Give my best love to my Mother and all the Family with you, and believe me ever, My Dear Father,

Your most affectionate son,
C. Grey.

Montreal,
December 12, 1838.

My Dear Father,

I have been longer without writing to you than usual, but it is so impossible in the discomfort of my present quarters when with the Regiment, to do *anything*, that it is only when I come into Montreal for a day or two that I have any opportunity of writing, and then I am generally engaged all the time I am in town.

I take for granted that you will have seen ample accounts in all the papers of everything that has been going on in both Provinces since the commencement of the disturbances on the 3rd November. The Pole who led the attempt on Prescott was hanged at Kingston last Thursday, and I hear today that warrants had also arrived there for the execution of the other two who have been already condemned. In the meantime there has been another miserable attempt at invasion made near Sandwich – 250 Sympathizers or thereabouts appear to have crossed over at Windsor, two miles below Sandwich. They were there attacked by the Militia, suffered some loss in killed and Prisoners, and afterwards dispersed in the woods, where they were being followed by a detachment of the 34th and the Militia.[14] This is the substance of dispatches received last night by Sir John Colborne. The Papers add that the Brigands on first crossing burnt two of our Steamers. General Brady is said to have behaved very well in seizing a schooner which was carrying over a second detachment and in otherwise frustrating the attempt.

But the question must be decided by our Government at home. There has not been a symptom of disaffection in Upper Canada and yet we are forced by the Acts of our neighbours to keep up a large war Establishment. It would be much better to have war at once, and then the inconveniences of this state of things would be felt on both sides, and there might be some chance of an end being put to them. But it is really not to be borne that the American Government should be allowed to laugh quietly in their

[14] The engagement popularly known as the Battle of Windsor took place on December 4, 1838, when a patriot force under L. V. Bierce attacked the town. Before coming into contact with the militia, the invaders set fire to the barracks, burning some of the occupants alive and shooting down others as they attempted to escape. They also shot and killed Dr. John Hume and burned the steamer *Thames*. When the militia arrived on the scene they killed several patriots with their first volley and the remainder soon fled into the woods. Most of the patriots might have been captured, but Colonel John Prince, a Sandwich lawyer who commanded the militia, feared that a second force was about to attack Sandwich and refused to permit active pursuit. When Prince ordered five of those who had been taken prisoner shot on the spot, repercussions occurred in both Great Britain and the United States.

sleeves at all the expense and annoyance we are put to by their unruly citizens. It is not enough to give the Government credit for good intentions. They ought to be made to show them by their Acts.

On this frontier too we hear endless reports of organization still going on. After the miserable failure of the Canadian insurrection, I cannot think they mean more than to keep us in a constant state of alarm. But of this I have no doubt, that if we were not prepared as we are, with an overwhelming force of Regular troops and volunteers daily becoming more efficient, the threat of invasion from the States would be carried into effect. The Home Government is the only one that can settle this and, in my opinion, only in one way.

We have had a further proof of the injurious effects produced by the interference at home with Lambton's Ordinances, in the declaration by two of the Judges (Canadians) at Quebec, that the suspension of the Habeas Corpus Act by Sir John Colborne and his Special Council was illegal.

The Judges after a long and, in my opinion, most unnecessary correspondence with them, have been suspended, but I do not think Sir John showed either the energy or decision which I should have expected from him. There could be no doubt of the Act – they had presumed to pronounce an Act of the only Legislature existing in the Province illegal. It *could* not be explained away and the consequences of Sir John's delay and hesitation in acting upon it have been that further proceedings arising out of it have been permitted at Quebec, causing increased embarrassment to the Government – that another Judge at Three Rivers[15] (also a Canadian) has been encouraged to follow their example – and that the confidence of the People in the energy of the Governor has been much shaken.

The manner in which the trials of the Prisoners have been hitherto conducted has increased this want of confidence. There were endless delays before the Court Martial commenced its

15 Joseph-Rémi Vallière de Saint-Réal.

sittings. Twelve men were arraigned, the trial dragged on very slowly, but did at length terminate last Thursday, a week ago tomorrow. The sentence is not yet known. The Court Martial has not since assembled, and there is today a report that the whole proceedings are to be quashed as illegal. In the meantime everybody is asking how they mean to get through the trials of near 700 more who are now in prison.

My Regiment is in a miserable little village about twelve miles from the opposite side of the river, where we have been, as elsewhere, engaged disarming the Inhabitants, making them take the oath of Allegiance, and arresting such as could be positively identified as having taken an active part in the outbreak. In the village of La Tortue, close to where we are, the only real outrage that I heard of was committed. A Farmer named Walker having been very brutally murdered in [the] presence of his wife, and another Yorkshire Farmer, of the name of Vitty, having been desperately wounded. I have taken up several men who are proved to have been very active in the attack on the house, three men in particular who are proved to have disputed for the honour of having killed Walker and acknowledge having fired. Sir John might make an example of these men at once for there can be no reason to hesitate about them, though there may about many others.

I have had a letter from Cavendish which has frightened me about my Equerryship and has determined me, unless I hear previously of a change of Government and that I have been turned out, to leave this Country next February, if everything, as I heartily trust it may, should then appear tolerably quiet. Of course I shall not ask for leave if there appears the least reason why I should stay, but we shall be able to judge pretty well then of our prospects for the remainder of the winter. The letter from Cavendish was to say it was contemplated to leave my name out of the roster for next year. I lost no time in writing to him and Lord Albemarle to beg that this might not be done, that it was my determination to be at home to take my waiting

in April, and that I had had Her Majesty's permission to miss
my waiting hitherto.

I hope Sir John Colborne will not make any objection to my
going on leave, and I do not think he will under the circumstances. However, I think it better to say nothing about it till
the time when I shall wish to go approaches nearer.

As soon as the Ice takes on the river my Regiment is to return
here. They tell me that may not be before the middle of January
which will be disagreeable to a degree as it is no easy matter at
present getting across, but I am also told it has been known to
set as early as the 27th December and hitherto the cold here
has been greater than ordinary. We have already had the
thermometer eight degrees below zero. But the extreme cold
seldom lasts more than two days when the frost gives again. To
give you some idea of the sudden changes: yesterday morning
the thermometer was 11 at nine o'clock, it rose gradually all
day, was 31 at ten last night, was 36 this morning at nine. At a
quarter past nine a sudden squall came on from the N.W., at
ten the thermometer had fallen to 24. At two it was 13. It has
since continued to fall, and is now (half past five) exactly at
zero! with a high piercing wind that makes it quite impossible
to put one's face outside the door. There is seldom so much wind
when the frost is so intense, and then I am told you do not feel
it much. I am keeping a register of the thermometer to send
Georgiana.

Give our best love to my Mother and all the Family. Ever, My
Dear Father,

Your most affectionate son,
C. Grey.

L'Acadie,
December 29, 1838.

My Dear Father,

I was in hopes that before this I should have been able to date my letters once more from Montreal, but our return there seems still as uncertain as ever.

This is a small village where we halted the night before we marched into Napierville, and about 20 miles from the lines. We were brought here about ten days ago in consequence of reports, which appeared at the time to deserve some attention, that a strong force of Sympathizers and Refugees meant to make an inroad into the Province before the end of the month. Côté, Gagnon,[16] Bouchette,[17] and Nelson were said to be at various points on both sides of Lake Champlain, and this day, the anniversary of the burning of the *Caroline*, was to be the commencement of new troubles. I never gave the least credit to these reports myself, but Sir John was certainly in the right to be prepared, and we must remember that it is in all probability this very state of preparation that prevents these reports from being verified. Charles Wellesley is with the 15th at Isle aux Noix, the 66th is at St. Johns. A Battalion of Guards [is] at Laprairie, six miles in my rear, with the King's Dragoon Guards at Chambly. So that in 24 hours a force of 3,000 Regular troops, exclusive of Volunteers, may be concentrated to oppose any attempts that may be made. A sufficient guarantee, in my opinion, that none will be ventured upon. There is no doubt that there are several Refugees, in numbers varying from 50 to 300 in Swanton, St. Albans, Champlain and other villages on the line, but I cannot make out that they get any active assistance from the Americans. There is a report, which does not seem to me so unlikely,

16 Lucien Gagnon, one of the leaders of the second insurrection.
17 R. S. M. Bouchette was among those banished to Bermuda by Lord Durham. With the disallowance of the ordinance he left Bermuda and went to the United States where he lived for a time in Vermont before returning to Canada.

that their object is to seize an opportunity of coming across the line to burn houses, or commit such outrages as may provoke the Volunteers to retaliate, and in that case it is thought that 'Sympathy' may become more active.

In the meantime Sir John has forbid anybody to cross into the States without passports and all People coming from them are forced to give a clear account of themselves before they are suffered to proceed.

There is nothing new from the Upper Province. I saw a letter from Colonel Airey commanding the 34th Regiment, from Sandwich, dated the 13th December, in which he says the Ice is now in such a state that there is no possibility of any landing being effected at present.

He seems at a loss to account for the attempt which had been made at Windsor, as they showed no fight, though attacked by a force not one-third of their own numbers. In fact they dispersed at the very first shot, the Volunteers following them up and shooting them as they ran, and they say they would have destroyed them all, if Colonel Prince, who came up after it was all over, had not ordered a retreat. A great many of them have since been brought in Prisoners and many more found frozen to death in the woods. It is since said that Detroit has been vacated by the Sympathizers, but Sir John Colborne seems to think that another effort will be made in that quarter when the Ice sets.

There is no evidence of a single man having joined either the Windsor or Prescott Brigands after their arrival in the Country, nor has there been a symptom of disturbance in any part of Upper Canada. It is for the Government at home to determine how long it will submit, under such circumstances, to the expense of a War Establishment here because the United States Government either cannot or will not control its Citizens. I am very much inclined to believe that nothing can settle the question but a war with that Country. At present they feel none of the inconveniences of this state of things.

Two men were hanged yesterday week at Montreal who were proved to have taken a lead in the insurrection. Several more have been sentenced to transportation. The trial of several of the Prisoners taken at Napierville was expected to terminate today, and next week the murderers of Walker, two of whom I sent in when stationed in that neighbourhood, are to be tried, and I should think there is no doubt of their being convicted and hanged. In Upper Canada the trials have proceeded with much more expedition and the executions have followed pretty rapidly.

I went into Montreal to spend Christmas and returned the day before yesterday. I wished most sincerely that we had been spending it at Howick instead and hope that next year it may be so. It is long since we have any accounts from England and I am told that at this time of year we are often two months without news. I hope the first arrivals may bring us some letters and that we may hear of your being all as well as I wish you.

With my best love to all, and wishing you a happy New Year, Believe me ever, My Dear Father,

Your affectionate son,
C. Grey.

CHAPTER VIII

A Winter at L'Acadie

Colonel Grey had expected that his regiment would be recalled to Montreal early in the new year, but in this he was to be disappointed. Repeated rumours of patriot attacks from the United States, together with the uneasy situation created by the Maine–New Brunswick boundary controversy, led Sir John Colborne to keep the regiment at L'Acadie throughout the winter and spring, despite his frequent promises to the contrary.

Grey's journal reveals that during these months he settled into a regular routine. Regimental business was handled in the middle of the week, and long weekends, from Friday or Saturday to Monday or Tuesday, were spent with his wife in Montreal. He now found himself with ample time to reflect on Lord Durham's mission and the events which followed. Frequently he speculated on the ideal solution for Canadian problems and invariably pronounced in favour of a legislative union of the two Canadas.

When Lord Durham's Report reached Canada, Grey was delighted to discover that his brother-in-law had recommended a legislative union and he enthusiastically endorsed all of Durham's observations on Lower Canada. He became less enthusiastic, however, when he read the Upper Canada section of the report for he realized that it was likely to benefit the disaffected in that province. He agreed with the widely-held suspicion that this section of the Report had been written by Charles Buller.

There had been little time for reading in the hectic weeks which followed Durham's departure, but during the early months of 1839 Grey was able to indulge extensively in his favourite pastime. Early in January he began reading Lockhart's 'Life of Sir Walter Scott' and was, at first, unfavourably impressed. By the time he finished the biography, however, he had completely revised his opinion and commented in his journal, 'I now pronounce it a most delightful work and the end inexpressibly affecting. Commencing with Scott's own account of his earliest years, and learning as one proceeds to know him from his works and his own letters and diaries, one feels almost to have lived with him throughout, and the changes from the vigour of health to sickness and death are so imperceptible and gradual that one is as little prepared for the final termination as if they had taken place under our own eyes.'

With his interest thus aroused Grey spent most of the winter reading Scott's works. Occasionally, for variety, he turned to other authors including Thomas Chandler Haliburton. Upon glancing at 'Sam Slick' he noted that it 'seems stupid enough . . . tho' the imitation of Yankee slang is excellent and a little of it amusing.'

Despite the rumours of patriot activity on the frontier the months at L'Acadie passed quietly. For the most part Grey's diary during this period presents a record of the daily routine and his regular weekend visits to Montreal. The few noteworthy events that occurred are fully discussed in his letters to his father which also contain, in greater detail, his reflections on the Durham mission and his comments on events in England. For these reasons only the letters are reproduced here.

Montreal,
January 7, 1839.

My Dear Father,

A Bag is to be made up tomorrow to go to New York for the

Royal William, of whose arrival we expect to hear every day. It is provoking that she is not arrived before it is necessary to write, as we must hear of Lambton's arrival by her and the effect it produces in England. We have news to the 24th and I have a letter from Henry of that date. I see all parties join in condemning Lambton's proclamation and his manner of resigning the Government. I am afraid it is too true that he consulted his own personal feelings of irritation against the Government and that he was not sorry to cause as much embarrassment to them as possible. I did not see the proclamation till it was out, and I told Louisa I was afraid that construction would be put upon parts of it, but I need not discuss its merits any more, for I believe I told you at the time how much I regretted it, and also the tone of some of his answers to the addresses presented to him.[1] I take the most objectionable parts of the proclamation to have been advised by Charles Buller whom I believe to be the most unfit man for such a situation as he filled that could have been found. His talents I believe to be overrated. I am sure he is a very weak man and he has not even the merit of being a good man of business.

As far as I knew of his Acts while in the Government of this Province, up to the arrival of the disallowance of his ordinances, I had thought Lambton deserved all the credit which People were disposed to give him. But I am rather inclined to think his system was too much one of 'management' and that he could not have gone on long without being more or less compromised. I do not think the account given by the Bermuda exiles of the manner in which they were induced to plead guilty, through the agency of a Mr. Simpson,[2] a notoriously bad character, is quite comfortable. I do not believe Roebuck's story of the

---

[1] *supra*, pp. 135-6, 139.

[2] John Simpson, the stepfather of J. A. Roebuck and collector of customs at Coteau du Lac, was the intermediary through whom the eight rebels, subsequently banished to Bermuda, were approached and persuaded to plead guilty.

tampering with Papineau through Gibbon Wakefield,[3] but I am afraid Lambton is too much one of the Mr. Ellice school, who think everything is to be done by intriguing and managing, even when a straightforward course would be safest and most effectual. A Mr. Derbishire[4] was brought out on purpose to write articles in praise of the Canadian Government, in doing which he was so indiscreet that they were forced to get him out of Quebec. Nor was an attempt to give a tone to the Public meetings called to address him on his departure more successful. A Mr. Thom, who had previously distinguished himself as a violent Partisan of the 'British Party', was sent to the meeting in this place to endeavour to get an expression of opinion favourable to the plan for a general confederation of all the North American Colonies. The result of which was that, having introduced a topic that had nothing to do with the object of the meeting, a resolution was passed, all but unanimously, condemning the scheme most strongly, and urging the Legislative Union of the two Canadas as the only remedy for existing evils. From

---

[3] On November 10, 1838, the *Spectator* published a letter from J. A. Roebuck in which he claimed that Wakefield, acting as Durham's agent, had gone to see Papineau at Saratoga. Wakefield replied, in a letter to the editor of the *Spectator* on November 25th, denying that he had acted on Durham's behalf or with his knowledge. He stated that after several discussions with La-Fontaine and other French-Canadian leaders he became convinced they were bent on following a misguided policy. He made a trip to Saratoga to see Papineau but found him absent. Wakefield's statements were contradicted in a letter published in *L'Aurore des Canadas* on January 22, 1839. See Chester W. New, *Lord Durham*, p. 418, n. 1.

[4] After having been a correspondent of the *Morning Chronicle*, Stewart Derbishire applied to Lord Durham for an appointment on his staff. On Durham's instructions he left for North America before the main party. He arrived in New York on April 20, 1838, and had interviews with Mackenzie, Rolph, and O'Callaghan before proceeding to Montreal where he conferred with D. B. Viger. When Durham arrived in Canada, Derbishire had a report ready for him on the causes of the rebellion and the state of French-Canadian opinion. During the month of August he travelled along the frontier of Lower Canada and made reports to Durham on the possibility of a second insurrection. Derbishire did not return with Durham, but remained in Canada and was elected the first member for Bytown in the legislative assembly of the Province of Canada. In 1841 he was also appointed Queen's Printer.

what I have seen here, and of the manner in which your Government was overturned by Mr. Ellice's 'leave it to me' system, I have a horror of all attempts to give a tone to the press, or to conduct a Government by 'management'.

Reports still come in of intended movements by the Sympathizers and Patriots at different points. The information received by Sir John Colborne of a contemplated attack near Missisquoi bay on the frontier of Vermont seemed so authentic that all the Regiments on the other side of the river were closed up towards the lines and Major Denny was sent with dispatches to General Eustace, commanding the United States Troops at Plattsburg. He returned last night, having had a most satisfactory interview with the General, as far as his wishes go, but his whole force, divided among the different villages, is only 160 men. However, from Denny's account I do not think there is any truth in the reports we had heard. He went along the line through Alburgh to Swanton and St. Albans, at which last place he attended a sympathizing meeting, and he describes everything as being perfectly quiet and says that as far as he could learn there are no great number[s] of Refugees in the States. I had before heard from a Canadian who had come in to L'Acadie, where my Regiment is now stationed, from Champlain, where he had been for the last two months, that most of the Leaders had dispersed, and that the Refugees could not be induced, by those who were still intent on mischief, to do anything – their object being to get back if possible into Canada. At the meeting at St. Albans Denny says there might have been 700 or 800 People present and the Speeches and Resolutions he describes as being violent, but he says on the whole it went off very flatly. They assert their *right*, after our example in Greece, South America, etc., to assist the cause of freedom wherever, whenever, and in whatever manner they please, and that the general Government has no right to interfere with them.

This is the language also of the Buffalo, Cleveland, and Detroit Papers who openly tell General Brady that they will fire upon him if he ventures to interfere with them. It seems certain, I think, that up there something more is in contemplation and that we shall have some more attempts at invasion as soon as ever the Ice will bear. The Probable explanation of the Reports we have had down here seems to be to prevent troops being sent to the Upper Province. But with eight complete Regiments there and the strong force of Volunteers now embodied, I think they may defy any force that is likely to come against them.

It will be quite impossible for me to ask leave, as I had intended in February, while these reports continue. I have therefore written to Cavendish to try and exchange my waiting from April to July or August and I shall make an attempt to get away the moment the navigation opens which will probably be about the middle of April – in which case I should hope to be at home by the first week in June.

I have been writing to you amid a thousand interruptions – scarcely five minutes having elapsed without somebody's coming in. I hope you will therefore excuse the carelessness of my letter which, on reading over, I can scarcely read or understand myself.

Very heavy snow this morning has turned to rain this evening, and it is now, to my astonishment, a rapid thaw.

Give my best love to all, and believe me ever, My Dear Father,

Your very affectionate son,
C. Grey.

Montreal,
January 14, 1839.

My Dear Father,

We received a great treat in the arrival of the *Royal William* mail yesterday, by which I got letters from you, my Mother, Georgiana, Henry, Frederick, George, Louisa, and Mary Lambton.

I need not say this must always be a pleasure, but it was particularly so at this time, and I was not a little rejoiced to find that you had received the news of the suppression of the Rebellion almost at the same time as the first accounts of its breaking out. You will not, therefore, have had much anxiety on our account and I think I may now relieve you from any that you might still feel by confidently expressing my belief that it is now really over for the winter. We are still kept on the other side of the water, but from all I can learn from those best acquainted with the movements and intentions of the Refugees on the lines, I do not think any aggression is to be apprehended and I am still in hopes Sir John Colborne may very shortly bring us back to Montreal.

The accounts from the Upper Province seem equally satisfactory and I see by this day's paper that great numbers of the Militia have been allowed to return to their homes.

We hear from Quarters that ought to know that there is a great deal of disaffection in Upper Canada so I suppose it is so. But it is somewhat remarkable in that case that not one solitary Individual joined the Brigands who crossed over either at Prescott or Sandwich[5] and that in both these cases the attack was frustrated entirely by the Militia of the Country and further, that nothing approaching to disturbances, or even to agitation, has taken place in any part of the Upper Province.

I believe I told you before that much as I disapproved of the course pursued by the Government in disallowing Lambton's Ordinances, and injurious as I thought their having done so would prove to the Colony, I did not in any way attribute to them the renewal of the rebellion. I was always convinced that Lambton was perfectly mistaken in thinking that it in any way increased the existing disaffection.

As little do I think that the outbreak was in any way caused by Lambton's proclamation and the conduct pursued by him in resigning the Government. I fully acquit both him and the Government at home of all such responsibility. I am perfectly

---

[5] References to the patriot raids that culminated in the Battle of the Windmill and the Battle of Windsor.

convinced that no set of Ministers in England, no Governor General in this Province, could by any measures have prevented this attempt. It was necessary to convince the People of the madness of their wishes and, also, that if they escaped punishment last year it did not proceed in any way from *fear* of them, as they had been studiously taught was the case, and some such lesson as they have now received was necessary. Sir John Colborne, in a long conversation which I had with him the other night, seems of the same opinion that, after what occurred last year, *nothing* could have prevented a second attempt at rebellion this year.

How to prevent it for the future is now the question and I do believe the best chance is that of at once uniting the Provinces, [and] of course abolishing the French Language [as] an official one, and disqualifying the districts which have been in open rebellion from returning members to the Provincial Parliament. They say there would be great opposition in the Upper Province to this measure as involving the removal of the seat of Government from Toronto. But in the Lower Province the 'British Party' is unanimous on the subject, and I am very much inclined to believe that the opposition in Upper Canada would be found to be confined almost entirely to the City of Toronto and that neighbourhood. If we do this and make our interference in the Government of the Country as much nominal as possible, I do not see why we should not keep the Country for ever. If we carry the British population with us in both Provinces, they have shown that they are perfectly able to take care of themselves and to resist successfully either foreign aggression or internal treason.

When I began to write I did not mean to say a word about Canada for I felt that I had nothing new to tell you and besides there is another subject that has been running in my head ever since I received your letters. It is the chance you mention of the railroad to Edinburgh being taken between the house and the sea! Surely this is impossible; I cannot even conceive its being the best line. Unless it crossed along the new road an immense viaduct would be required to get across the long walk. But I really cannot bear to think even of the possibility of such ruin to the place. I can quite fancy it looking beautiful when you wrote, and I rejoice beyond measure to hear that the exchange with the Duke is likely to be effected at last. I hope it will take in enough to keep the Alnwick Poachers at least one field from the covers.

I had been in hopes of seeing Howick again sooner than I shall probably be able to do now. Everything seemed so quiet that I was thinking seriously of asking Sir John's leave to start, as I had at first proposed, in February. But unfortunately, by the *Royal William*, Major Denny has received the news of the sudden death of his only Brother which makes it necessary for him to go home at once to arrange about the guardianship of his Nephew, etc. Of course under such circumstances I could not object and he has promised to be back in April so as to allow me to get away then.

It will be decided long before that time whether I am to retain my Equerryship or not. If I should be so fortunate, I think I should certainly lose no time in going on half-pay to prevent the possibility of being forced to come out here again, for which I have no desire.

I am glad you did not tell Henry my suspicions of Lambton's having communicated the dispatches he wrote, on resigning the Government, to Count Nesselrode and the King of the Belgians for, though the shape and nature of the Packets leave little doubt in my mind of what they contained, it is merely a suspicion and I am not sure I ought to have given utterance to it.

Louisa's letter to me seems to anticipate nothing but vexation and discomfort and the course Lambton has hitherto pursued since his return seems well calculated to ensure it.

I have just read the 'letter to the Queen'.[6] If I had not been told it was Brougham's it would have been impossible not to recognize him in it, and to be sure it is impudent enough not only in its language as addressed to the Queen, but in the

---

[6] The 'letter to the Queen' urged the necessity of extending the franchise in Great Britain.

measures it recommends, considering he was one of the Authors of the Reform Bill, and as a Final measure. Nothing would astonish me less than, notwithstanding what has occurred in Canada, to see him and Lambton sitting on the same bench.

Caroline has written to my Mother. I would have done so too if I had had time, but Major Denny, who takes this, starts early tomorrow morning. Give her my best love, therefore, as also to Georgiana, George, etc., and believe me ever, My Dear Father,

Your most affectionate son,
C. Grey.

L'Acadie,
January 29, 1839.

My Dear Father,

Since I wrote last we have not even had a report and I really believe there is no more probability, now, of anything fresh this winter, and, from what I see in the Papers, it seems as if the American Border population were really disposed to be quiet for the future – I ought perhaps to say for the present. For I have no doubt that their present peaceful demeanour only proceeds from the fear of similar failures to those of Prescott and Sandwich and that if we were not prepared for them as we are, we should soon hear of them again. This being so, all the interest is transferred to your side of the water, to know what steps the Government means to take to obviate the probability of a recurrence of similar events next, and every winter, till the objects of the Sympathizers are obtained.

After repeating his views in favour of a legislative union of the Canadas as opposed to a federal union of British North America Grey continued:

In the meantime, I begin to be heartily sick of my quarters here – though I have the advantage of being able to dine at home four times a week – and I cannot see the least reason now for our being kept out here. Sir John Colborne said on Sunday that he hoped to relieve us from our suspense in a few days, but he has said the same ever since the beginning of last December and here we are still.

The Court Martial goes on slowly with its proceedings and if no other mode is substituted of getting rid of the Prisoners, they will not have finished by this time next year. I believe the Law Officers here to be dreadfully inefficient and the manner in which the evidence appears to be got up, in the cases of which I know anything, seems to me very disgraceful. I heard the French Officer Hindenlang's[7] defence which he rested entirely upon his being a Foreigner and that, therefore, he could not be guilty of High Treason. So far they seem, in Upper Canada, to have had doubts on the subject for they passed a special Act to meet the case of Foreigners who might be taken in Arms. He seemed very indignant at being called a 'Brigand' and considered himself in the same position as Lord Byron, Lord Cochrane, and Evans. Boyd, who was executed at Malaga with Torrijos by Moreno, seems to me certainly an exactly similar case.[8] He said a true bill was found against Moreno, when he came to England with Don Carlos, for the murder, but if I remember right our Government thought the Spanish Government justified in what they did and made no demand for explanation. I have not heard whether he will be hanged or not, but all this *ought* to have been considered before he was tried.

I was very glad to read today in the *Standard* of the 17th December Lambton's answer to the Westminster Reform Associa-

---

7 Charles Hindenlang, together with Robert Nelson and Médard Hébert, led the *patriote* force at Odelltown, November 9, 1838. He was captured the next day while endeavouring to reach the United States. On February 15, 1839, he was executed after being tried and sentenced to death by court martial.

8 On November 28, 1831, the Spanish revolutionary José Maria Torrijos sailed from Gibraltar with a party of fifty-three including Robert Boyd, a British subject. Torrijos' force was pursued by the Spanish coastguard and their small vessel ran ashore near Malaga on December 2nd. They took refuge in a farmhouse but were surrounded and, on December 5th, they surrendered to Don Vincente Gonzales Moreno. Despite the protests of the British consul at Malaga, Robert Boyd and his companions were executed by a firing squad on December 11th. Boyd's body was handed over to the British consul for burial.

tion.[9] I only hope he will act firmly upon such principles. If he knew what I could tell him of some of his Agents here, he would not be much flattered. You will probably have seen M. LaFontaine's letter in answer to Mr. Wakefield's.[10] It certainly proves him to have been a most improper man to employ.

You will be very sorry to hear of Colonel Maitland's death at London in Upper Canada. He has been a long while in bad health and Sir John Colborne had only sent him leave a few days before to come down to Montreal.

The weather has been quite detestable for the last eight or nine days. Constant high wind, which was the last thing I was taught to expect in Canada, and so variable that the thermometer has been as high as 42° and as low as 18 below zero! On both these days I drove into Montreal, a cutting wind and driving snow in my face one time, and drenching rain the other. Yesterday and today have been perfectly detestable – a gale of wind, and so cold last night that a glass of water in my bedroom was frozen perfectly *solid*.

The *Great Western* was to sail on the 19th so that I shall have an opportunity of writing again in a few days, though in our present quiet position I am almost ashamed of sending such stupid letters.

Give my best love to my Mother, Georgiana and all who are at home, and believe me ever, My Dear Father,

Your most affectionate son,
C. Grey.

---

9 The Westminster Reform Association passed an address to Lord Durham shortly after his return to England. The address contained nothing objectionable, but speakers at the meeting at which it was carried had expressed their opposition to the government in the most violent terms and had looked to Durham as their champion. Durham declined to receive the address until officers of the Association declared that they did not endorse the opinions expressed at the meeting. See Chester W. New, *Lord Durham*, pp. 485-6.

10 In a letter published in *L'Aurore des Canadas* of January 22, 1839, LaFontaine asserted that Wakefield had given him to understand that in seeking his support he was acting as an agent of Lord Durham. He also added that as a consequence of his conversation with Wakefield he was interviewed by Charles Buller.

Montreal,

February 8, 1839.

My Dear Father,

Having written to you only a few days ago by the bag sent for the *Liverpool* Steamer to take home, I have little to add to what I then wrote. Everything has remained perfectly quiet, with the exception of an outrage of an aggravated nature committed on Sunday morning last by some Refugee Canadians and Americans from Vermont,[11] of which I send you the official Report. This, added to some information which Sir John Colborne has received from the States, of intended movements among the Refugees and Patriots in Vermont, have induced him to alter his intention of recalling us to Montreal and we may now, I fear, expect to remain where we are till the Navigation of the St. Lawrence opens again. It is provoking for I had fully expected to find myself comfortably settled by the beginning of next week for the remainder of the winter.

I have just been reading the Article in the *Westminster Review* about Lord Durham[12] and think I never read a greater display of nonsense and ignorance of everything connected with this Country. The object is too apparent – to get Lambton to put himself at the head of the Radicals, in which case they are quite prepared to give up any sympathy for the 'suffering Canadians'. I fear from the tone of his answers to the different addresses presented to him they will succeed in this. I know this was Wakefield's sole object in this Country. Colonel Clive dined with me last night and told me he had seen Wakefield the morn-

11 Early in the morning of Sunday, February 3rd, a band of about twenty crossed the border from Vermont, burned the house and barn of a farmer, Vosburg, at Caldwell's Manor, and inflicted bayonet wounds on him and his son. Some reports state that the attack was led by a man who had been previously in Vosburg's employ and that it was based on personal rather than political motives.

12 In the hope of producing a union of liberal Whigs and Radicals under Durham's leadership, John Stuart Mill wrote a stirring article for the December issue of the *Westminster Review* defending Durham's administration in Canada and advocating his leadership of a new Liberal party.

ing after the Proclamation had been settled – that he could not contain his exultation, boasted of the share he had had in getting it, and said he had now accomplished all he wanted. That Lord Durham had quarrelled with the Government beyond the possibility of reconciliation and that he should now write to the leading Radicals at Birmingham, etc. to ply him with addresses on his return and 'that he was their own'. Clive told me not to mention it and I shall not to anyone but you, but I do not think Lambton would be much flattered if he knew the manner in which these People boasted of making him their tool.

I hope in a few days to hear something of you. Our last letters are of the 13th December, two months ago nearly, an unusually long while to be without intelligence from home. I have read Mr. Stevenson's report about the proposed Railroad. I suppose by his saying he leaves the grounds of Howick perfectly undisturbed, he means it to go close along the sea-shore, but I cannot imagine that or any other line to the east of the House being so good as to the west of the Heugh and I think even that would be an intolerable nuisance. In little more than two months I hope to be thinking of my Homeward Journey. I wish to leave this [country] about the 1st of May, when the lease of my house expires, and to sail from New York about the beginning of June which will give me time to take Caroline to Boston, Philadelphia and Washington so that she may see a little of the States, but of course this will depend upon my hearing from Colonel Cavendish that he has changed my waiting, as I asked him, till August next. Believe me ever, My Dear Father,

Your most affectionate son,
C. Grey.

February 18, 1839.

My Dear Father,

The *Cambridge* is arrived at New York, having left Liverpool on the 19th January, but I have no letters by her, my last being of the 13th and 14th December. She brings the melancholy news of the loss on the same day of three New York Packets, two of them outward bound, which might probably have had letters for us, though that is of very little consequence compared to the unfortunate loss of life on board of one of them, the *Pennsylvania*. I have not yet seen the English Papers, but if we hear of the loss of such Vessels as these I fear we may expect dreadful accounts of the loss occasioned by this storm.

We remain in the same quarters. The wish of the Leaders of the Refugees is not doubtful – to keep up a state of things on the lines which may lead ultimately to collision between the two Governments. But on the west side of Lake Champlain there is great indisposition among the Refugees to attempt anything and, even if they were so disposed, there is plenty of force to repel them without keeping us out there, for which I certainly see little necessity. This day week six of the Refugee Leaders, Wolfred Nelson,[13] and two other returned exiles from Bermuda, with Côté, etc., had a meeting in the Village of Champlain, but failed in doing anything, and though Côté succeeded the next day, Tuesday last, in collecting 30 or 40 People at a place called Corbeau, about a league further back, I hear since that he is gone back to the east side of Lake Champlain.

But it is now a question between the two Governments and I gather, from the tone of the resolutions adopted in Congress on the motion of Mr. Cushing,[14] that they are more disposed in the States to insist upon every alleged ground of complaint they may have against us than to give us any satisfaction, which

[13] After the disallowance of Durham's ordinance the Bermuda exiles were informed on October 26, 1838, that they were free to leave the island. Dr. Wolfred Nelson landed at Hampton Roads, Virginia, on December 8th. He practised medicine in the United States until he returned to Canada in 1842.

[14] On January 28, 1839, Cushing proposed and carried a series of anti-British resolutions concerning violations of neutrality during the rebellions, the *Caroline* incident, presents given to Indians residing in the United States, Hudson's Bay Company posts west of the Rocky Mountains, and the free navigation of rivers forming part of the boundary between the United States and British North America.

we certainly have a right to demand, for the repeated and un-provoked attacks upon our Territory.

Mr. Clay, the Candidate in opposition to Van Buren for the next turn as President, is decidedly hostile to us. He told Colonel Clive, when he went to present letters of introduction which he had to him, that he would not disguise from him his hope to see the day when the British would be finally expelled from this Continent. He was also very uncompromising about the N.E. Boundary – said he would not consent to cede an inch and that the utmost he would grant would be a right of way between our Provinces.

Five more of the Rebels were executed last Friday – making twelve in all,[15] including Walker's murderers. Two of this last batch were men who were acquitted last autumn of the murder of Chartrand.[16] Sir John has consented to these executions with great reluctance. I do not think he could have done less and those who have been hanged have been well chosen. De Lori-mier[17] was a man of very good family and his execution has had a great effect. But a horrid murder committed below Quebec has been the chief subject of interest lately. A Monsieur Taché, Seigneur of Kamouraska, had quarrelled with and separated from his wife, a beautiful woman, I am told, of about 20. She was living since her separation with a Dr. Holmes at Sorel. They appear to have concerted the murder of her husband between them and Dr. Holmes actually drove 200 miles in his Carriole to perpetrate the murder, returning quietly home, and thence going on to the States where he has been arrested. But it seems

---

[15] The twelve executed were Joseph-Narcisse Cardinal, Amable Daunais, Pierre Théophile Decoigne, Chevalier de Lorimier, Joseph Duquette, François-Xavier Hamelin, Charles Hindenlang, Pierre-Rémi Narbonne, François Nicolas, Joseph Robert, Ambroise Sanguinet, and Charles Sanguinet.

[16] François Nicolas and Amable Daunais were tried for the murder of Chartrand and acquitted on September 7, 1838.

[17] Chevalier de Lorimier was implicated by the testimony of Dr. Jean-Baptiste-Henri Brien and other *patriotes* as one of the leaders in the second insurrection. He was a 'brigadier-general' at Lacolle Mill. On February 15, 1839, he was hanged after being sentenced to death by court-martial.

doubtful whether or not the Governor of Vermont will give him up. He has already refused to give up the perpetrators of the outrage on Vosburg, and it seems that the laws of this State will not allow him to act otherwise.

I have not yet seen more than the extracts from the English Papers published in the Montreal Papers and I have seen nobody this morning so am ignorant what news there may be. I am just returning to L'Acadie, but shall be back in town the day after tomorrow. Our best love to my Mother, etc., and believe me ever, My Dear Father,

Your most affectionate son,
C. Grey.

Montreal,
February 25, 1839.

My Dear Father,

By the *Great Western* I had letters from Henry and Lambton and I have also another from Henry by yesterday's mail for an earlier date. Lambton seems to write in good spirits and says he has no fear of the issue of the appeal to the judgment of the Public, which will be made at the opening of Parliament by the production before both houses of his Report, and of his and Lord Glenelg's dispatches. If his Proclamation is not taken into the consideration of his case, I certainly think he has a good one – indeed a triumphant one. But I much fear he is going to weaken it still more by his Report. What his plan is I do not know for he never told me more than that it was a very comprehensive one; but it is generally supposed, on apparently good grounds, that it embraces a plan for a Federal Union of all the North American Provinces and I do not believe there is any shape in which such a plan, however plausible it may be in theory, will be acceptable to the People of this Province, and I can hardly conceive his being so deceived in their feelings as not to know this.

Henry seems to me to have formed a correct opinion of what will be the best course if they are not prepared with such a plan for the future Government of these Provinces as would obtain the support of the British Party, without which I can only repeat my conviction *nothing* could be safely attempted. He tells me he should propose to extend the period for which the Act of last year is to continue – to increase the powers of the Governor General and Council, enabling them to pass any Laws which could have been passed by the late Legislature, provided that no Act should remain in force for more than twelve months unless specially confirmed by the Queen in Council after being submitted to Parliament. He would then use these powers for all the local improvements which have been so long demanded, abolishing the French as an official language, employing the Provincial Revenue in the improvement of communications, opening roads, canals, etc., encouraging emigration, extending education, amending the laws of tenure for landed Property, creating municipal corporations, etc., etc. In short he would do what Lambton, if he had been supported as he had a right to expect in the exercise of the powers which he had, would already have done. We know that he had a Registration Act ready, and that all his enquiries towards effecting the other measures which Henry mentions were in a state of great for-wardness, and I am much deceived if he would not at once have followed the suppression of the Rebellion by the suppression of the French as an official language. That was the proper moment for doing it. Now it would not look so much like the merited punishment of their crime and might possibly excite the French to a third insurrection.

After criticizing the absence of any provision for a legislative union of the Canadas in his brother's plan Grey's letter continues:

My objection to Henry's plan is that you cannot be sure how long the Governor in Council might be supported by the British

Inhabitants, without whose support we could not now keep the Colony a day. It is not to be supposed that *they* will be long satisfied with being governed despotically – at all events I feel sure that they would become discontented long before it would be possible to revert to constitutional Government in Lower Canada by itself, so as to give them, *fairly*, the preponderance which they *must* have over the French party – particularly when they think there is an easy mode at this moment of returning to the principles of Self-Government by doing little more than repealing the Act of [17]91. We should probably then be driven to adopt this very measure, if we had not previously lost the Colony, when it could not be so advantageously attempted either with regard to one Party or the other.

People have been so constantly in and out of my room, inter-rupting me, that I fear I may have made a sad jumble, and failed in explaining what I mean. It is this – that the British Party will not be long content without governing themselves, that we can-not keep the Colony without their support, that the present opportunity is the best for uniting the two Provinces, which experiment (for I take everything that can be suggested only as an experiment) will be the safest, as uniting the most powerful body of supporters; and that if we do not seize this opportunity, either such a measure, or perhaps a recognition of their *inde-pendence*, will be forced from us at no distant period.

February 26th.

I dined last night with Sir John Colborne and had a long con-versation with him in the evening. I see he inclines decidedly to Henry's opinion of the best course to be adopted for the present. From his long experience of Canada his opinion must have great weight, but I am not yet convinced that steps ought not at once to be taken by the Government for preparing the way for a Union of the Provinces within a certain time, and my opinion rests simply upon this: that the object of the British

Party is not to deprive the Country of Constitutional Government, but to exclude the French from any share in it, or at all events to deprive them of the preponderence which their numerical majority has hitherto given them in this Province; and this they think, unanimously, may be effected by the Union of the Provinces. The only objection to the plan seems to me [to be] the opposition of the Upper Canadians, and if we are wrong here in supposing it can be overcome, I certainly do not see how the difficulty is to be removed.

Sir John tells me that this Maine business has created great excitement on the lines. The invaders had not dispersed entirely as was at first said, they had merely retreated 50 miles up the Aroostook where they had taken a position and were waiting for reinforcements. I like Sir John Harvey's proclamation and I am told his letter to the Governor of Maine, who by all accounts has behaved infamously, is excellent.[18] The best possible spirit animates the New Brunswickers, and instead of one-fourth of the Militia that Sir J[ohn] Harvey calls upon to be ready, the whole have begged to be allowed to muster. It seems

18 On February 11, 1839, an armed party from Maine advanced into the disputed territory for the purpose of expelling New Brunswick lumbermen whom Maine regarded as trespassers. Upon learning of the Maine expedition, a group of New Brunswick lumbermen broke into the military stores at Woodstock, armed themselves, and proceeded to take into custody the Maine land agent and two other officials who had accompanied the expedition. The Maine force then withdrew to a point just inside the disputed territory taking with them four or five British subjects whom they had arrested. When Sir John Harvey learned of these events on February 13th, he issued a proclamation ordering the return of arms which had been taken from the government stores at Woodstock, and instructing the commanding officers of the 1st and 2nd Battalions of the Carleton County Militia to have one-quarter of their effective force stand ready for active service. On the same day he wrote a letter to Governor Fairfield of Maine expressing 'surprise and regret' at the occupation of the disputed territory, and stating that the United States had agreed that the territory should remain in the 'exclusive possession and jurisdiction' of Great Britain until the claim was settled. He entreated Fairfield to order the recall of the Maine force and cautioned him that, if this were not done, he had a strong force ready to protect British subjects in the disputed territory. For a time the Maine–New Brunswick boundary dispute threatened to lead to war but it was eventually settled by the Webster-Ashburton Treaty in 1842.

that this must bring these questions to a crisis which will be one advantage at all events.

It seems impossible to say, in the present state of things, whether I may not be prevented returning home in May. I can only hope not.

We have had the most extraordinary weather for the last ten days – a constant thaw, which is almost unknown at this season of the year. Today the thermometer is up to 45, and there seems, at present, every prospect of the navigation being open at an unusually early period. In 1801, I am told, a Vessel arrived here from England on the 23rd March. The usual time is the first week in May.

We are now looking anxiously for the arrival of the *Liverpool*. It is provoking that they have not detained her a few days longer. She will merely be able to bring us the Queen's speech.

Give my best love to my Mother, and believe me, My Dear Father,

Your most affectionate son,
C. Grey.

Montreal,
March 13, 1839.

My Dear Father,

I do not know when there may be an opportunity of sending this, but I cannot let the day pass without writing to say how anxiously I hope that it has found you perfectly recovered from the effects of the very disagreeable accident which I heard of from Henry and Frederick.[19] I cannot tell you how anxiously I am looking for the next accounts which it will still be weeks probably before we receive. Dr. Skey, the Staff Surgeon here, tells me that one can never be perfectly safe against inflammation for ten days, but he encourages me to think that where care

19 Lord Grey was struck on the head by a falling picture and suffered a deep gash.

is taken from the first there is not much danger of it. I will not think it possible it can be otherwise and most sincerely hope that next year at this time I may be able to wish you joy in person of the return of another and a happy birthday. I am indeed most anxious to get home again. I hate being at this distance from those I love, the long intervals that occur in hearing from home keeping one in a constant state of anxiety. It would have been much more comfortable if there had been no Steamers across the Atlantic till they could be established in regular and rapid succession.

I cannot but fear this Maine business may oblige me to remain where I am. We have not heard what the State Authorities have done on the receipt of the joint memorandum from Mr. Fox and Mr. Forsyth.[20] Our last accounts left 700 men fortifying themselves on the Aroostook, about 80 miles from its confluence with the St. John, and 15 from the undisputed boundary of Maine. Sir John Colborne thinks they will retire, which seems probable, I think, from the difficulty they find in provisioning them, but there appears to be a Party in Maine who are disposed, if possible, to push things at all hazards to a rupture with England. We shall see before the first of May how things look, and if it should then appear possible I shall ask for leave for seven months, viz: to the end of November. It is provoking, this Maine embarrassment having sprung up, when every difficulty to getting away owing to the state of Canada, was completely removed.

Everything now is *really* quite peaceable and even from the lines we get no fresh reports. My own belief is that even a war with the United States would not encourage the French Cana-

[20] In an effort to prevent war Fox and Forsyth drew up a joint memorandum, dated February 27, 1839, which recognized the existing difference of opinion between the United States and Great Britain concerning jurisdiction over the disputed territory, and stated that the question could only be solved by friendly discussion. The memorandum added that the Maine force should be withdrawn but New Brunswick should not attempt to expel it. It also stated that civil officers who had been taken into custody should be released.

dians to rise again at the present moment. I have seen a good
many lately of those who fled to Champlain after the assemblage
at Napierville was dispersed, Sir John Colborne having allowed
me to exercise a discretion in readmitting, on bail for their
future conduct, those, belonging to the Parish in which my
Regiment is quartered, of whose behaviour since they became
Refugees we should receive satisfactory accounts. I have brought
seven respectable farmers in on these conditions and, though I
would be sorry to answer for them if a *good* opportunity should
offer, it is hard to doubt men who seem so very sincere in their
promises. Previous to this outbreak they were all men of good
character, all well off, without a single cause of complaint that
one can discover. Nor can I make out the least from any of them
what it was they expected, beyond a vague idea of the establishment of a Republic. I much fear that the People who have
been the cause of it all are still undiscovered and that they
remain in the Province for further mischief. It is impossible to
believe, though it failed in the execution, that any of those who
have been hitherto taken and tried should have been able to
devise and conduct with such secrecy, up to the very last
moment, so well planned a scheme for a general and simultaneous rising.

I will not close my letter till my return from my Regiment
the day after tomorrow. We ought to have further news from
Maine before that.

                              March 17th.

The bag is to be made up tomorrow at nine o'clock, so I must
close the letter I began on the 13th.

There has been a wonderful dearth of news since, considering
the apparently imminent danger that then existed of collision
between the New Brunswick and Maine troops. We have nothing
further than that the Americans, in spite of the joint recommendation of the Messrs. Fox and Forsyth, remain in position

on the Aroostook and that the 11th Regiment is in occupation of Madawaska, also in the disputed territory. From what I hear of the nature of the Country it does not seem probable that Sir John Harvey will make any attack, in which case the expense and difficulty of provisioning their men will probably induce the Maine Authorities to withdraw them, when, of course, we should also withdraw whatever we may have in the disputed territory, and then a long negotiation between the two Governments may again be entered into.

While the result of all this remains uncertain, of course I shall not ask leave, but should Maine and New Brunswick mutually withdraw from the disputed territory, as is generally expected, I see nothing to prevent my returning home for a few months. Anxious as I am to do this, I must wish for a peaceable termination of the dispute, otherwise I think the conduct of the United States has been so abominable throughout – their Government (if Government it can be called) so odious, and their language so intolerable – that I should like to see them chastised as their insolence deserves. I do hope our Government will not let down its tone at all before all the bluster of Congress. We must have the best of a war, properly conducted. My idea would be to make it purely defensive in Canada, indulging our Volunteers perhaps with the burning of their frontier towns, and working their seacoast with a fleet of Steamers, etc. that should defy the possibility of attack from their miserable Navy.

Good-bye, my Dear Father, I do hope to hear soon of your perfect recovery from your accident and, in spite of Governor Fairfield, that things may appear on the 1st of May in such a state as to admit of my asking leave.

I need hardly say that Caroline joins me in every affectionate wish for many, many happy returns to you of the 13th, and in sending our best love to my Mother, and I am ever, My Dear Father,

Your most affectionate son,
C. Grey.

L'Acadie,
April 17, 1839.

My Dear Father,

My latest letters at present are to the 9th February, from Frederick, and the 4th from Harry, but Lady Farquhar fortunately sent on a letter of my Mother's to her written on the 14th, which, with a paragraph I have since seen in a still later Paper, has greatly relieved the anxiety I have been under since I first heard of your accident. But I shall not feel quite happy till the *Great Western* has arrived and I have received the good accounts which I confidently expect. It has happened too that never since I have been in Canada have I been so long without letters – just at the moment when I was most anxious to receive them, for none of the later packets which we have to the 2nd March have brought me a line.

The papers tell us that the anxiety for her arrival at New York is intense and that, in the fear of the news she may bring being warlike, all business is at a stand. This has revived the interest in the Maine question here which, since the pacific arrangement entered into between Sir John Harvey and General Scott,[21] had completely died away; and the idea of a war, which seemed to me to have been completely given up by everybody, has returned in full force. I believe a war would be extremely popular in these Provinces with the people who compose the Volunteer force, from the unsettled habits which they have acquired, and their desire to be kept on pay; with the merchants in the hope of increased activity in the St. Lawrence and a lucrative smuggling trade all along the line; and with many from sheer hatred of the Americans and desire of revenge. It is very little use speculating either as to the probability of a war, or the probable result of one if it should occur. But if properly conducted I should have

21 After an exchange of conciliatory letters between Major-General Winfield Scott and Sir John Harvey (March 21 and 23, 1839), the Maine militia force was withdrawn from the disputed territory and the New Brunswick militia which had been called up was permitted to return home.

very little fear of it. A defensive system along the frontier of this Country and an offensive one on the Coast of America would be sure, I think, to bring it to an end very soon. I should have no fear of Canada either from Rebels within, or from the enemy from without. I firmly believe the Americans to have very little offensive power. Their whole system is one of defence and as such very effective, I believe, as we should find if we were fools enough to march far into their territory. But I much doubt their ability to get any considerable Army on foot for offensive measures and they would find the People in this Country nearly as good at defensive warfare as themselves.

I need not tell you that Lambton's Report has been the all-absorbing topic here, till within these few days that the idea has again gained ground that we are to have a war. I may safely tell you that I have not heard from anybody in any situation, or of any party, the slightest difference of opinion as to that part of it which relates to Lower Canada. They say, one and all, that it is the fairest, most impartial and at the same time the fullest, clearest and truest account of the state of things here that *could* have been put together. Their only fear seems to be lest the Government at home should not be convinced of the *extent* to which it is true. Whatever mistakes he may have committed in his proclamation, or in intemperate dispatches on the Turton and other disputes, he has amply made up for them all in this most valuable Report. I defy anybody that has been any time in this Country not to concur most completely in every word he says, on almost every subject of his enquiry. I think perhaps the hatred of the Races in the Country districts may be a little exaggerated, but then nothing can be more correct than the account he gives of the influence obtained by the shoals of Doctors and Notaries in every parish, and I do believe that they hate us most cordially. Nor do I agree in thinking there is any decrease of sympathy. I believe the feeling the whole way along the line to be as bad as possible and, whatever the wishes of the General Government may be they are quite powerless, and the

feeling of the States' Governments may be gathered from the
fact of the Pirate Johnston and his daughter,[22] whose sole merit
is having burnt the *Sir Robert Peel*, having had a 'crowded
benefit' at the theatre at Albany since his liberation. From Governor Fairfield in Maine, to the man in Michigan, whoever he
may be, I think they and their subordinate officers one more
rascally than another.

In his remedial measures I most entirely agree, which I need
hardly tell you, as I believe I have constantly advocated a legislative Union of the Provinces. Whatever you try must be more
or less an experiment, and probably a dangerous one, but everybody agrees that you must try something and surely that is the
safest which unites the greatest number of those to whom we
must now look for the preservation of the Colony. And that is
certainly this Union of the Canadas, unanimously desired by the
British Party in Lower Canada and by a very strong Party in
Upper Canada as is proved by a resolution in favour of it having
been carried, though joined to some absurd conditions, in the
House of Assembly in that Province. It has been thrown out in
the Legislative Council as was to be expected, as their importance would, of course, be lessened by such a measure, and
they will oppose it on the same principles that Lambton's proposition of giving a responsible Executive will probably be
objected to here and in the other Colonies, that it touches them
personally. I rather think this feeling may account for the
Upper Canada part of the Report not having been so favourably
received. I have not read that part of it attentively myself, so
will give no opinion upon it. They say all the information in it
is taken from one side, and that the Radical or Republican one,
and ascribe it entirely to Charles Buller. But there is nothing
I agree with Lambton in more completely than in his opinion

[22] Bill Johnston's attractive daughter, Kate, was devoted to her father. She
lived at French Creek but visited him frequently in the Thousand Islands.
When an Albany court sentenced him to a year in prison for his piratical
activities, Kate obtained permission to share his confinement. Johnston
escaped within six months and was pardoned by President Harrison after a
previous application had been refused by the Van Buren administration.

of the absolute necessity of a responsible Executive and the folly of ever granting a representative form of Government if you were not prepared to go this length.

We continue perfectly quiet in this Province, without the slightest chance, in my opinion, of the Habitans trying it again. I doubt their moving even in the event of a war with the States. Having been instrumental in getting a great number of them allowed to return home – on giving bail for their future conduct – from the States, I have lately seen a great deal of them and if you are to believe their professions, made with the greatest sincerity of manner, they will remain quiet for the future. But it is rather discouraging that last summer they all came forward voluntarily to take the Oath of Allegiance, and yet within two months had begun to take the secret oath of the Rebels.

Our neighbours on the other side of line 45[23] are also beginning to get tired of the present state of things. The burnings, which had so long been occurring nightly on this side, have at last extended to the other and they now begin to discover, for the first time, that there is nothing very praiseworthy or Patriotic in such proceedings.

I must now finish my letter or I may be too late to catch Sir John's messenger at St. Johns, where he takes the Steamer up Lake Champlain. Should the *Great Western*'s day of sailing from New York have been altered I will write again and tell you what my plans are, which will greatly depend upon the news she brings. The only thing that can keep me in this Country beyond the summer is the chance of war with the States, and of that I cannot think – considering the pacific disposition lately shown on both sides by the Local Authorities in Maine and New Brunswick – there is now much chance.

With my best love to my Mother, believe me ever, My Dear Father,

Your most affectionate son,

C. Grey.

[23] The 45th parallel formed the boundary between the United States and Canada from the Connecticut River west to the St. Lawrence.

Montreal,

May 13, 1839.

My Dear Father,

I cannot tell you how delighted I was once more to see your handwriting after so long an interval during the whole of which, as I had not received a single letter from anyone of the Family, I had felt not a little anxious. Considering that there are weekly sailing Packets from Liverpool, which are not on an average more than ten days longer making the passage than the Steamers, I do not think the excuse that the *Great Western* sailed sooner than was expected is quite enough to justify none of them writing, from the 9th February till the 6th April, at a moment when I was naturally so anxious for a letter. However, they all say they are sorry for it and I can say no more though I still think it inexcusable. Your letter was the greatest possible comfort as the best proof that you had recovered from the effects of your accident. And the Packet was farther satisfactory as bringing me long letters from nearly all my usual correspondents. But it did not bring any intelligence which enables me to say whether or not I shall be able to get home, being quite silent as to the manner in which the Maine occurrences have been taken up in England. As I told Henry my movements must now necessarily depend upon the greater or less probability that it may lead to a war with the United States, I conclude he had nothing satisfactory to tell me: and I hear further from Sir John Colborne that the Government seems very little disposed to give up anything, so that there is a chance of its drawing out into a fight. However, the *Great Western* will be out again the first week in June and surely by that time we shall be better able to form a judgment. I gather from what Sir John said that he is in favour of a conventional line giving the Americans all the territory south of the upper part of the St. John as far as the Eagle Lakes, turning south through Three Lakes so as to secure the Madawaska Settlement to us, and he says he thinks the

People of Maine would agree to it. This would give them what they are most anxious for, the Valuable Pine Woods on the Aroostook, and would, at the same time, give us a satisfactory Boundary with a clear communication between New Brunswick and Canada.

There is great anxiety here to know the nature of the Government's Plan for the Settlement of these Provinces. The part of Lord Durham's Report which is most objected to is that which recommends a responsible Executive and I fear that is more generally disliked by the British Party in this Province than I had supposed. With respect to the rest of his report on Lower Canada, I should still say it is generally approved, though parts of it have been violently attacked, and continue to be so in the different Papers, while his friends are silent. But nobody can deny that, however People may have since cooled, it was received here at first with universal approbation. I have heard or read nothing to induce me to change the opinion I then formed, and trust, with perhaps some modification of his recommendation of a responsible Executive, that it may be made the foundation of whatever measure the Government may introduce.

I have no Canadian news of any interest. The Court Martial for the trial of the State Prisoners has at last closed its proceedings and been dissolved, and People are now waiting anxiously to see what Sir John Colborne means to do with all the Prisoners against whom sentence of death has been recorded, but whom it is not his intention to execute.[24] I hope myself that he will transport the greater number if not all. I do not think it would be prudent entirely to disregard the opinion of the British Inhabitants of this Province who are loud and violent in their demands for their punishment and I also think the example necessary for the Canadians. I have had considerable experience

---

24 As a result of the second insurrection, 108 were tried by court martial. Nine were acquitted and ninety-nine were sentenced to death. Of these only twelve were executed, fifty-eight were transported to Van Diemen's Land, two were banished, and twenty-seven were released after posting a bond for good behaviour.

of these People during the last six months and am convinced that nothing was ever more true than what Lambton says, that we must not expect that the Canadians of the present generation will ever now be loyal or well affected. But if the greater part of these Convicts are transported, I shall have little fear of a renewal of disturbances next winter.

It was provoking that the *Liverpool* could not wait a few days so as to bring us the account of the introduction of the Canadian measure and also of the division on Lord John's motion. Certainly a majority, composed as his majority will be, must be most unsatisfactory to any Minister, but surely it must strengthen the Government. It will be a formal approval by a majority of the House of their Irish policy, on which alone their difference with Sir Robert Peel seems very marked; and the news from India with the Russian correspondence, must, I think, give a little credit to their Foreign Policy. If they are whitewashed in Ireland, I do not well see on what question the Tories and Radicals can combine to turn them out.

We are thinking of making a tour through the Eastern Townships early next month and, as soon as the Inspection is over, we propose a tour in the States so as to hang on in this Country till towards the end of the Session, when we shall be better able to judge of what is likely to happen, both as respects the probability of war with America, and the stability of the Government. If I should lose my Equerryship on a change of Government, I had rather stay here another winter and come home, probably for good, next spring, than return home to have to come out again, and if there is war of course I must stay. As therefore the fate of the Government must be decided long before I could get home under any circumstances, I think it better to make up my mind to hold on here a little longer. I shall be disappointed to a degree if it does not end in my being with you at Howick by the end of September.

I have written this in a great hurry so pray excuse bad writing and blunders. The bag is made up tonight – 48 hours sooner than I expected, or than is necessary – for which I was not prepared.

Our best love to my Mother, etc., and believe me ever, My Dear Father,

Ever your most affectionate son,
C. Grey.

Montreal,
May 29, 1839.

My Dear Father,

Since I wrote last we have news from England to the 25th of April, but I do not see anything of much interest in the Extracts from the Papers (for I have not seen the English Papers themselves) except the majority in favour of Government on the Irish Question which is better than I expected, and a report that 10 sail of the line are to go to the Baltic.

Here everything remains quiet though the excitement still appears great on both sides of the lines in the Upper Province. You will see an account of a very foolish business at Brockville where the Collector of Customs yielded to the Mob and seized a Schooner for having a dismounted gun on board, consigned to somebody at Ogdensburg, but which was again given up, if the accounts are true, on Colonel Worth coming to demand it with an armed Steamer from Sackets Harbor. The seizure may have been wrong, but to yield to an appearance of bullying by Colonel Worth was making it worse. Altogether, I think the accounts look like more trouble from the violent on both sides next winter. Then Lambton's report has caused the greatest excitement and I fear the disaffected are the People who will be assisted by it. It is the test by which the Candidates will be tried at the next Election and it is thought that there will be a large majority in favour of it. In the meantime the present House of Assembly has published an answer to it, in their report on the state of the Province, which upsets, certainly, most of his facts. There is but one feeling here with respect to it and also to many parts of the Lower Canada Report that, even if true, it was most inexpedient to have it published and disseminated in Canada. The Rebellion had united, to a certain degree, all parties in Upper Canada. This Report has made them more bitter against each other than ever. I cannot have a doubt in my own mind of its having been written by Charles Buller and the absurd statement he made in the House of Commons of neutrality having been better enforced by the Americans than by us, and of sympathizing meetings not being allowed to be held, which he must have known to be untrue, shows how little, like other Radicals and Tories too, he cares about the truth of his facts.

I think my plans are nearly made up – that is, I think I have decided on asking leave as soon as Denny returns, which will probably be next week as I expect him to come out by the *Great Western*. I should then probably take six weeks or two months in the States, and so sail from New York about the end of July or beginning of August. I am very much tempted to make a tour, when I leave this, up again to Niagara, to Buffalo, and by Cleveland to Pittsburgh, down the Ohio to Cincinnati, and thence by the direct line of stages to Washington. I am told the Country is quite beautiful. The objection will be the heat of the weather and the badness of the roads, the railroads not having yet extended far enough west, but I think these inconveniences must be borne. Should I decide upon this we shall make a ten days' trip, starting next week, into the Eastern Townships which one ought not to leave Canada without seeing.

May 30th.

I believe I may now say my plans are made up, and that I shall sail from New York on the 19th August in the *Oxford*, unless, in the meantime any news comes from England, or anything happens in this Country to prevent me.

I start on Monday next for the Eastern Townships. Before the end of the month I shall also visit Bytown – the Inspection will be over – Major Denny out – and on the 1st July shall start on the trip I have mentioned to you which, if everything goes smoothly, will bring me to New York, having seen all I wish, in time for the 19th August Packet. All I have, therefore, now got to hope for is that nothing will occur between this and then to prevent my sailing for England.

I hope to be written to, if by sailing Packets, as late as the 13th July, which is one of their sailing days from Liverpool; if by a Steamer, any time before the end of July; and my letters should be directed under cover to the Consul at New York to be kept till asked for.

I will write again by the *Great Western* if I have anything to say. At present I have quite exhausted my budget.

With our best love to my Mother, etc., believe me ever, My Dear Father,

Your most affectionate son,
C. Grey.

CHAPTER IX

A Visit to Bytown

*Colonel Grey had consoled himself during the wearisome winter
at L'Acadie by making plans to visit different regions in the
Canadas when spring came and Major Denny returned. He
enjoyed travelling and was anxious to see more of the country
before returning to England on leave in late summer.*

*On the first Saturday in June he and his wife set out for a brief
visit to Bytown. His journal describes their trip through the
Rideau Canal, completed just seven years previously, to the site
of Canada's future capital, and back down the Ottawa River to
Montreal.*

KINGSTON, U.C., JUNE 5, 1839

On Saturday last after a great deal of wavering I made up my
mind for a trip to Bytown. Asked and obtained Leave on Sunday for a week, and on Monday morning at seven started with
Caroline, in Denny's jaunting car, for Lachine (sending Trounce
with the baggage per coach) with the intention of going up the
Ottawa in the *Ottawa* Steamer, but finding that she had nine
heavy barges to tow up, and that she did not expect to reach
Carillon before one in the morning, where we should have to be
transferred at that hour to stages to go twelve miles to Grenville,
I determined to go round by Kingston and down the Rideau to
Bytown, and accordingly we take our passage in the *Chieftain*

(late *Henry Brougham* – name changed since last year's rebellion when she was seized by the Rebels) for Cascades. A number of passengers on board. Three officers of the Royal Regiment en route for Niagara, Captain E[vans] of the King's Dragoon Guards ditto, Mister C., wife, wife's sister, and three children on their way to some place in the Upper Province where the gentleman is to leave his encumbrances. It is an odd story. I fancy he is to be separated from his wife in consequence of having taken illegitimate means, with the assistance of his wife's maid, to increase his family. He is son of the Bishop of St.— and is a Lieutenant in the 66th Regiment.

There is also a Mr. Roy, agent for a Madeira House, from whom we receive the greatest possible civility; Dr. Rolph,[1] formerly an Essex Reformer, now an Upper Canadian High Tory and converted Catholic – tho' which way he is converted I know not – Probably to, not from, Catholicism as he is about going to England with Macdonell, the Catholic Bishop of Kingston, to preach emigration etc. Also Dr. Gilder of the Coldstream Guards, as I find out afterwards, on a matrimonial trip to Prescott. A lot of Raftsmen returning from Quebec and several 'Loafers'. What does the term mean? Mrs. Brown of Beauharnois with her two sisters is also on board the *Chieftain* and tells me that the Canadians are again getting very insolent about Ste. Martine, etc. where I had had dealings with them in the winter. Believe there is more fear than Danger. Nevertheless they have a right to protection even from fear, if possible. At Cascades, which we reach a few minutes under two hours, we are all transferred to stages, five in number, having each nine inside. Captain Whipple fortunately takes us under his special protection and arranges one

1 Grey would appear to have confused Dr. Thomas Rolph with Dr. John Rolph. Dr. Thomas Rolph came to Canada in 1833 and practised medicine at Ancaster. In 1839 he was appointed Canadian immigration agent in Great Britain and retained this position until 1843. Dr. John Rolph represented Middlesex in the legislative assembly from 1824 to 1830, and Norfolk from 1836 to 1837. He was one of the reformers who became implicated in the rebellion and fled to the United States. He did not return to Canada until 1843.

coach for myself and Caroline, the three Royals, the Dragoon and the marrying Medico of the Coldstream, seven in all, and we get over the 16 miles to Coteau du Lac tolerably comfortably, tho' the road is execrable from the late Heavy rain. Embark in the *Neptune*, 44 Cabin Passengers in all – and lots of steerage ones. Leave Coteau at three. Dine on board at four and arrive at Cornwall at half past eight. Here we are again transferred to stages to go 12 miles to Dickinson's Landing. But there being only four coaches they are all crammed full, inside and out, and one coach contains ourselves, the C— family and maid, two Royals and the Dragoon, in all nine grown up People and three children. A dreadful road and being dark do not reach the Landing till half past eleven, when we turn in tolerably comfortably on board the *Brockville*.

At Cornwall Colonel Turner tells me that Bill Johnston had been seen two days before to pass Brockville with five boats, containing between 50 and 60 armed men, in consequence of which he had sent an extra Picquet to the Landing. The boats all going armed. Consequently we find a strong guard on board the *Brockville*, all on the alert, and we turn in in perfect security. At three get under way. Reach Prescott at half past nine where I land with Caroline and walk up to the Church. It is a wretched place showing great symptoms of ruin and decay. It was flourishing before the opening of the Rideau Canal, when everything went up and down the St. Lawrence in bateaux, but that work has been its deathblow. About a mile and a half below we passed close under the windmill where Von Schoultz landed with his unfortunate sympathizers. The strength of his position consisted in the windmill and houses flanking each other and being all of stone, with an open country which made it impossible to turn them out without heavy guns. The Houses are all burnt and the windmill, I conclude, occupied as a Picquet house, at least the English Ensign was hoisted on the top as we went by.

Between Prescott and Brockville we passed Maitland, a very pretty thriving village which has risen up of late years under the auspices of a Scotchman named Langley.[2] He came out about 20 years ago not worth more than 100 Pounds. Now the greatest part of this village belongs to him, where he has built a very neat Presbyterian Church, at his own expense, an immense flour mill, and has a beautiful farm with 300 acres under cultivation. Nothing could look more snug or substantial than the whole establishment and after being so long in the Lower Province, and seeing nothing but the wretched cultivation of the French Canadians, it was quite refreshing to see something like good home farming. But nothing can be more thriving looking or better cultivated than the Canada bank of the river the whole way up from Matilda, and [it] affords a most striking contrast to the South or American bank which is by no means, in spite of Mr. Buller, so far advanced.[3] Where Mr. Buller found the deserted farms and symptoms of decay and want of enterprise which he says characterizes the Upper Canadians, as distinguished from the 'go ahead' Yankees, I have not been able to discover, but Mr. Roy tells me that while he was detained by illness at Kingston, he got most of his information from a Mr. Manahan,[4] a disappointed applicant to Government, and who vents his spite by abasing everything and everybody belonging to the Province.

Stop half an hour at Brockville where we land – the prettiest village I have seen in Canada, with the greatest air of comfort about it. Caroline and I take a delightful walk up to the Court house and through a grove of American Pines on the hill close behind it, whence there is a very pretty view. Our next stopping

---

2 Maitland was originally settled by United Empire Loyalists. George Langley built his grist mill in 1828.

3 Grey apparently felt that the numerous references to the progressive character of the United States which appear in Lord Durham's *Report* could be attributed to Buller.

4 Anthony Manahan. Manahan was subsequently elected for Kingston in 1841 but resigned in order to permit one of Lord Sydenham's favourites to gain a seat. For this he was rewarded with the appointment of inspector of customs. He returned to politics, however, and unsuccessfully contested the Kingston seat against John A. Macdonald in the election of 1844.

place is Gananoque, 25 miles below Kingston, which we reach a little after three, after a most lovely sail through the Thousand Islands. The *Montreal* Armed Schooner is lying here on the look out to protect the People against Bill Johnston. Thought we saw an armed schooner a little lower down running up the river before the wind on the American side. This lake and river work must be a new life for Jack, and the Lieutenant commanding the *Montreal* thinks it is a good excuse for growing a very imposing pair of mustachios. Reach Kingston a little after six. Find every place full, but fortunately stumble upon my old friend Captain Bourchier of the 93rd who, in the most good natured way possible, gives us up his rooms at Macdonald's 'North American' Hotel. Dress and dine with the 83rd.

This morning, as there is no boat down the Rideau today, spend forenoon calling on the Old Bishop [and] Dundas of the 83rd, etc. The latter lends us his gig, and I drive Caroline out to the Penitentiary which is being built on the Auburn plan.[5] Only one division of the building is yet finished. It is to be in the shape of a Cross. Three limbs of the Cross being each divided into two rows of Cells of five tiers, a gallery, from whence the Cells on both sides can be overlooked, running down the middle of the space between the rows of Cells. The fourth limb of the Cross is for Offices and Apartments for the Officers. The division already finished, which is the smallest and is calculated for 210 convicts,

---

5 The provincial penitentiary at Portsmouth, just outside Kingston, was built on the same plan as the one in Auburn, New York. It was also operated on the Auburn system under which the convicts were confined in separate cells during the night and employed at various trades during the day. William Powers, who had experience at Auburn, was engaged as superintendent of building and was later appointed deputy warden. The original building is still the nucleus of the Kingston penitentiary, but fires and additions have modified its appearance. At the end of September 1839, there were 148 convicts in the penitentiary. Visitors were admitted at a charge of 1s. 3d. for men and 7½d. for women and children. When Charles Dickens visited the penitentiary in 1842 he observed that it was 'well and wisely governed and excellently regulated in every respect', but the evidence presented to the Penitentiary Commission of 1848-9 justifies Grey's suspicion that penitentiary officers frequently abused their disciplinary powers. Even women and children were flogged on numerous occasions.

was built by hired labour. The remainder, two other divisions being in a state of great forwardness, is to be built by the Convicts themselves, and we found Masons, Carpenters, Blacksmiths, etc. all in full and apparently very hard labour. Shoemaker's and Tailor's Shops, Soap Makers, etc., etc. seemed all in full employment. I need not say that the most perfect silence is enforced. So many Convicts could not otherwise be safely allowed to work together and the slightest disobedience is punished by flogging with a thong of Bull's hide. Any under-keeper may give from six to a dozen lashes and the probability is this power is constantly abused. However, enough has been said and written by others on the silent system and I will only add I cannot bear the idea of the flogging power. Tho' I must say the convicts all looked well and as cheerful as their situation would allow. From the Penitentiary we crossed by a bad concession road, thro' a Country only beginning to be cleared, to a McAdamized road which goes about nine miles from Kingston towards Toronto. Delighted at having to pay a regular turnpike. The *Cataraqui* Steamer arrived this forenoon and will start again with us tomorrow morning at six for Bytown. She brought up a reinforcement of 30 men for Captain Sandom. Raining all the afternoon which is spent, after our return from our drive, in writing this journal and in an interminable visit from Dundas, Bourchier and Lieutenant Maclure, R.N., appointed last year from the *Hastings* to Captain Sandom's force.

BYTOWN, U.C., JUNE 7, 1839

Before I say anything about our journey down the Rideau and our arrival at this place, I must mention for the information of myself, in case I should ever return to Kingston, that there is great difficulty in getting accommodation, and that when you do get the best it is no great things. . . . I think I also forgot to say that the extraordinary news of the resignation of Government brought out by one Packet, and of their being reinstated, brought out by another, greeted us on our arrival; with no particulars, however, except that the resignation was in consequence of the smallness of the Majority on the Jamaica Constitution Suspension Bill, and that their recall was owing to a difference between Peel and the Queen on the Household appointments.⁶ It is said the Government will be remodelled, but it is no use speculating on newspaper reports which are always one more absurd than another. When I get hold of an authentic account in any Paper I will cut it out and insert it. At present I will return to my journey.

Yesterday morning at six o'clock, according to our arrangement with the Captain, we embarked on board the *Cataraqui* for this place and arrived here this afternoon at two o'clock. I do not think I ever was more pleased with any excursion and rejoice beyond measure at having come round by Kingston, which has saved me from returning to England without seeing the thing, in my opinion the best worth seeing in it, the Rideau Canal. But this splendid work is miscalled, and the term Canal is apt to deceive those who have not seen it and who merely fancy something of the same nature as our Canals at home. On somewhat a larger scale perhaps, but still they do not get beyond a 'Canal' with its towing path, etc. — such at least was my idea of it; and I never was more surprised and delighted in my life than to find its only resemblance to a Canal is in its magnificent locks by which an internal water communication from the Ottawa to the St. Lawrence — leading for half the distance through a chain of most beautiful lakes, and for the other half down the Rideau River to Bytown — has been improved and completed. This has been done by building a series of dams heading the water back to a greater or less height, according to the length of the rapid to be overcome, and the depth of water required to

⁶ When their majority on a bill for the suspension of the constitution of Jamaica was reduced to five, the Whigs resigned and Queen Victoria called upon Sir Robert Peel to form a government. The Queen refused, however, to dismiss the ladies of her household, among whom were included the wives and daughters of several Whig members, and Peel declined to take office. The episode was popularly known as 'the bedchamber crisis'.

be raised; at each dam locks being built through which you ascend to the next Level. The whole of these locks are beautifully finished of solid masonry, with steps cut on each side, but some are perfectly magnificent. At Kingston Mills you rise 42 feet in four successive locks and at Jones falls 62 feet in the same number. This is the finest work on the line. The dam is 62 feet high, faced with solid stone, being 300 feet wide at bottom and 60 at top. It drowns a rapid of one mile in length and adds three feet in depth to the lakes above. This is the most interesting part of the route.

The situation of Jones falls is beautiful, and the passage thro' Sand, Opinicon, Indian, Clear, Mud and Upper Rideau Lakes, generally connected by a narrow Creek where there is one lock, most interesting. Upper Rideau lake is the summit Level of the Line. Here you commence descending and, after passing a lock of only two feet at the narrows where you pass into Rideau lake, you have 19 miles through one of the most splendid sheets of water possible. Formerly Rideau Lake and Upper Rideau Lake were in one and it was intended originally to keep them so, in which case there would have been a stretch of about 40 miles in the terminal Level without a Lock. But to do this it would have been necessary to excavate the passage which leads into the Upper Rideau Lake about four feet four, in order to get sufficient depth of water, and so many lives had been lost by accidents in blasting, in excavating it to its present depth, that Colonel By[7] preferred raising the upper part of Rideau Lake by dams, for which the ground gave every facility. Mr. Burrows,[8]

[7] Lieutenant-Colonel John By was sent out to Canada in 1826 to direct the construction of the Rideau Canal. He established his headquarters at the junction of the Ottawa and Rideau rivers and the settlement which developed became known as Bytown (now Ottawa). In 1832 a British Treasury minute censured By for having exceeded his estimates on the canal and requested his recall. Upon his return to England, By testified before a parliamentary committee and was completely exonerated, but he never received the acclaim he might have expected for so significant an achievement as the construction of the Rideau Canal.

[8] John Burrows was overseer of works while the Rideau Canal was under construction. A diary and sketch book kept by Burrows, while working on the canal, is in the Bytown Museum, Ottawa.

Clerk of the Works to Colonel By during the whole time, was fortunately on board with us and gave most interesting information respecting the progress of the work. It was really almost impossible to believe when sailing over a magnificent sheet of water, extending for miles in every direction, that this was formerly nothing but a marsh with a narrow winding stream running through it. They call this part to which I allude the 'drowned Lands' and it is the only drawback to the Beauty of the scenery that the trees, which have been killed by the flooding, are still standing naked and rotten in the water, and it must be years probably still before they are got rid of. For seven miles above Kingston Mills the effect of these dead trees is particularly disagreeable, but in the lakes above Jones falls you have not this drawback and the scene is one of unmixed beauty – on all sides sloping banks covered to the water's edge with magnificent timber – endless wooded or rocky Islands, bays and outlets to the right and left, appearing to recede, as in many cases they do, into other lakes running east and west. At present it is all a wilderness!

Till you come towards the lower end of Rideau Lake, no attempt even at clearing and yet, with the facility of internal communication given by these lakes, what a Country this ought to be – and that before a great many years have passed. The first step towards it is the Rideau Navigation, and it is melancholy to think that Colonel By, who planned and executed it under difficulties that few men would have borne up against, should have died, some say of a broken heart, at seeing his exertions undervalued, and from meeting with blame for having exceeded his estimates instead of reward for having completed one of the greatest works ever undertaken. The cost of money signifies nothing. The loss of life is a more serious consideration. Mr. Burrows tells me that 40 or 50 lives were lost by accident alone, while the numbers that died by disease is quite incalculable. Dr. Barker[9] estimates those who died from the works at

---

[9] Dr. Edward John Barker, the editor and owner of the Kingston *British Whig*.

Kingston Mills alone as 500 and Mr. Burrows says he thinks it is very possible! It is satisfactory, however, to know that since the completion of the work the Country is less unhealthy than it was before it was begun. The water being now kept up to a certain Level prevents the exhalations which used to follow the rise of the waters in the spring and fall.

The Steamboat was clean and comfortable and the eating very fair. I am told, however, she is the only one tolerable and that the others on the line are as bad as possible. From Bytown to Kingston they generally take Barges in tow and are four or five days making the Passage. It seems to me disgraceful, considering that Government has made the Province a present of the work, requiring no interest even for the money expended, that they have not put tolls enough upon it even to keep it up, and that it is still allowed to cost Government from four to five thousand a year. We had very few Passengers on board. A Mr. McMartin, a Barrister belonging to Perth, came from Kingston as far as Oliver's ferry – strongly in favour of Lord Durham's Report and violently opposed to the present House of Assembly and the 'Family Compact' – a Radical I should think by his dislike to the name. Mr. Mathewson,[10] M.P.P. for the County of Frontenac and a large Mill Proprietor and Lumberer, also came on board for a short distance – a fat, vulgar man – violent in his abuse of the Yankees and 'the Family Compact'. While on the Rideau Lake we have a tremendous thunder shower with two violent claps of thunder. One of them seemed to burst exactly over the vessel and sounded like a salvo of 32 Pounders.

We got here at two o'clock having been detained considerably since we got to the last locks by rafts of timber. The Locksmen told me they had never known anything like the quantity taken down. It seems the most hopeless thing in the world to expect that one of these rafts should ever work its way as far as Quebec, but in the Ottawa or St. Lawrence, however, they make rapid progress.

10 James Mathewson.

Doran's Hotel here is *excellent* – as clean and comfortable as any I ever saw at home. The misfortune is that it cannot pay and will therefore probably not last long. Dine at half past three, after which Mr. Stevenson,[11] agent for the Commercial Bank, with whom I make acquaintance in the street, takes us in a car as far as the falls of the Chaudiere. Too strong a glare of sun upon it, and the day too hot to enjoy it as we should otherwise have done. From thence we drive to Mr. Stevenson's house at New Edinburgh, just beyond the Rideau falls, where we have tea and coffee, and remain till half past eight, walking to see the falls, etc. Mr. Stevenson settled here about four years ago. He has a farm of 600 acres – about 120 cleared – and has built himself a very nice cottage with a pretty view down the Ottawa, which might have been prettier if he had put his cottage nearer the Bank. One of his sons drove the car, who had lost an arm, having had it bit off (!) last year by a horse. He would probably have been killed if a dog had not seized the horse by the hip and made him drop the boy whom he was shaking as a terrier would do a rat! His daughters are pretty.

I have been terribly punished by mosquitoes and my left eye is almost a vanishing quantity. We had not had one till we got to Oliver's ferry where we landed while they were taking in wood and walked into a wood. Here I was immediately assailed in gathering some water lilies and the brutes came back with me on board and never left me all night. They certainly have succeeded in making a figure of me.

BYTOWN, JUNE 8,1839

We had intended starting this morning at four o'clock to go to Aylmer to take the Steamer which leaves that place every other morning at six A.M. for the Lac des Chats, returning the same evening, but there was a difficulty about procuring a conveyance from the Ferry house which prevented us, and, as it

11 James Stevenson, the collector of timber duties on the Ottawa River.

has been raining the whole morning, I cannot say I regret it. Tomorrow after Church if I can procure a waggon I shall content myself with driving to Aylmer and back. At present there is no communication with the other side except by the Ferry boat. A Bridge which crossed to a small rocky Island at the foot of the Falls, whence there is a stone bridge to the other bank, broke down two years ago and there is no money forthcoming to replace it. For tho' Mr. Stevenson tells me that the Lower Province has consented to give £1,500 towards rebuilding it, the Upper Province has refused to come forward. The Legislative Council has thrown out the bill passed with this view by the House of Assembly. Two other wooden bridges over two narrow offsets of the river are also in a very precarious condition, one half of one of them having actually fallen last year. Hull on the opposite side of the river is a much older settlement than Bytown – a Mr. Wright,[12] an American, having settled there 40 years ago. He has one or two well cleared farms, having got rid of the eternal stumps. He died last Monday and is to be buried on Sunday next. His Property is immense – consists of 75,000 [sic] acres. There seems a good Church at Hull and some few scattered substantial houses, which compose the whole village. Nine P.M. – It has been raining nearly the whole day. Caroline and I took advantage of a clear interval to walk to Government Hill whence there is a magnificent view up and down the Ottawa and over the back Forest to the north of the river. To the east of the Hill the Rideau Canal is brought down a natural chasm, through eight locks, to the Ottawa.

In the event of the Union of the Provinces the Bytown People put in their claim to have it made the Capital and I am inclined to think it would be the best situation. If not quite so central

12 Philemon Wright settled on the present site of Hull, Quebec, with a party of twenty-five associates in 1800. Wright had substantial capital and the settlement made rapid progress. Within four years a grist mill, a sawmill, a smithy, a tailor shop, a bake-house, and a tannery were in operation. In 1807 Wright floated the first timber raft down the Ottawa and St. Lawrence rivers to Quebec.

as Kingston it is farther removed from the frontier, which is an advantage, and I am told the navigation might easily be extended well up the Ottawa.

From Government Hill we walked down to the Chaudiere falls and were consequently caught in the rain. After taking shelter for half an hour under a rock, we were forced to leave it and got home tolerably wet. Dine at three, and at six o'clock, the rain having ceased, I walk out and watch a large raft for a long while in the hope of seeing it start. Mr. Stevenson collects the duties for the Province. One of the rafts lying below, as he told me, had paid £225 duty and its value was probably about £1,300. It belonged to an old Scotchman who had been up the River all the winter collecting the timber for it, and whose all was probably embarked in it. A gale of wind in Lake St. Peter will frequently break up these rafts which, as in this case it would be, often ruins the owner. The Raftsmen are mostly French Canadians, half-caste Indians and Irishmen − a Lawless uncivilized race. They are often nine years in the woods without coming down. Artificial 'Slides', as they call them, have been made on each side of the falls here, down which the rafts are brought in detached portions called cribs, which are again collected below and locked together again, to be again detached at the Long Sault rapids. It is a service of some danger for the men who come down the Slides on the cribs, it sometimes happening that the stream takes them down the Fall itself. In which case there is no hope for the men, unless they can get off in their canoes in time. A Raft hence will get to Quebec in about three weeks on an average, but the distance has been done in 10 days. Tea at eight and read very comfortably to Caroline afterwards till ten.

BYTOWN, JUNE 9, 1839

A Rainy day with fair intervals sufficient to allow us to go to Church morning and evening. Evening Service is at half past six, a much better time than three, in my opinion, which comes too quick after morning Service. Good sermons morning and evening from Mr. Strong, the Clergyman of the Place, and a neighbouring Clergyman who had come to assist in consequence of the funeral of Mr. Wright. Meant to have gone over to Hull after morning Church if it had not rained. In spite of the weather a great crowd followed Mr. Wright to the grave as the first settler in the District. The sound of an axe had never been heard so high up the river when he first squatted on the other side.

Had a long conversation with Mr. Doran, the Keeper of the Inn, [who] complains like everybody else I have met of the Monopoly which the forwarding Company is allowed to retain by their having the only lock, at present, by which the rapids of Ste. Anne's below Grenville can be passed.[13] Also very indignant at the refusal of the Legislative Council to sanction the grant proposed by the House of Assembly for building a new Bridge over the river to Hull. Full of regret that Lord Durham did not visit the place, in which I join, for I feel convinced that he would have agreed that such a place for the Capital of a Country never existed – within a day's journey of Montreal – not 24 hours distant from Kingston – under 50 miles from Cornwall, Prescott, and Brockville – and with the possibility of having an uninterrupted water communication opened to Lake Huron – The Centre of the Lumber trade – With thousands upon thousands of acres of excellent uncleared land all round – Rich, as Mr. Stevenson tells me, in iron ore of the finest quality. It seems intended by nature from its magnificent situation, finer in my opinion than that of Quebec, to be the first place in British North America.[14]

13 McPherson and Crane owned the only lock at Ste. Anne's Rapids and thus enjoyed a monopoly of the Ottawa River forwarding trade. A canal was started at Ste. Anne's in 1840 and was completed in 1843.

14 When Queen Victoria was considering the location of the seat of government for the Province of Canada in 1857, Charles Grey was Prince Albert's secretary. The Prince's memorandum in favour of Ottawa is written in Grey's hand. Public Archives of Canada, *Letters to Queen Victoria, 1837-1867* (Typewritten copies). Manuscript Group 24, A 29, pp. 59-60.

CARILLON, JUNE 10, HALF PAST EIGHT P.M.

Just arrived by the stage from Grenville en route for Montreal, having left Bytown this morning at half past ten in the *Shannon* Steamer. We are now detained here in a miserable pothouse, where we may have to wait till three tomorrow morning for the *Ottawa* Steamer before we can go on to Lachine, without even the possibility of even lying down. And this because, having completed the Rideau Navigation at an immense expense, the Government have not thought it worthwhile to make a lock at the Ste. Anne's Rapids below, without which the monoply of the whole line has been given to one Forwarding Company who, having a private lock by which these Rapids can be passed, will allow no Steamers to ply but their own. Having thus no fear of competition, the last thing they consider is the comfort or convenience of their Passengers, of which we are at this moment a wretched and a fractious group. Our inconvenience and discomfort, however, is nothing compared with the injurious effect this monopoly has otherwise, retarding, as it does most effectually, the progress of the fine Country we have passed through since we left Kingston. I have heard nothing but complaints of it ever since I left that place from men of all parties I ask before we sailed from Bytown. After we were actually on board the Steamer, Major Bolton of the Engineers, the Superintendent of the Canal, came on board and gave me two packets of Papers which I had been on the point of leaving behind. He had been away so that my letters had lain in his office. I learned from them that the same Government is come in for the moment, whether to remain as they are or not seems uncertain, and the adjournment of 18 days moved for by Lord J[ohn] Russell looks like some changes. I hear the satisfactory news that the situations in the Household of the subordinate officers who were not in Parliament were not intended to be touched.

Sixty-one miles down to Grenville. Beautifully wooded Banks and a most splendid river all the way, but no variety of scenery.

One wretched stage to take us 12 miles to Carillon through an uninteresting Country and here we are waiting for the *Ottawa*. I was very sorry to leave Bytown without going higher up. But I am told the scenery is much the same as what we have seen elsewhere and I am anxious to get back in order to make another trip, through the Townships, before the end of the month.

MONTREAL, JUNE 16, 1839

It is in vain trying to keep a journal regularly from day to day. When one proposes to do so, one generally lies most tremendously in dates, a week's journal being constantly written in one day. The best way is whenever one feels inclined to sit down and to fancy oneself writing on to some friend an account of what has happened since we last wrote, and, like letter writing itself, it will be found easier in proportion to the regularity with which it is done. To bring up a week's journal is almost as difficult as to write to a neglected correspondent. One does not know where to begin.

Our movements have been brought down as far as the pothouse at Carillon where I wrote the last of my journal by way of passing the time. We had not to wait, however, as long as usual. The *Ottawa*, having a light tow – only three barges – arrived at eleven o'clock, much earlier, the Carillon Authorities tell you, than usual. Tho' at Lachine they do not mind telling the monstrous lie that you will arrive at five in the evening! Before twelve we are all turned in. Between sleeping and waking I hear the Boat get under way at three. Wake at daylight, and having a window close to my berth get a tolerable view of the Lake of Two Mountains. The morning is wet, and the Hills from which it takes its name are covered with thick mist. The Indian village seems very pretty and also the little village where we shoot the rapid of Ste. Anne's. It is here that Government ought to build a lock in order to destroy the monopoly of this line. ... There is no difficulty in the way except the want of money, a

trifling one after the large sum already paid out on the Rideau
Navigation which is incomplete without this. The Company's
lock is on the other side of Ile Perrot and is besides 10 miles
longer than the passage would be through one constructed at
Ste. Anne's. The day clears up by the time we are dressed and
we have barely time to Breakfast before we arrive (eight
o'clock A.M.) at Lachine. A coach with six grey horses driven
in hand lands us at our own door in Montreal before half past
nine on Tuesday morning.

No particular news awaits our arrival. I read the debates in
the English Papers, but learn nothing more than I had already
heard. On Wednesday I call upon Sir John Colborne and ask him
about going to England. He does not think there is anything to
prevent me going though he does not seem sure of the winter
passing over quietly. Other People are convinced it will *not*,
tho' nobody seems to think it will this year assume the form of
an open insurrection. Still there is enough to make me hesitate
about asking leave. Colonel Clive of the Guards advises me
decidedly to go. So does Colonel Ellison. Still I cannot make up
my mind and shall probably, I think, hang on here till towards
the middle of July. At all events I shall give up our long western
tour. It will be much too hot to enjoy anything.

Hear on our arrival at Lachine on Tuesday morning of the
burning of the *John Bull* Steamer, which is confirmed, tho' up
to this moment it seems doubtful whether it occurred acci-
dentally or not. The Second Engineer and two sailors who were
on duty are missing, whether burnt or escaped after doing it
wilfully no one knows. The Captain (Vaughan) says on the
alarm being given he found his cabin door locked on the outside, which looks like purpose, but it is also said there was a
good deal of spirits on board and that these men had been drink-
ing, which would account for the accident. It probably will
never be cleared up.

On Friday there is a Cricket Match at St. Helen's. On Saturday
a Field day at the Old Race Course. Today we are just come back

from Church to which we went, in spite of heavy rain, to assist in enabling the Church of Toronto to rise 'like a Phoenix from its Ashes'.[15] Dr. Bethune told us it was the largest Church in British North America. I regret that I gave anything when I think that it is the People of Toronto who have prevented the outlay of the necessary sum for rebuilding the bridge over the Ottawa at Bytown.

Montreal,
June 14, 1839.

My Dear Father,

I had started on Monday the 3rd of June on an excursion with Caroline to Bytown, and do not think I was ever much more provoked than, on my arrival on Tuesday afternoon at Kingston, to be met with the information that the *Great Western* had arrived, after an extraordinary passage of only 13 days, bringing out such strange news. The intelligence of the resignation of the Government arrived in the morning by the *Orpheus* and had hardly time to be copied into the Provincial Papers, under the heading of 'Glorious and Important News from England', when the mail by the *Great Western* arrived to stop their rejoicings with the news that the Government was reinstated. I dined with Henry Dundas at the 83rd mess, who received a letter from Lord Melville during dinner, and, from an extract which he read from it, I gather that Peel's own party blame him for having thrown up the Government on such a question. I confess I do not quite understand it, but it does seem to me that it would only have been reasonable to expect some change among the immediate Attendants on the Queen, and that if the whole of the Ladies of the Bedchamber retained their places, related as they were so nearly to the going-out Ministers, the Country never would have believed that Sir Robert had the real confidence of the Queen. I conclude, however, that he asked this

---

15 St. James Cathedral in Toronto was destroyed by fire on January 5, 1839.

in an improper manner, and gather, from what you and Henry tell me, that he would have attained the object, which he professes to have had in view, without commencing beforehand with a demand which had the appearance of harshness and disrespect. Judging at this distance, and from Peel's general conduct, I should certainly say he had done it on purpose, in the hope that this Government may be driven to dissolve, in which case he would probably have a majority in the House of Commons which would of course give him the Government. His whole speech seemed to me an apology to his own Party for not going on with the formation of the Government. The way in which he dwelt on the difficulty he would experience from having a minority in the House of Commons to commence with, and his intention of not dissolving seems to confirm this.

I have spoken to Sir John Colborne about my leave and he says I may go when I like. If I say I am again doubting about it, it will look as if – the moment every difficulty is smoothed, by Denny's return, as far as the Regiment is concerned – I *wished* to find some other reason for delaying my return. But Reports have, within the last few days, gathered such strength of a more extended and better combined rebellion this next winter than ever that I begin to doubt whether or not I am right in asking leave. These reports have arisen very much from some of the Refugees having been lately caught on this side of the lines with Pistols and Bowie knives, and the knowledge that they have been secretly into the heart of the Country, also from fires suspected to be the work of Incendiaries having occurred in various places, and, lastly, from the Burning of this fine Steamer, the *John Bull*, and the Brutal behaviour of the Habitans towards the Crew and Passengers.[16] Sir John Colborne does not

16 The steamer *John Bull* burst into flames in the early hours of the morning on June 10, 1839, while on her way to Quebec from Montreal. The inhabitants of Lanoraie were criticized by the Montreal *Gazette* for refusing to come to the aid of the passengers until promised financial remuneration, and for being more interested in plunder than in rescuing the victims. This was denied, however, by the French-language press.

attach much faith to the reports he hears, nor do I believe that the Canadians will again move in open insurrection unless they see an actual force of Americans in the Country. But there is no doubt their feeling against everything British is more bitter than ever, and I hear that the Message of the Queen, recommending the Union of the Provinces, has indisposed many of the Priests who have hitherto behaved well. This was sure whenever it happened, and I am convinced that the danger would not have been lessened by delaying the measure. Everything considered, therefore, added to the great heat of the weather in July and August, I have determined to give up the Western tour which I announced in my last letter, and, instead, to take an excursion after the 1st July through the Eastern Townships, the Green Hills and White Hills of Vermont and New Hampshire, and to return here, so as to start, if Sir John Colborne shall think I *can* do so, after the 1st August; and then content myself, before embarkation, with the usual trip through the Eastern Towns of the States. This letter is wanted to go down to Quebec so I must finish now. I have written it in the greatest hurry, not having been aware of the opportunity in time, but I have no doubt I shall be able to write again in a few days when I will give you some account of our late delightful excursion.

My very best love to my Mother and all with you. Caroline also desires not to be forgotten. Believe me ever, My Dear Father,

Your most affectionate son,
C. Grey.

Montreal,
June 24, 1839.

My Dear Father,

I wrote to you 10 days ago, thinking a bag was to go by the *Racehorse*, but have heard since that that was not the case, so that in all probability you will receive this letter at the same time as the other. I believe I threw out some doubts in that letter as to whether we should get back to England as we had intended or not. I am glad, however, to be able to say now that I have much better hopes on the subject.

The body of the Second Engineer who had been on duty at the time, and who had been suspected, having been found, it seems now almost certain that the fire on board the *John Bull* was accidental, and that most of the other reports, which were afloat at the time I wrote last, appear to have been equally unfounded.

From the Upper Province they constantly write word that the Sympathizers are active on the frontier and the disaffected at work within. But with respect to the latter it merely appears that the question of a responsible Executive is much agitated and is gaining ground, and that a majority of the next House of Assembly will be favourable to it. And with respect to the former I hear General Scott writes word to Sir J[ohn] Colborne that he has now more means, both in men and money, at his disposal, and that he has no doubt he shall be able to prevent any serious attempts to disturb the Peace of the Country.

I should also mention that though Dundas who commands at Kingston seems convinced, from the information he has received, that serious troubles are in store for us, the Agents of the Steam Packets and other People whom I saw when I was there, and who ought to know, did not attach much credit to the reports in question. The *Great Britain* Steamer had made her first trip to Oswego and Lewiston when I was at Kingston, and had been well received.

With regard to the question of a responsible Executive I cannot say I exactly know what it is that has been demanded. But if it is merely that the Executive Officers, nominated by the Governor, shall be so far responsible to the House of Assembly that they shall be changed like the Government at home when proved not to have the confidence of the People as expressed through their Representatives, I must say that it seems to me the inevitable consequence of giving Representative Government at all, and that I do not think it will be long *possible* to withhold so much. More, of course, could not be granted, nor do I believe more would be required.

As the time for the arrival of the *Liverpool* draws near, the anxiety of everybody is increasing to know the nature of the Government measure for the future Government of these Provinces, and I think Sir John Colborne seems to be of opinion that it will greatly influence our prospects for the winter.

I think myself they attach undue importance to the expected news. If the Provinces are to be united I take it that the French party and their Leaders will not care much about the details, and the Queen's message having announced that this is to be the principle of the measure, I do not see why their hostility should be either diminished or increased by the news we may receive. It is not to be expected that they will ever acquiesce cordially in the Union, come when it may, or that their opposition to it in '41 will be less than it is in '39. On the contrary, I believe, as seeming to be the consequence of their own conduct, that it will be more readily submitted to at present.

It is certainly evident that the British Population themselves will not agree as to the details, and that there will be a Party strongly opposed to whatever measure the present Government introduces, particularly in the Upper Province. But here again I cannot see that their opposition will be weakened, or any other advantage gained, by delay. Long discussion beforehand does not appear to me to have ever facilitated the passing of any measure.

I expect the Regiment to be inspected this day or tomorrow week, and I hope to start on our travels the next day, should the *Liverpool* have arrived. As her time is so near I shall certainly wait for her, and hope that the letter I mean to write by her may be the last I shall have to date from Montreal. Caroline tells me she has told my Mother the route we mean to take, so that I will not repeat it, particularly as I know from experience how liable all such plans are to change up to the last moment. I will only say that I hope nothing may prevent our travels ending on board the *Oxford* Packet which is advertised to sail from New York on the 19th August.

Give my best love to my Mother, and all at home, and believe me ever, My Dear Father,

Your most affectionate son,

C. Grey.

MONTREAL, JUNE 30, 1839

I had nearly made up my mind yesterday to start on our long projected trip to the Townships. I had got the General's leave, ordered my things to be packed up, given parting Regimental directions to Major Denny and actually taken places in the *Canada* Steamer for Port St. Francis, when, talking the matter over with Colonel Clive who happened to call, I changed my mind once more. In the first place the weather was rainy and unsettled, and in the second, as we have given up the *western* tour and mean now to visit instead the Green and White Hills of Vermont and New Hampshire, the best part of the Townships comes naturally in as part of the tour, and we save both time and money by doing it all in one. I am glad we did so decide, as, with a few fair Intervals, it has been raining all the morning. . . . On the 18th there was a grand field day, in commemoration of Waterloo, under General Clitherow and a grand dinner in the evening by Sir John Colborne, at both of which we officiated – 16 Waterloo Medals at table. Yesterday I drove my new waggon round the mountain and was delighted with it. I only wish I had had it sooner.

CHAPTER X

Epilogue

On July 5th the Greys left Montreal with little expectation of
ever returning. Although he was eager to be off, Colonel Grey
had delayed his departure until his regiment had been inspected
and the fourth of July had passed without producing any patriot
disturbances. Now he was free to take his leave and proceed to
England after a brief tour of the eastern United States. At the
last moment his original plan of including the Eastern Townships in the tour was abandoned in favour of a route by way of
Burlington and the White Mountains of New Hampshire.

After stopping for the night at St. Johns, Grey and his wife
set out for the United States on a trip which was to take them
to Boston, New York, Philadelphia, Baltimore, Washington, and
numerous smaller cities and towns. In Philadelphia he was introduced to James Fenimore Cooper, with whom he had an
enjoyable conversation.

By August 6th they were at Caldwell on Lake George, where
they planned to spend a quiet week before returning to New
York to embark for England. Although he complained that the
fishing was 'no great things', Grey enjoyed his rest at Caldwell
in the company of fellow officers from Canada who were also
taking a short holiday.

They had expected to sail on August 19th, but unfavourable
winds delayed them. While waiting for a change in the weather

Grey wrote to inform his father of his immediate plans, upon his return to England, and to give him the latest news from Canada.

New York,
August 19, 1839.

My Dear Father,

Being detained by a foul wind, I have an opportunity of writing to you by the *Liverpool*, which will probably arrive some days before us as she sails on Saturday next and it seems uncertain whether we shall go tomorrow or not – at least the wind shows little inclination to change.

The *Liverpool* arrived this morning, and brought me letters from Henry and Frederick by which I was delighted to hear that you had got as far as Darlington on your way to Howick. I hope we shall now very soon join you there as, after the Easterly winds that have been blowing for the last week, we may hope, when we do start, for a good run. I have no desire to remain an instant longer than necessary in London, and if I hear from you that you are at Howick, we should come on as soon as possible. But I should be vexed beyond measure to think that we interfered in any way with your excursion to Scotland, which I was glad to hear was in contemplation, and there is no reason why we should for Caroline has many relations that she would be very glad to visit, if I would only give her time, or, what I should like better myself, we could steam down to Edinburgh and take our chance of getting invitations to join you. But I do hope that the prospect of our being in England by the middle of September will not interfere with any of your plans. Anxious as I am to see you all, I cannot tell you how sorry I should be to think we had done so.

We have all sorts of reports here, of the recall of Sir John Colborne, and of the nomination of his successor, some say Lord

Clarendon – others the late Speaker[1] (!) – I sincerely hope this is without foundation. For wretchedly managed as I think the whole business has been, there seems to me little chance of peace, even if we are able to preserve the Colony, if one who has got the entire confidence of the British Population were at this moment withdrawn.

At present nobody seems to anticipate any fresh outbreak in Lower Canada this year – on the strength of which opinion I have applied for, and obtained Leave of Absence till the 1st May next. But I wish I could feel as certain of the Upper Province – though I think it probable that things may go on quietly till the period of the next election. What may be the probable consequences of the *Constitutional* Agitation which the Movement Party will then commence, I do not think anyone can say, and I will not say what I think lest I should be called an evil Prophet.

I will reserve all account of my travels and what we have seen in this Country till I see you. I trust a change of wind may enable us tomorrow to make some approach towards that time, by letting us get clear of this Country, and that then a succession of fair winds may blow us over close upon the steps of the *Liverpool.* I will keep my letter open till I see our prospects tomorrow and hope sincerely to announce our embarkation. In the meantime, with our best love to my Mother, Georgiana, and all who are at Howick, believe me ever, My Dear Father,

Your most affectionate son,

C. Grey.

Tuesday Evening, 20th.

The North East Storm is over and the wind has changed to the west with beautiful weather. I think, therefore, there is no doubt of our sailing tomorrow. I will, therefore, close my letter and will not open it again unless we are unexpectedly detained.

---

[1] James Abercromby, who retired as speaker of the House of Commons on June 7, 1839, and was raised to the peerage as Baron Dunfermline.

On September 17th, a few days after he had arrived back in England, Grey reported to Windsor Castle and learned that his period of waiting would begin in October. At a party in the evening he was surprised to discover that dancing had become socially acceptable at court, 'but,' he observed to his father, 'I am sure there was nothing in it last night to which the most fastidious person could object.' He added that the Queen 'dances beautifully . . . and certainly seems to enjoy it excessively.' Personally he found 'the long interval between the dances, planted round that large room, . . . really awful.'[2]

When Grey took up his position as equerry-in-waiting he found the duties had increased somewhat since he had last served in that capacity. The Duchess of Kent had suffered a fall the previous year and as a result the equerry was required to accompany her, as well as the Queen, whenever she went riding.

He had been at Windsor less than a fortnight when the arrival of Prince Albert and his brother Ernest on a visit from Saxe-Coburg produced a state of excitement in the royal household. 'Report says one of them is to be our future King,' he informed Lord Grey, 'and I thought the Queen seemed a little flurried when she heard they were coming. They are both good looking and gentlemanlike looking – particularly the youngest.'[3] By early November he was beginning to doubt the matrimonial rumours and noted that 'the courtship, if courtship it is, seems to go on coldly, at all events on the gentleman's part.' His doubts were soon dispelled, however, for within two weeks his letters began to include references to plans for the Queen's marriage and he observed that she was wearing a miniature of Prince Albert in her bracelet. When the wedding arrangements had been completed, Colonel Grey was chosen to go to Saxe-Coburg and accompany Prince Albert on his return to England. It was the beginning of a close connection with the Prince which was to last until the latter's death in 1861.

[2] Charles Grey to the 2nd Earl Grey, September 18, 1839.
[3] Charles Grey to the 2nd Earl Grey, October 11, 1839.

In November, 1840, Colonel Grey returned to his regiment in Canada for one last tour of duty before going on half-pay. The following June he and his wife visited the Eastern Townships, as they had planned to do in 1839, and Grey found many opportunities to enjoy his favourite sport of fishing. In one remote area his angling equipment created quite a sensation:

> ... the astonishment of the natives of Cuba and St. Domingo on their first discovery by Columbus, at everything belonging to the White Men could not be greater than that of these people at my Fishing rod and tackle. One woman asked me if my reel was a compass, and it was impossible to prevent the boys seizing, to its manifest danger, what they 'guessed' was the funniest 'Pole' they ever 'seed'.[4]

Grey returned to England in August and when his leave expired in April 1842, he went on half-pay. He was made a brevet-colonel in 1846, a major-general in 1854, a lieutenant-general in 1861 and a general in 1865. From 1860 to 1863 he was Colonel of the 3rd Buffs. In 1863 he became the Colonel of the regiment with which he served in Canada, the 71st Light Infantry.

His career in the royal household also continued to advance and in 1849 he became Prince Albert's private secretary. It is quite possible that Queen Victoria's selection of Ottawa as the capital of the Province of Canada in 1857 was indirectly influenced by the favourable impression Grey had formed during his brief visit to Bytown (later renamed Ottawa) in 1839. Prince Albert's memorandum recommending the choice of Ottawa to the Queen is in Grey's hand. When Prince Albert died, in 1861, Grey became the Queen's private secretary, and in 1866 he was given the additional appointment of joint keeper of the privy purse.

In recognition of the close bond which had existed between her husband and his secretary the Queen selected Grey to com-

4 Journal, June 12, 1841.

pile, with her assistance, the first of a projected two-volume biography of Prince Albert. This work was published in 1867 under the title 'The Early Years of his Royal Highness the Prince Consort', and was translated into French, German, and Italian. Previously, in 1861, he had published a biography of his father entitled 'Some Account of the Life and Opinions of Charles, second Earl Grey'.

On March 31, 1870, just a little more than two weeks after his sixty-sixth birthday, Charles Grey died of a paralytic seizure.

The family connection with Canada was renewed in 1904 when Grey's son, Albert, who had succeeded to the title as the fourth Earl Grey, was appointed Governor General. Lord Grey was extremely popular with the Canadian people and remained in office until 1911. It is impossible to say whether or not Charles Grey's memories of Canada had any indirect influence on his son, but certainly the active role which Lord Grey played in the celebration of Quebec's tercentenary and the preservation of the Plains of Abraham, and his presentation of the Grey Cup for the Canadian football championship, reflected his father's interest in historical and military tradition and in sporting activity.

INDEX

Regiments of military personnel are given in brackets whenever they could be obtained.